ULTIMATE X-MEN

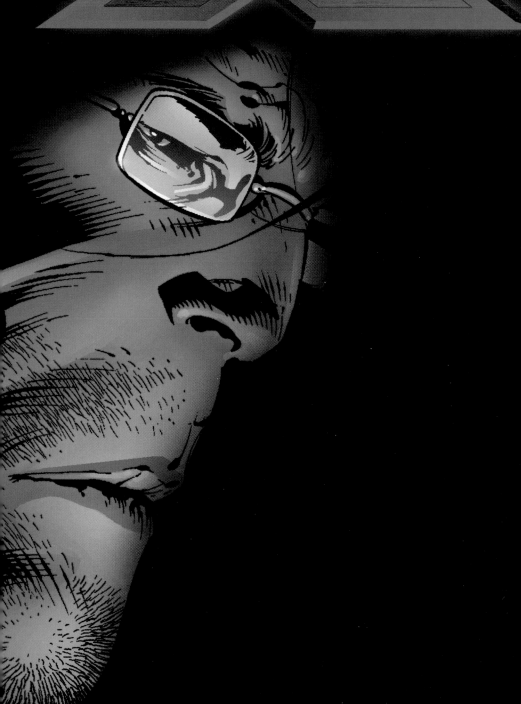

ULTIMATE X-MEN

writer:
BRIAN MICHAEL BENDIS

pencils:
DAVID FINCH

inks:
**ART THIBERT WITH DANNY MIKI,
JOHN DELL & JON SIBAL**

colors:
**FRANK D'ARMATA
WITH MORRY HOLLOWELL
& JUSTIN PONSOR**

letters:
CHRIS ELIOPOULOS

assistant editors:
**NICK LOWE &
MACKENZIE CADENHEAD**

associate editor:
C.B. CEBULSKI

editor:
RALPH MACCHIO

collections editor:
JEFF YOUNGQUIST

assistant editor:
JENNIFER GRÜNWALD

book designer:
CARRIE BEADLE

creative director:
TOM MARVELLI

editor in chief:
JOE QUESADA

publisher:
DAN BUCKLEY

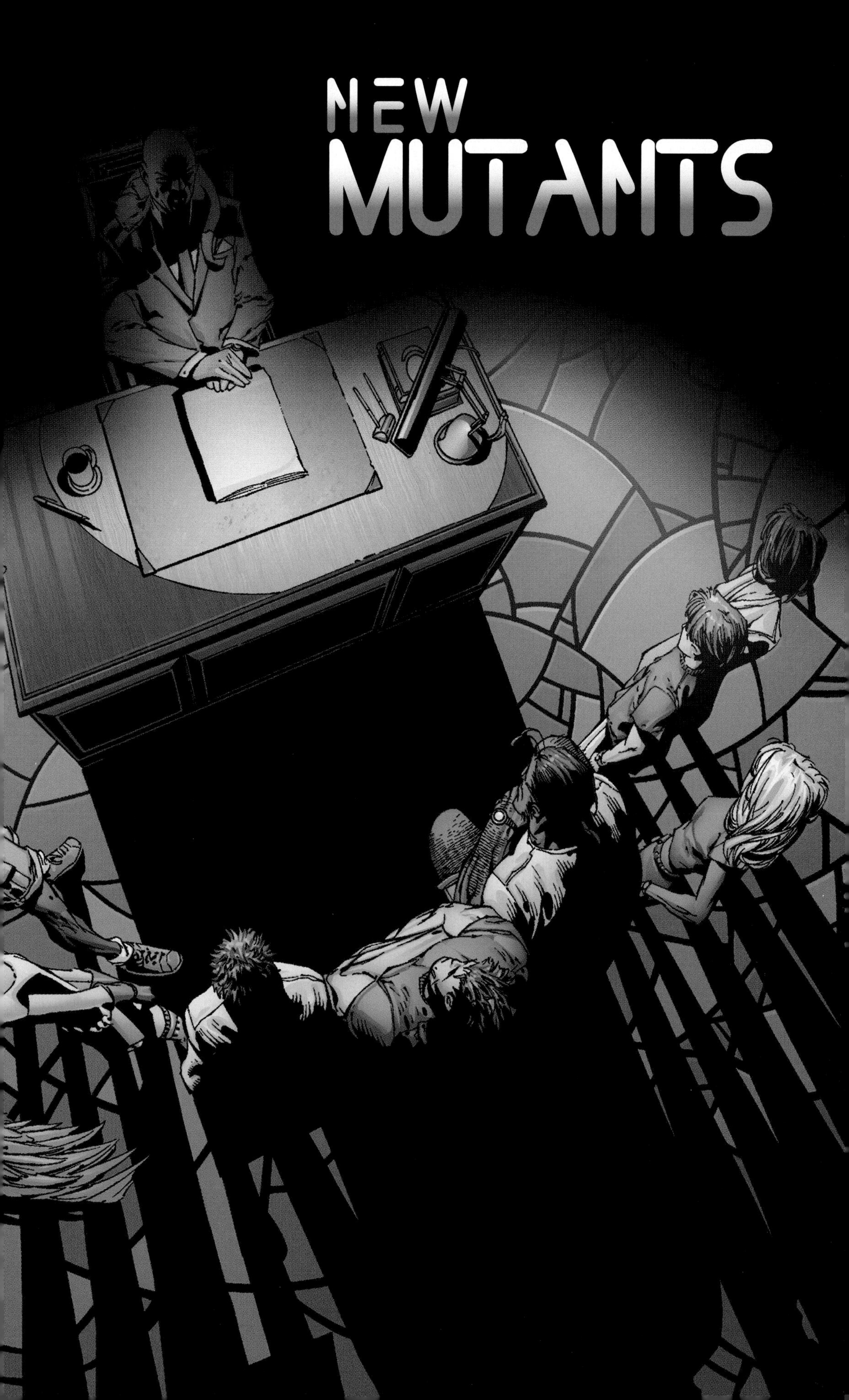
NEW
MUTANTS

ULTIMATE X-MEN

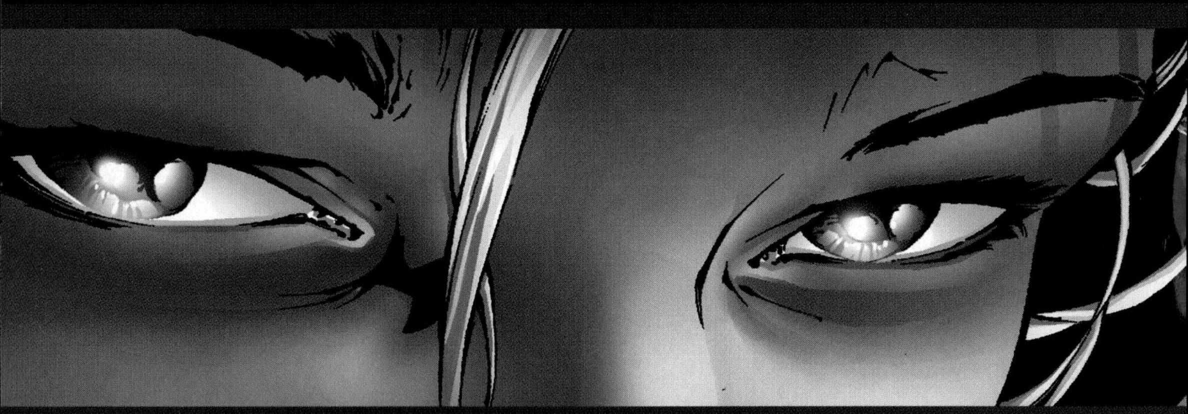

PREVIOUSLY IN ULTIMATE X-MEN:

Professor Charles Xavier brought them together to bridge the gap between humanity and those born with strange and amazing powers: Cyclops, Marvel Girl, Storm, Iceman, Beast, Colossus and Wolverine. They are the X-Men, soldiers in Xavier's war to bring peace between man and mutant!

The X-Men have gone public in an attempt to carry their pro-mutant/human relations messages forward. The X-Men now fall under the jurisdiction of world security leader Nick Fury with both the government and Xavier trying to figure out exactly how this will work.

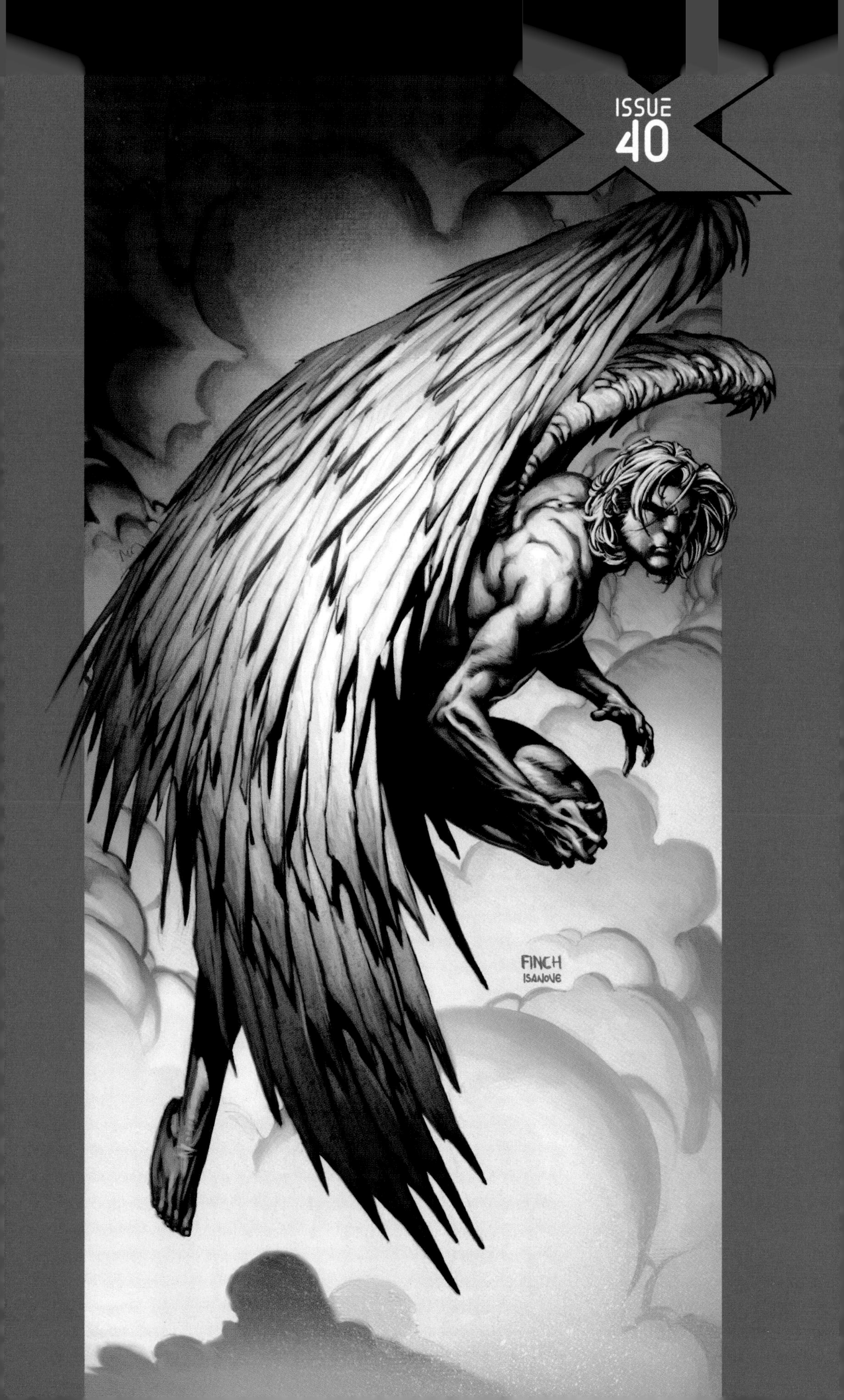
ISSUE
40
FINCH
ISANOVE

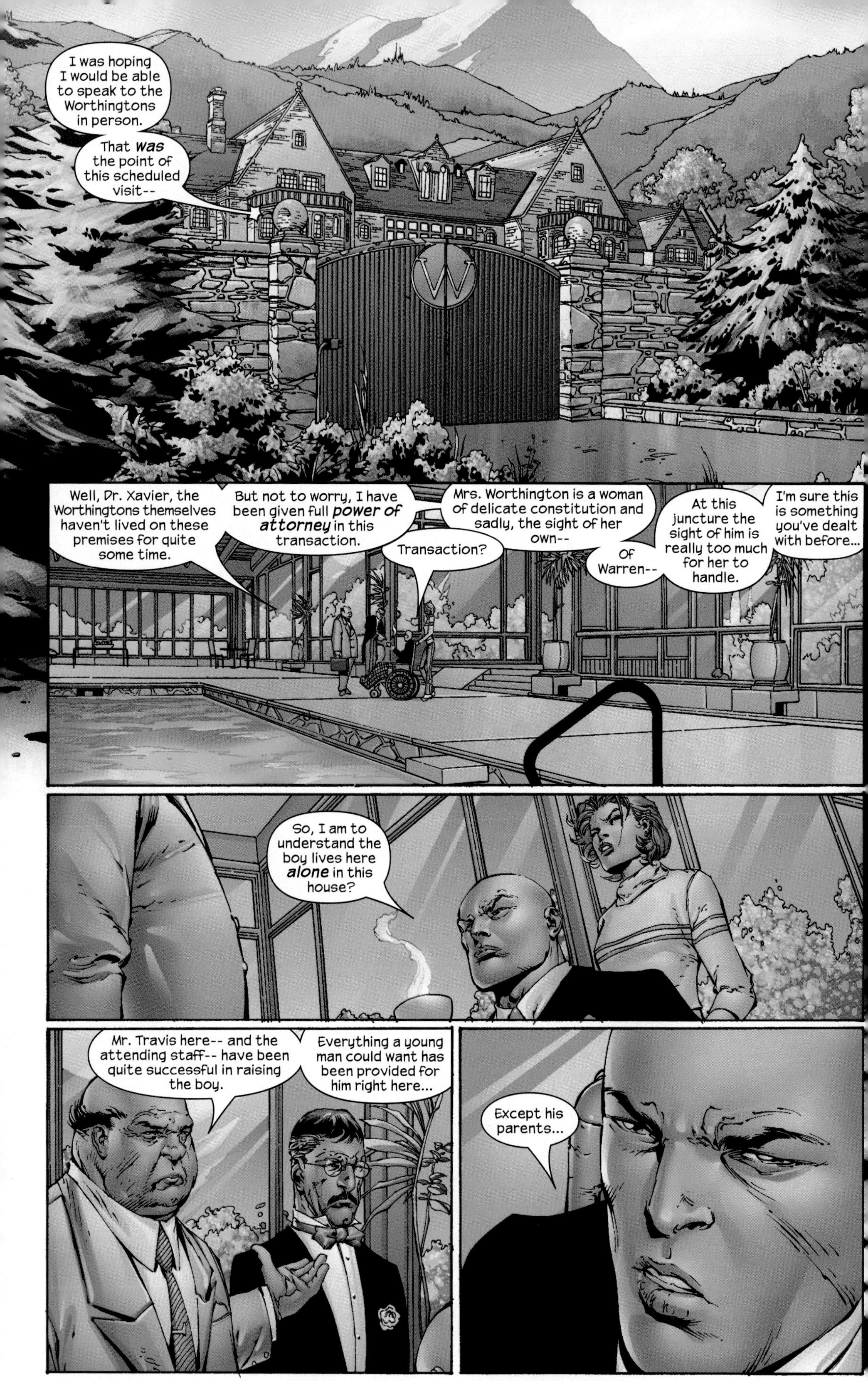
I was hoping I would be able to speak to the Worthingtons in person.
That **was** the point of this scheduled visit--
Well, Dr. Xavier, the Worthingtons themselves haven't lived on these premises for quite some time.
But not to worry, I have been given full **power of attorney** in this transaction.
Transaction?
Mrs. Worthington is a woman of delicate constitution and sadly, the sight of her own--
Of Warren--
At this juncture the sight of him is really too much for her to handle.
I'm sure this is something you've dealt with before...
So, I am to understand the boy lives here **alone** in this house?
Mr. Travis here-- and the attending staff-- have been quite successful in raising the boy.
Everything a young man could want has been provided for him right here...
Except his parents...

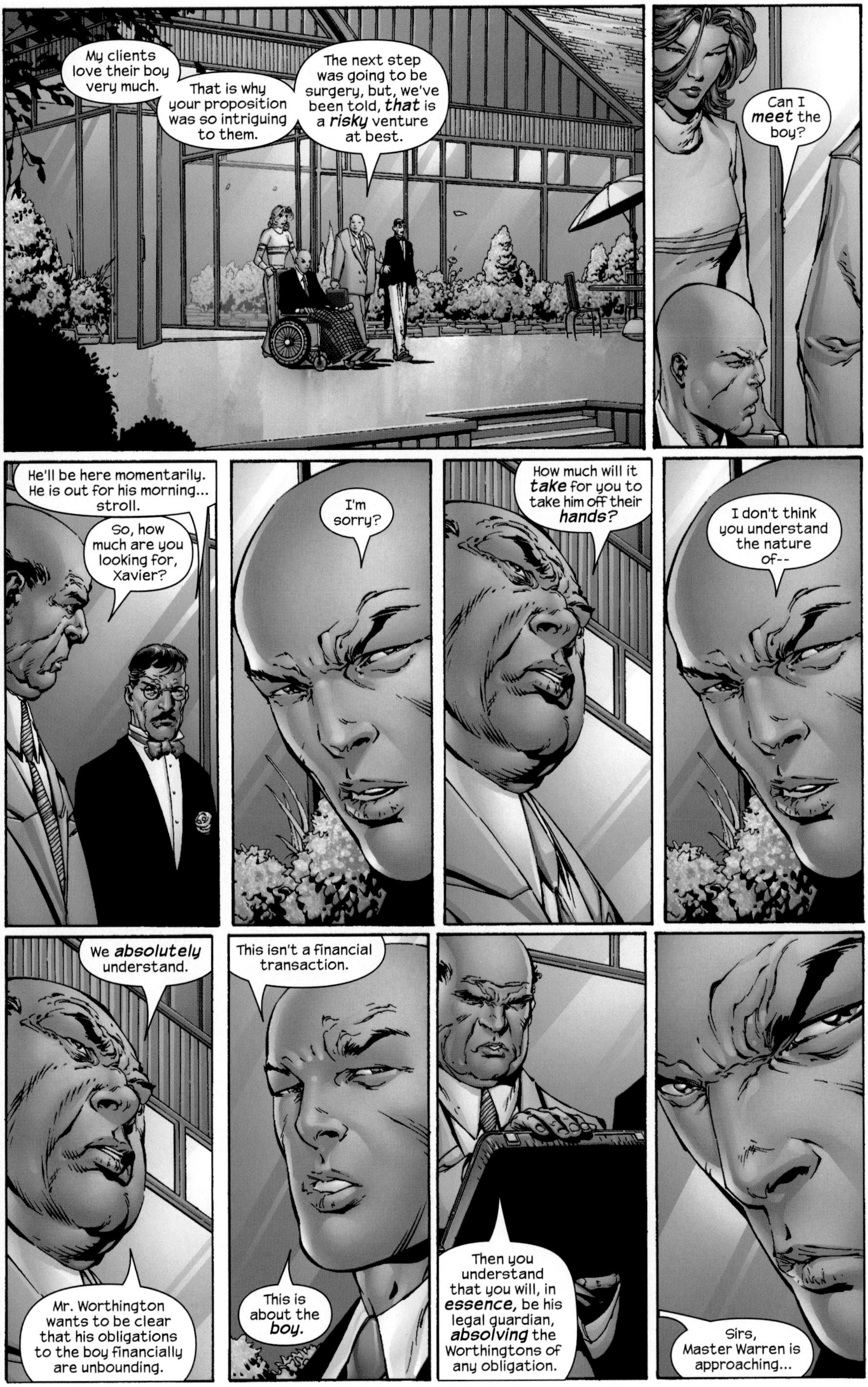
My clients love their boy very much.
That is why your proposition was so intriguing to them.
The next step was going to be surgery, but, we've been told, *that* is a *risky* venture at best.
Can I *meet* the boy?
He'll be here momentarily. He is out for his morning... stroll.
So, how much are you looking for, Xavier?
I'm sorry?
How much will it *take* for you to take him off their *hands?*
I don't think you understand the nature of--
We *absolutely* understand.
Mr. Worthington wants to be clear that his obligations to the boy financially are unbounding.
This isn't a financial transaction.
This is about the *boy.*
Then you understand that you will, in *essence,* be his legal guardian, *absolving* the Worthingtons of any obligation.
Sirs, Master Warren is approaching...

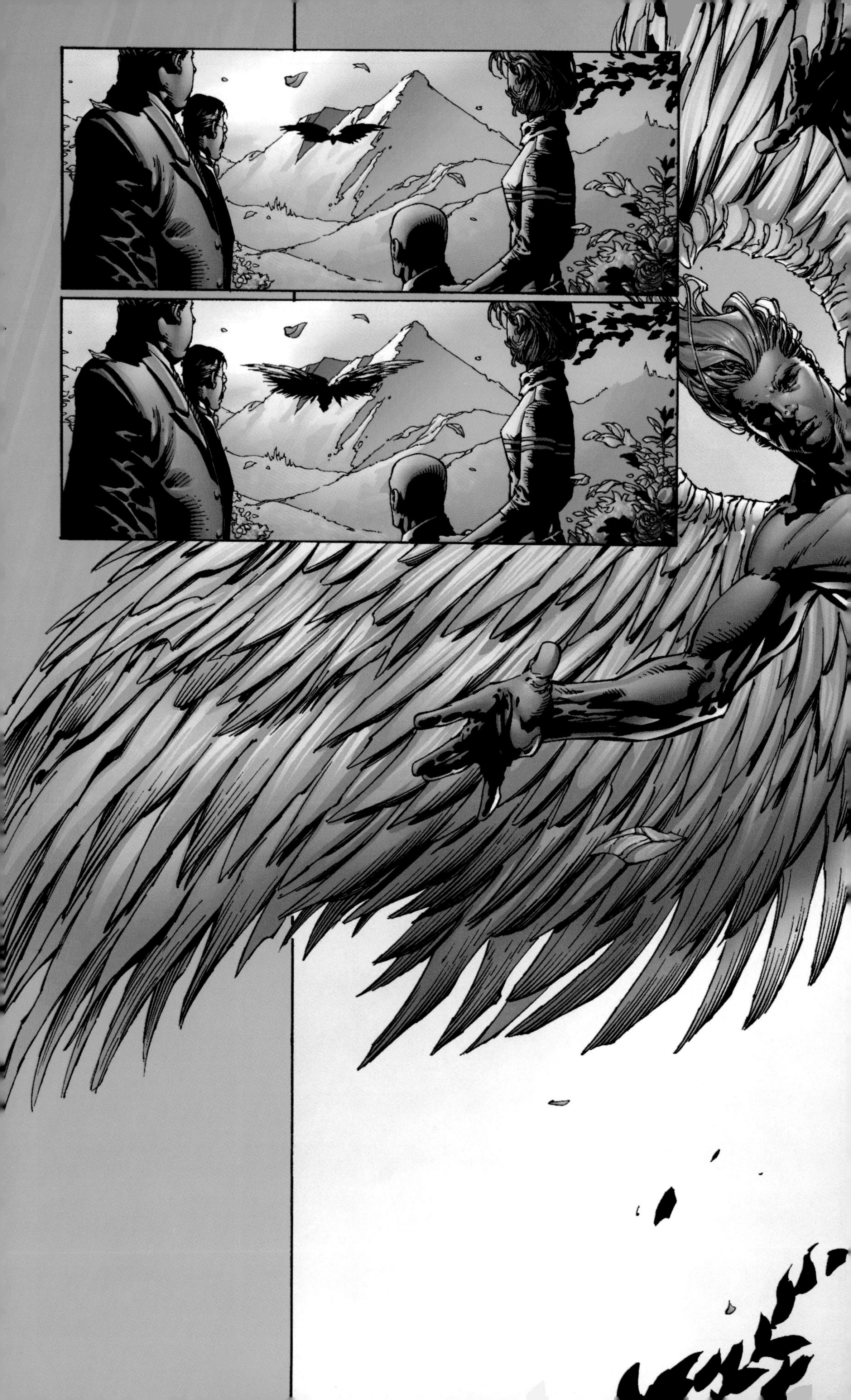

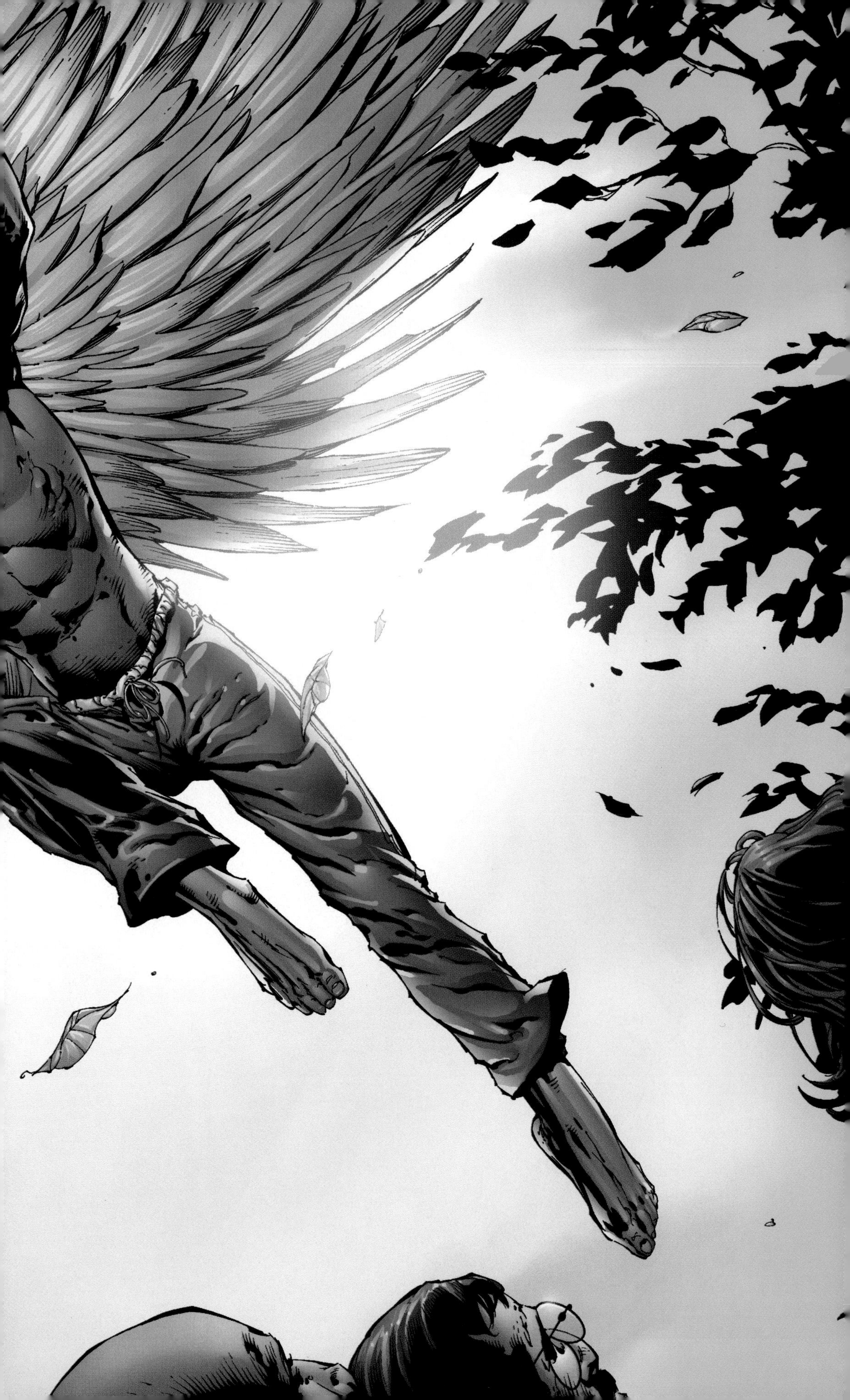

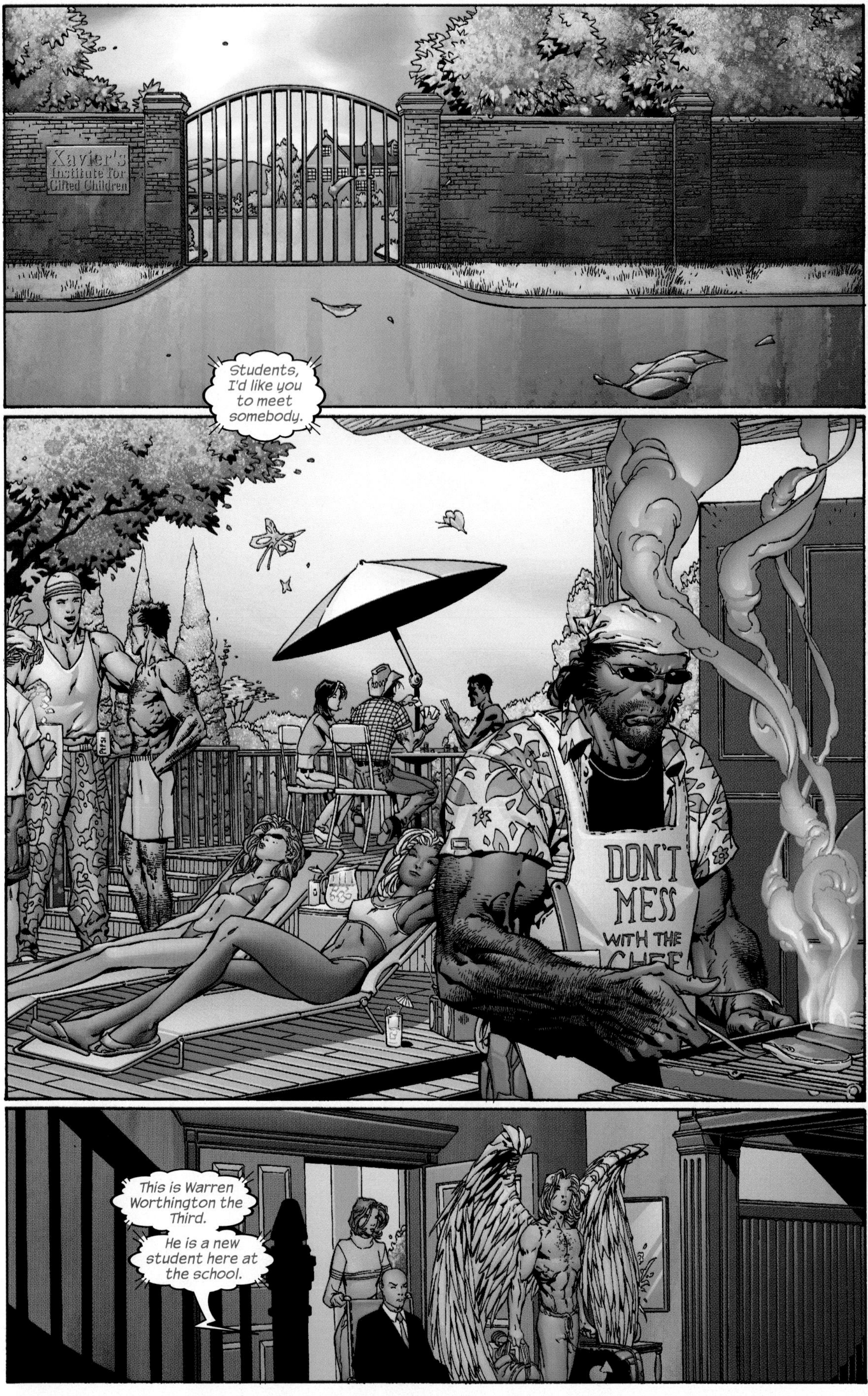
Xavier's Institute for Gifted Children
Students, I'd like you to meet somebody.
PEPSI
DON'T MESS WITH THE
This is Warren Worthington the Third.
He is a new student here at the school.

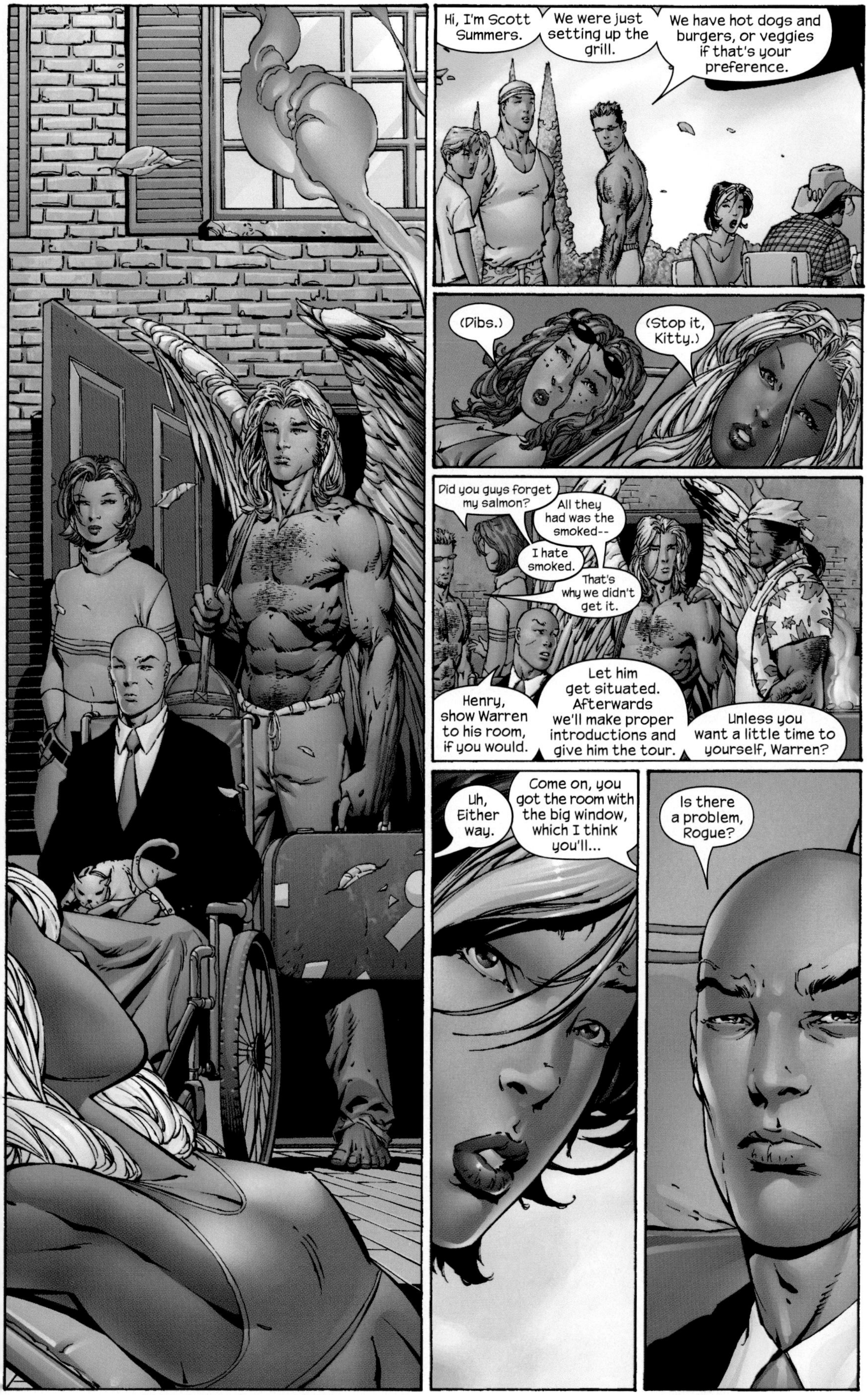

Hi, I'm Scott Summers.
We were just setting up the grill.
We have hot dogs and burgers, or veggies if that's your preference.
(Dibs.)
(Stop it, Kitty.)
Did you guys forget my salmon?
All they had was the smoked--
I hate smoked.
That's why we didn't get it.
Henry, show Warren to his room, if you would.
Let him get situated. Afterwards we'll make proper introductions and give him the tour.
Unless you want a little time to yourself, Warren?
Uh, Either way.
Come on, you got the room with the big window, which I think you'll...
Is there a problem, Rogue?

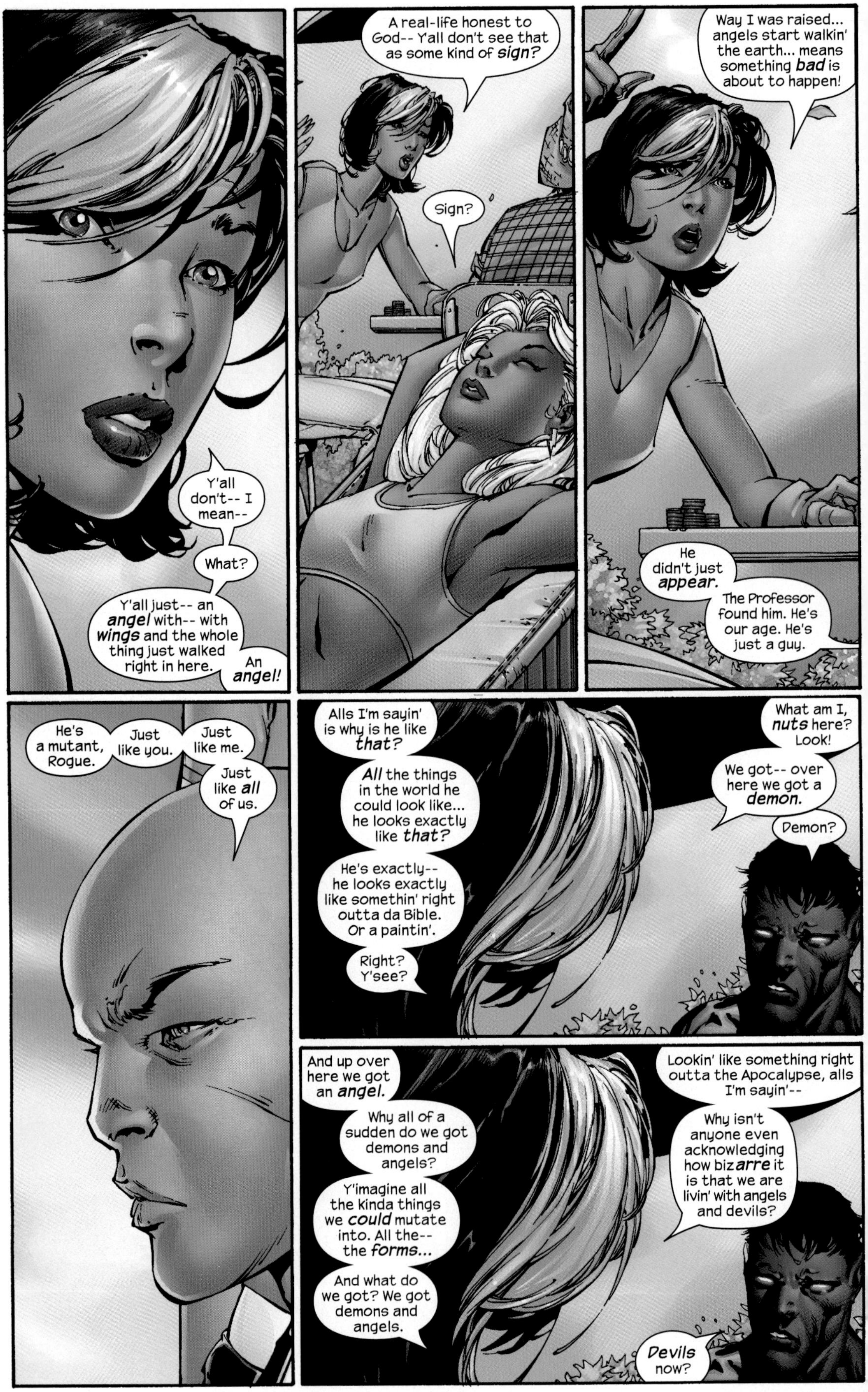
Y'all don't-- I mean--
What?
Y'all just-- an angel with-- with wings and the whole thing just walked right in here.
An angel!
A real-life honest to God-- Y'all don't see that as some kind of sign?
Sign?
Way I was raised... angels start walkin' the earth... means something bad is about to happen!
He didn't just appear.
The Professor found him. He's our age. He's just a guy.
He's a mutant, Rogue.
Just like you.
Just like me.
Just like all of us.
Alls I'm sayin' is why is he like that?
All the things in the world he could look like... he looks exactly like that?
He's exactly-- he looks exactly like somethin' right outta da Bible. Or a paintin'.
Right? Y'see?
What am I, nuts here? Look!
We got-- over here we got a demon.
Demon?
And up over here we got an angel.
Why all of a sudden do we got demons and angels?
Y'imagine all the kinda things we could mutate into. All the-- the forms...
And what do we got? We got demons and angels.
Lookin' like something right outta the Apocalypse, alls I'm sayin'--
Why isn't anyone even acknowledging how bizarre it is that we are livin' with angels and devils?
Devils now?

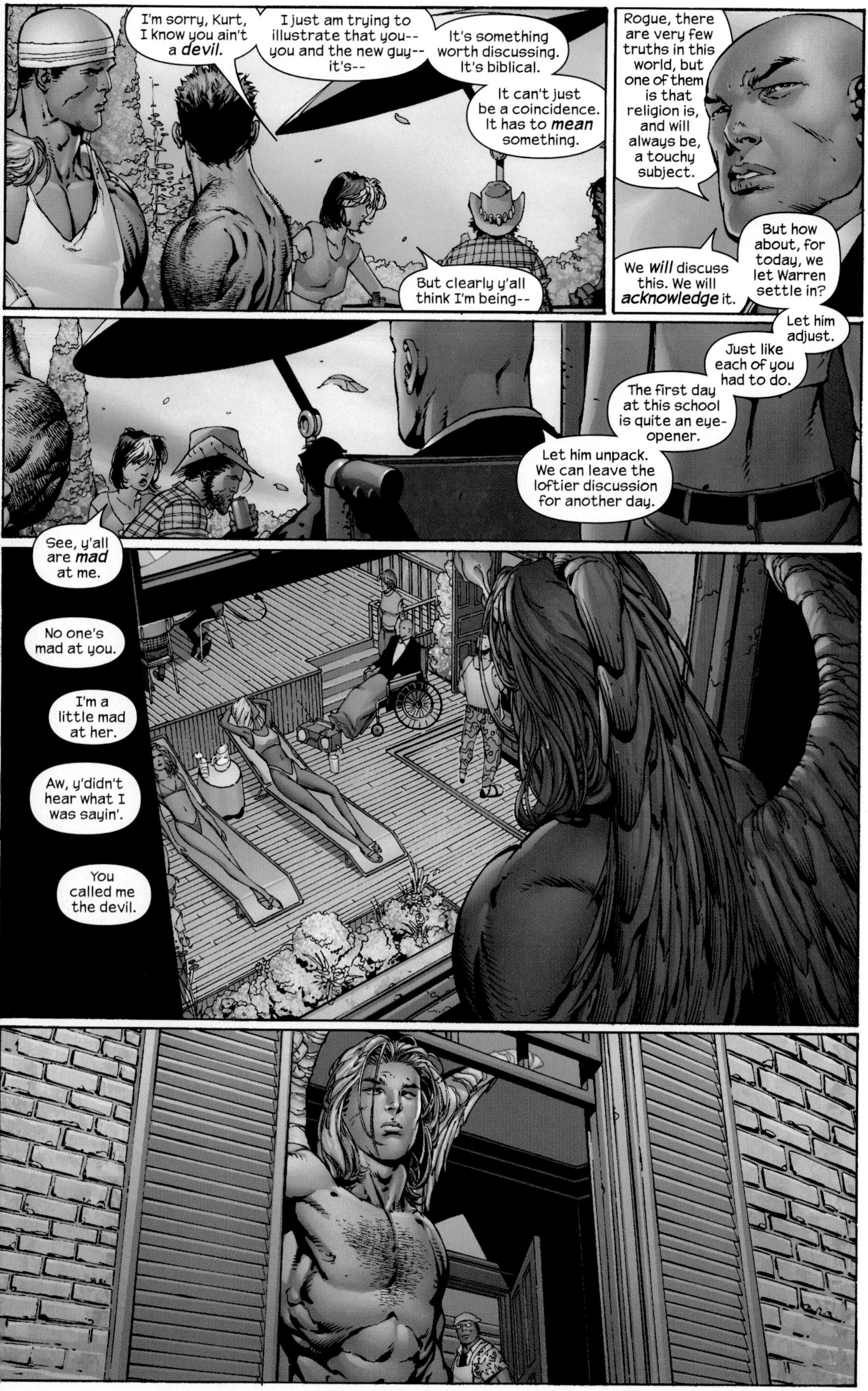
I'm sorry, Kurt, I know you ain't a *devil.*
I just am trying to illustrate that you-- you and the new guy-- it's--
It's something worth discussing. It's biblical.
It can't just be a coincidence. It has to *mean* something.
But clearly y'all think I'm being--
Rogue, there are very few truths in this world, but one of them is that religion is, and will always be, a touchy subject.
We *will* discuss this. We will *acknowledge* it.
But how about, for today, we let Warren settle in?
Let him adjust.
Just like each of you had to do.
The first day at this school is quite an eye-opener.
Let him unpack. We can leave the loftier discussion for another day.
See, y'all are *mad* at me.
No one's mad at you.
I'm a little mad at her.
Aw, y'didn't hear what I was sayin'.
You called me the devil.

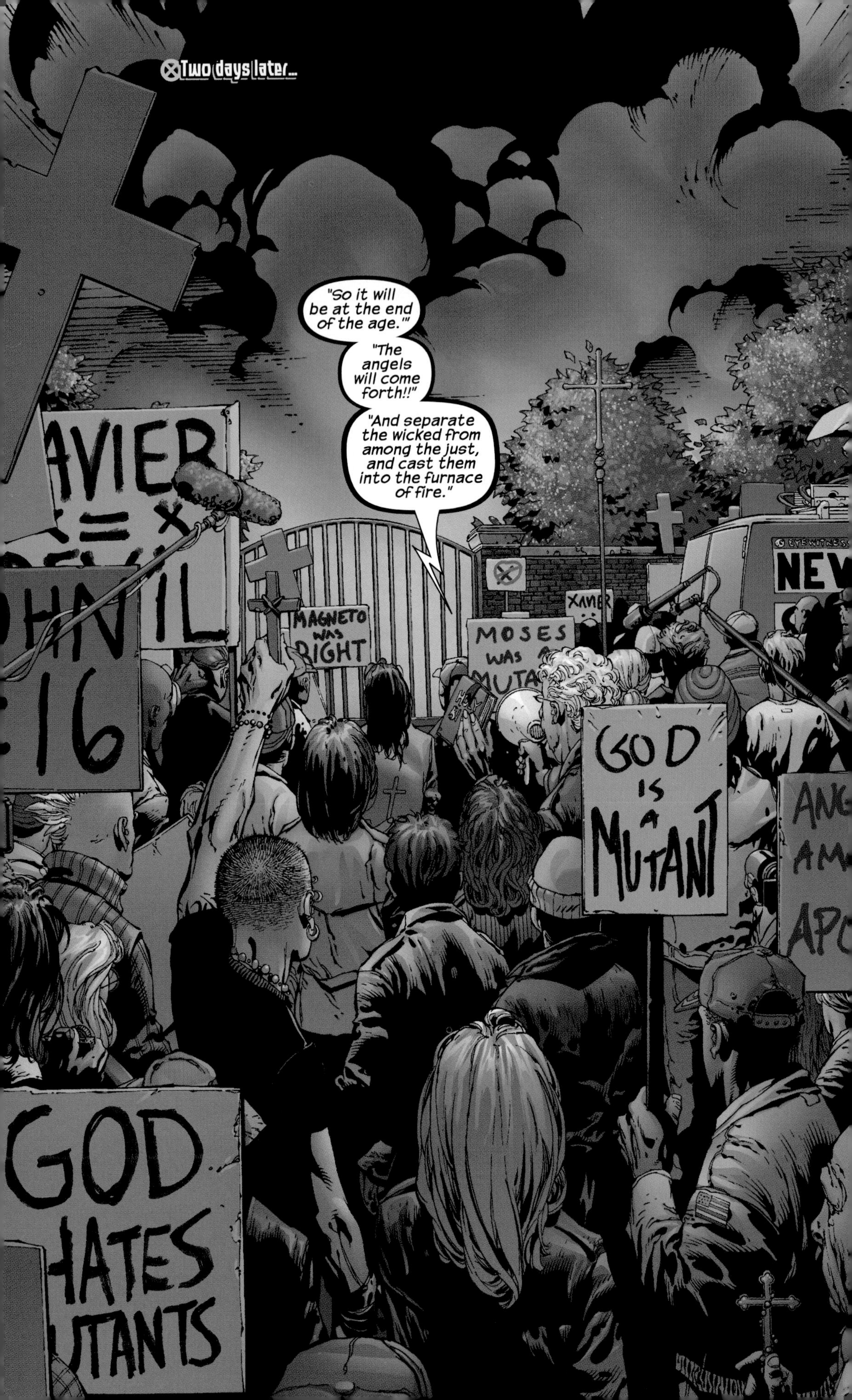
Two days later...
"So it will be at the end of the age.'"
"The angels will come forth!!"
"And separate the wicked from among the just, and cast them into the furnace of fire."
MAGNETO WAS RIGHT
GOD IS A MUTANT
XAVIER
GOD

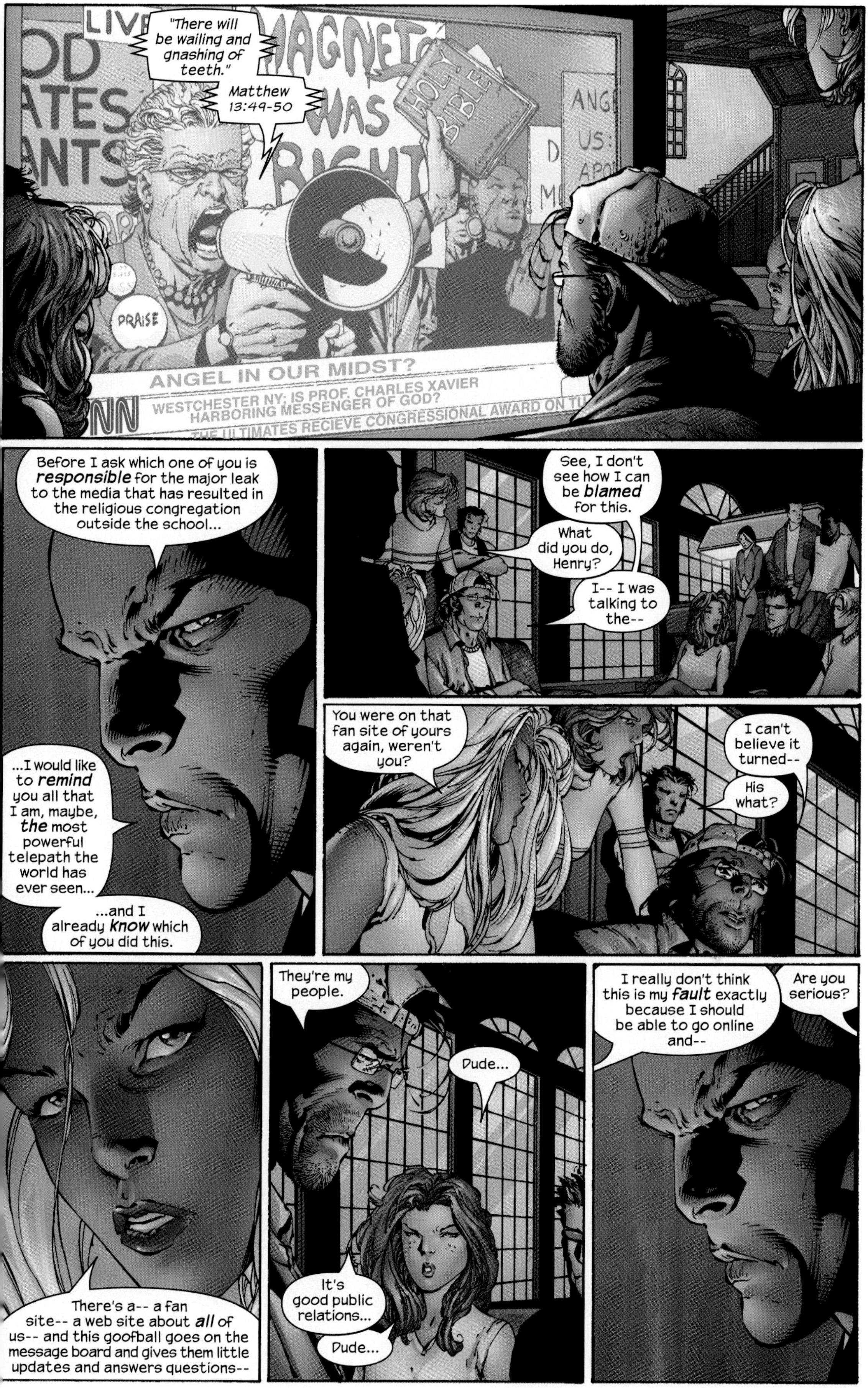
LIVE
"There will be wailing and gnashing of teeth."
Matthew 13:49-50
HOLY BIBLE
PRAISE
ANGEL IN OUR MIDST?
WESTCHESTER NY: IS PROF. CHARLES XAVIER HARBORING MESSENGER OF GOD?
THE ULTIMATES RECIEVE CONGRESSIONAL AWARD ON TU
Before I ask which one of you is *responsible* for the major leak to the media that has resulted in the religious congregation outside the school...
...I would like to *remind* you all that I am, maybe, *the* most powerful telepath the world has ever seen...
...and I already *know* which of you did this.
See, I don't see how I can be *blamed* for this.
What did you do, Henry?
I-- I was talking to the--
You were on that fan site of yours again, weren't you?
I can't believe it turned--
His what?
There's a-- a fan site-- a web site about *all* of us-- and this goofball goes on the message board and gives them little updates and answers questions--
They're my people.
Dude...
It's good public relations...
Dude...
I really don't think this is my *fault* exactly because I should be able to go online and--
Are you serious?

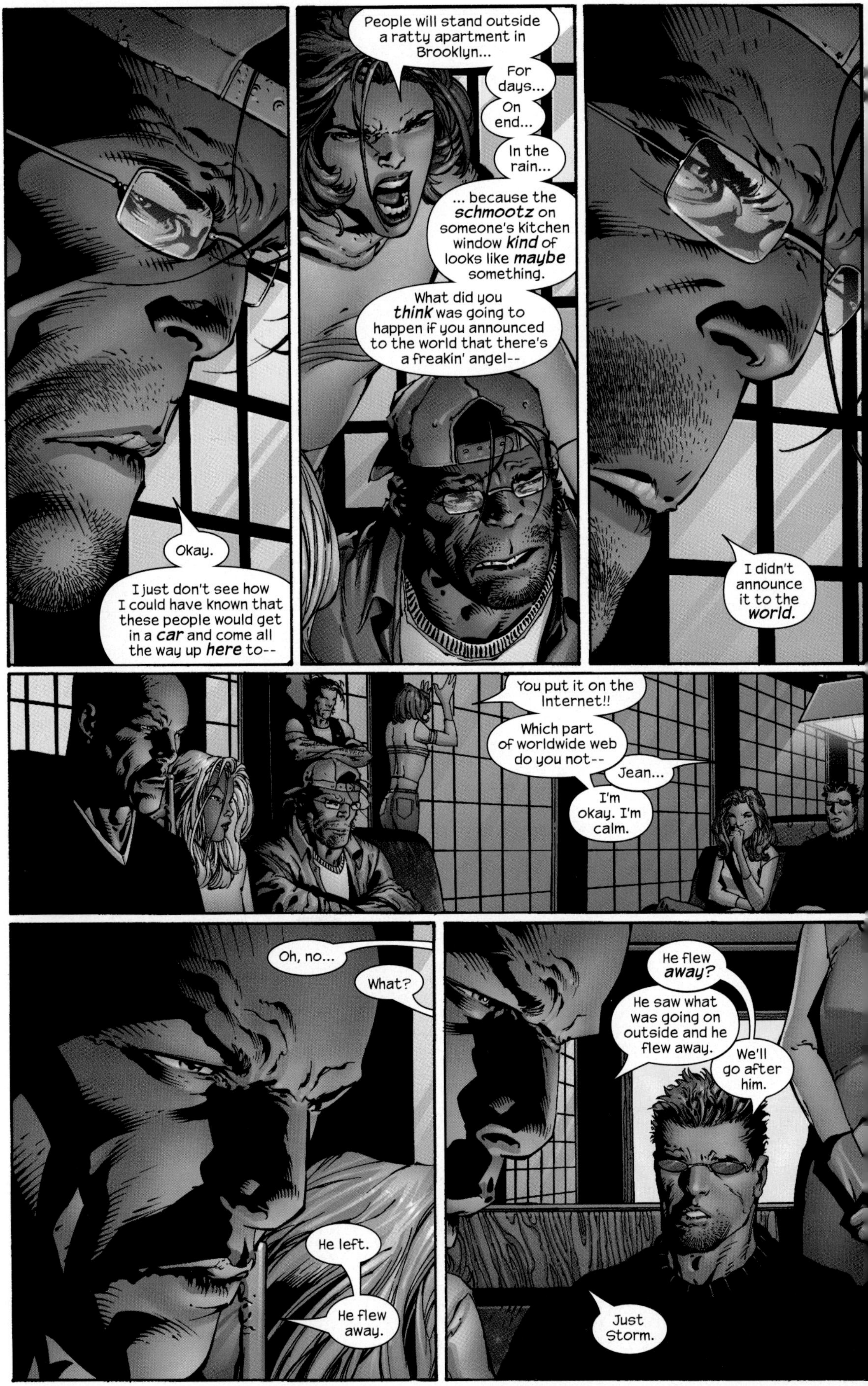
Okay.
I just don't see how I could have known that these people would get in a car and come all the way up here to--
People will stand outside a ratty apartment in Brooklyn...
For days...
On end...
In the rain...
... because the schmootz on someone's kitchen window kind of looks like maybe something.
What did you think was going to happen if you announced to the world that there's a freakin' angel--
I didn't announce it to the world.
You put it on the Internet!!
Which part of worldwide web do you not--
Jean...
I'm okay. I'm calm.
Oh, no...
What?
He left.
He flew away.
He flew away?
He saw what was going on outside and he flew away.
We'll go after him.
Just Storm.

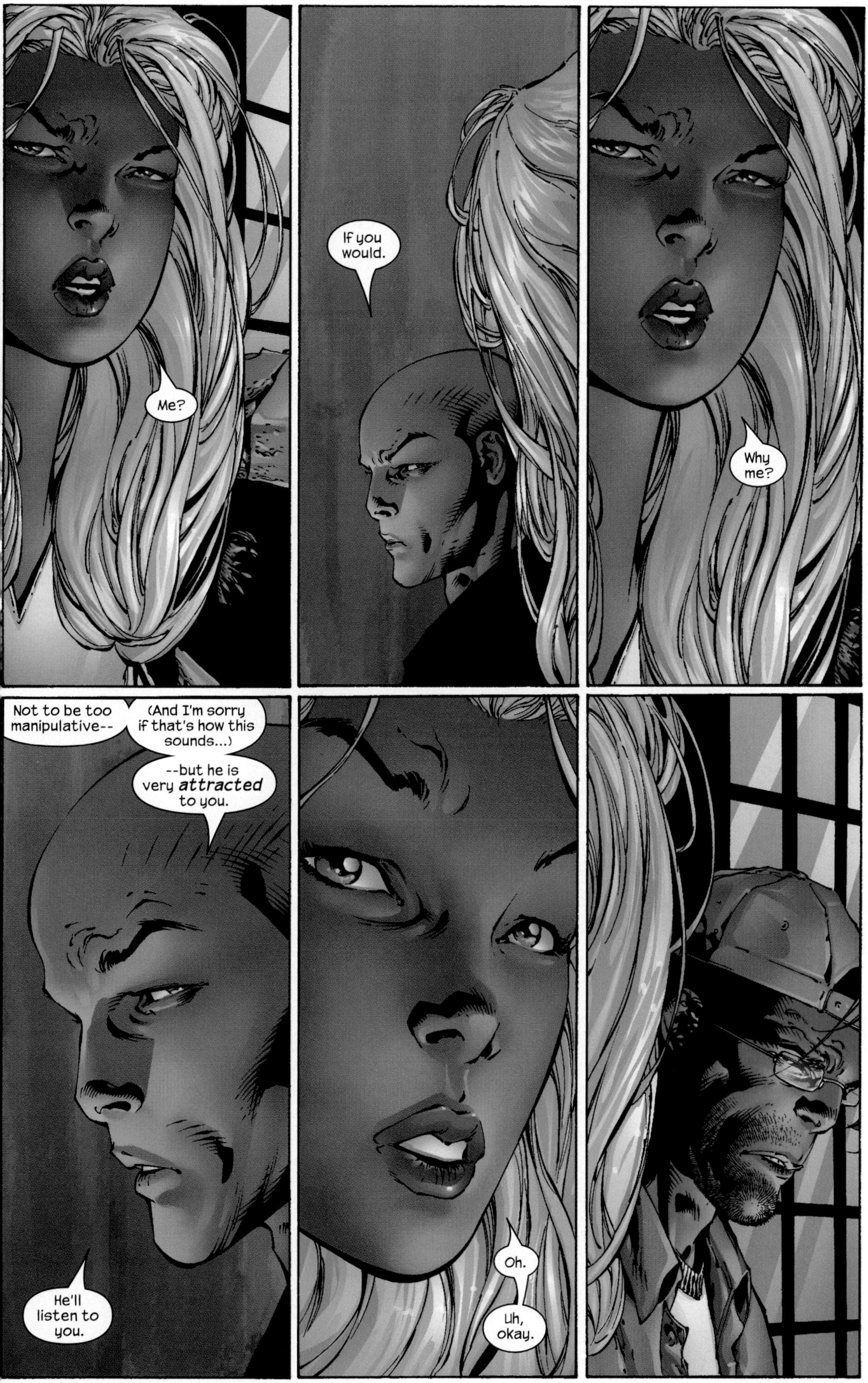
Me?
If you would.
Why me?
Not to be too manipulative--
(And I'm sorry if that's how this sounds...)
--but he is very *attracted* to you.
He'll listen to you.
Oh.
Uh, okay.

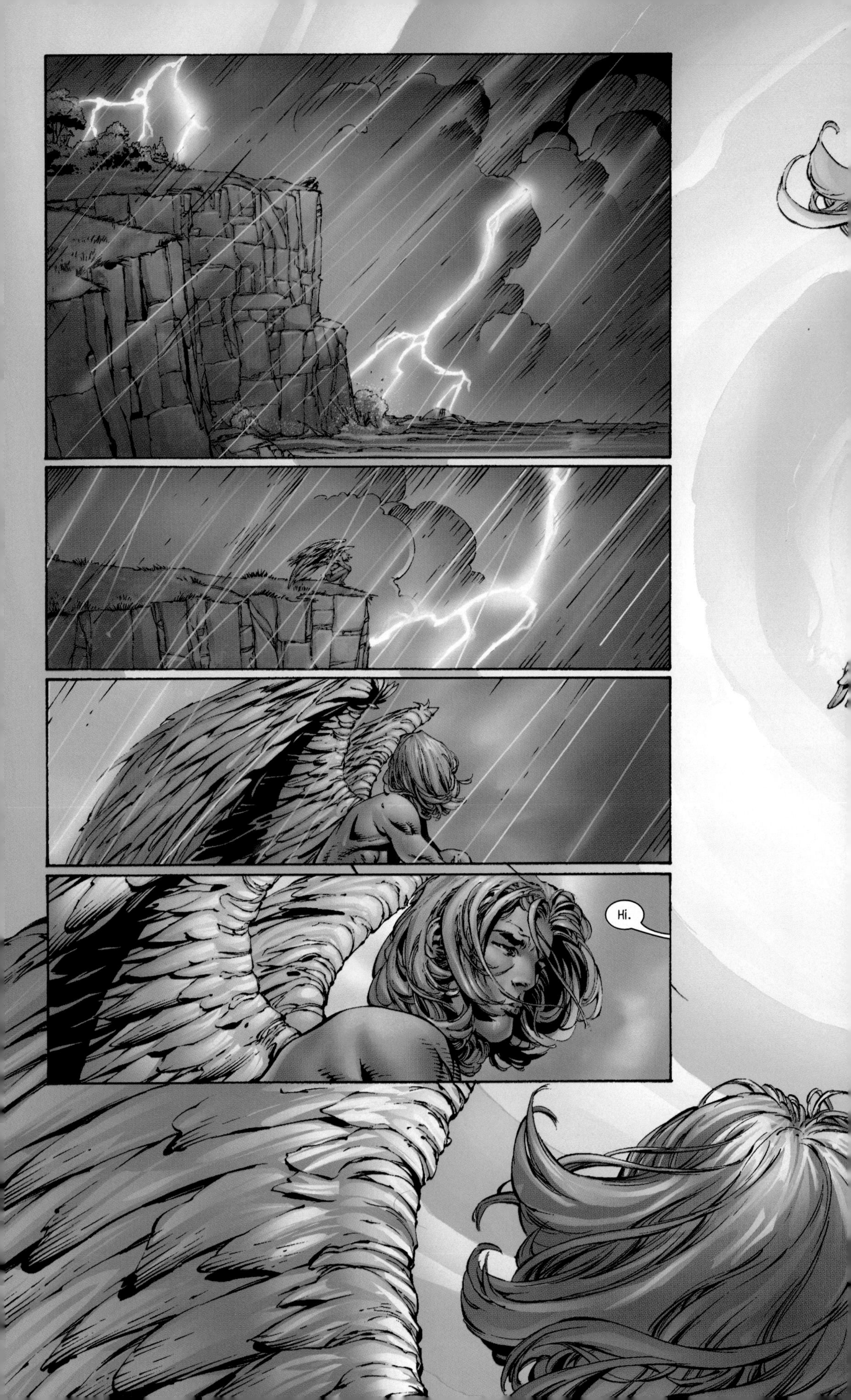
Hi.

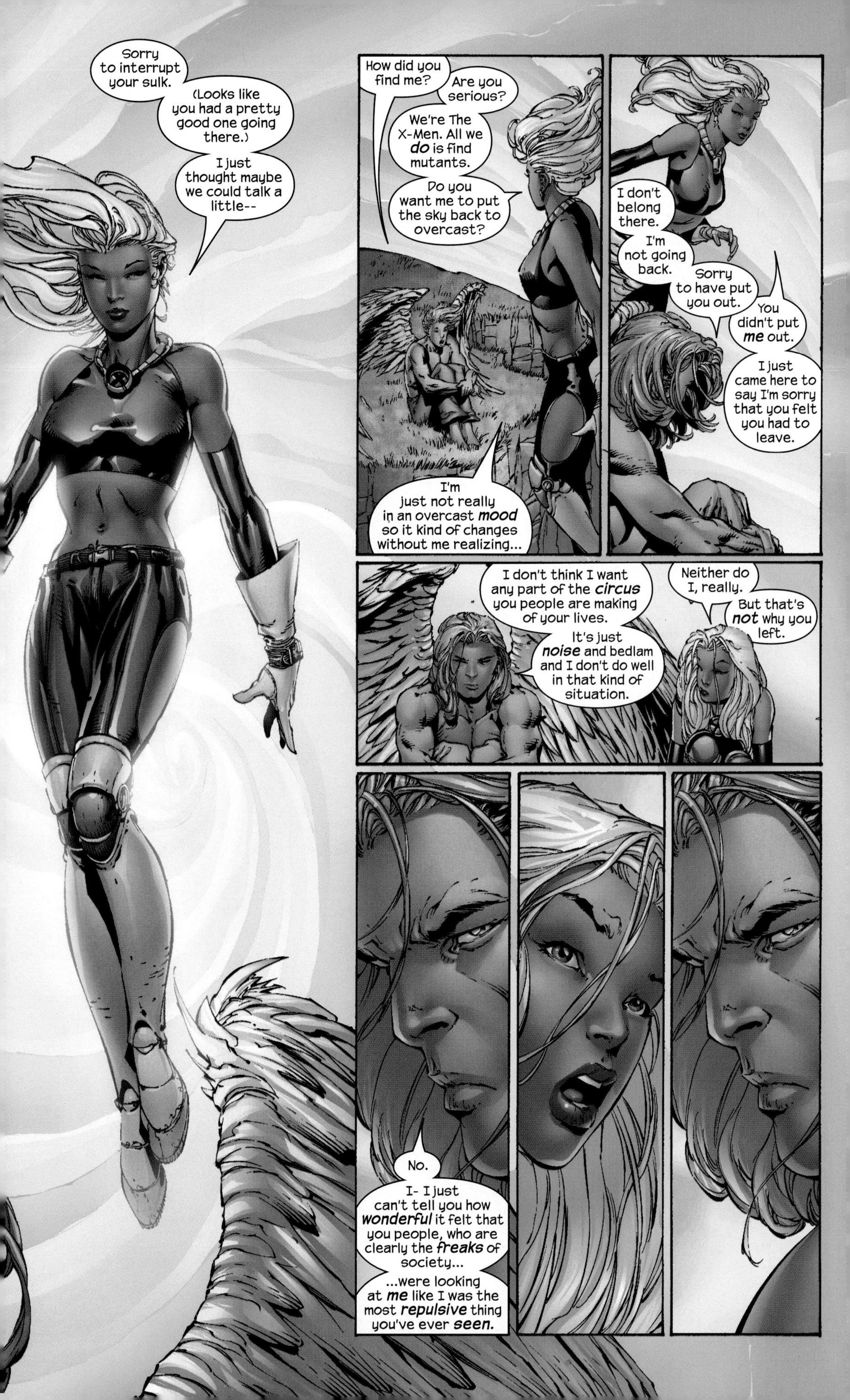

Sorry to interrupt your sulk.
(Looks like you had a pretty good one going there.)
I just thought maybe we could talk a little--
How did you find me?
Are you serious?
We're The X-Men. All we do is find mutants.
Do you want me to put the sky back to overcast?
I'm just not really in an overcast mood so it kind of changes without me realizing...
I don't belong there.
I'm not going back.
Sorry to have put you out.
You didn't put me out.
I just came here to say I'm sorry that you felt you had to leave.
I don't think I want any part of the circus you people are making of your lives.
It's just noise and bedlam and I don't do well in that kind of situation.
Neither do I, really.
But that's not why you left.
No.
I- I just can't tell you how wonderful it felt that you people, who are clearly the freaks of society...
...were looking at me like I was the most repulsive thing you've ever seen.

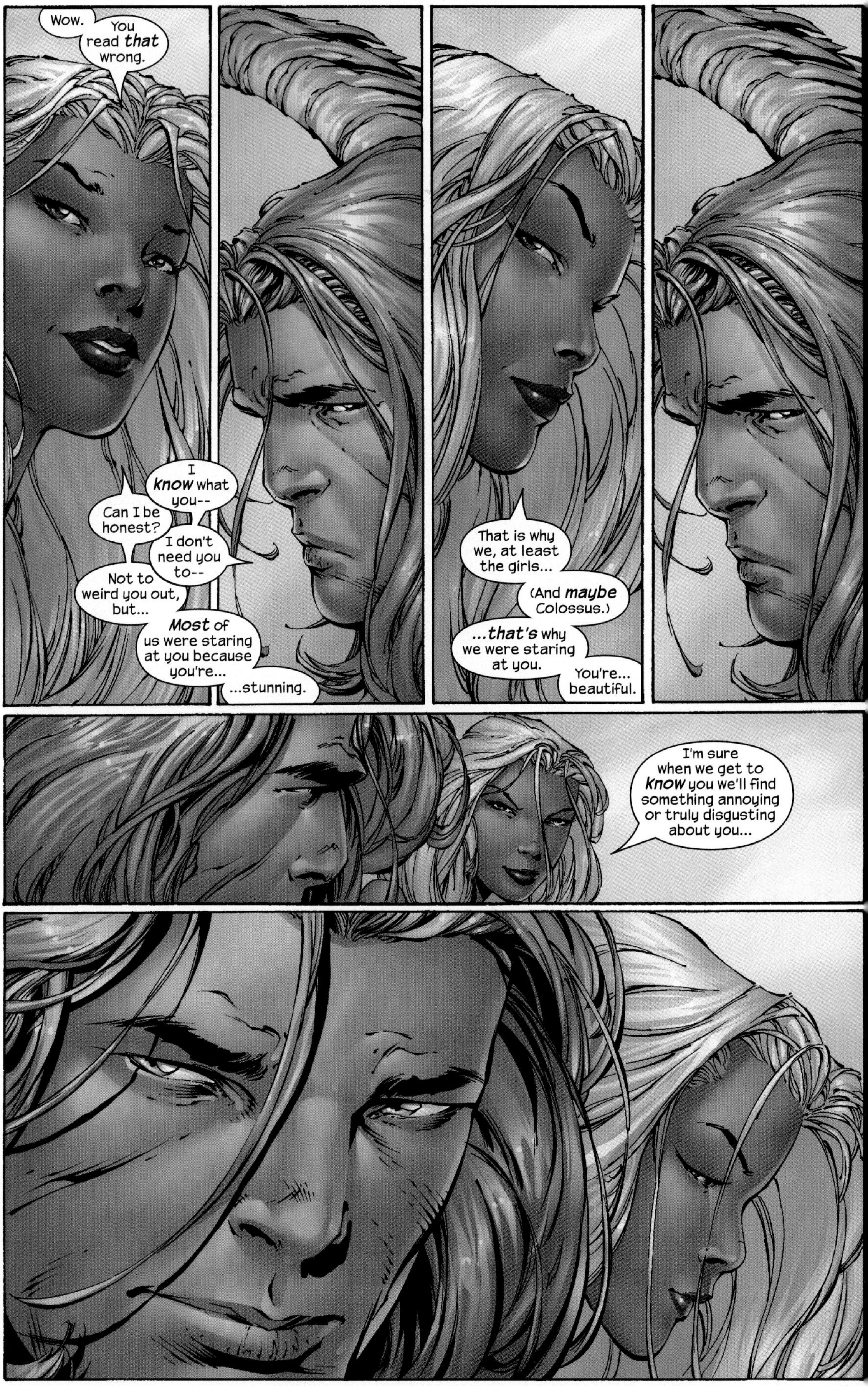

Wow.
You read *that* wrong.
Can I be honest?
I *know* what you--
I don't need you to--
Not to weird you out, but...
Most of us were staring at you because you're...
...stunning.
That is why we, at least the girls...
(And *maybe* Colossus.)
...that's why we were staring at you.
You're... beautiful.
I'm sure when we get to *know* you we'll find something annoying or truly disgusting about you...

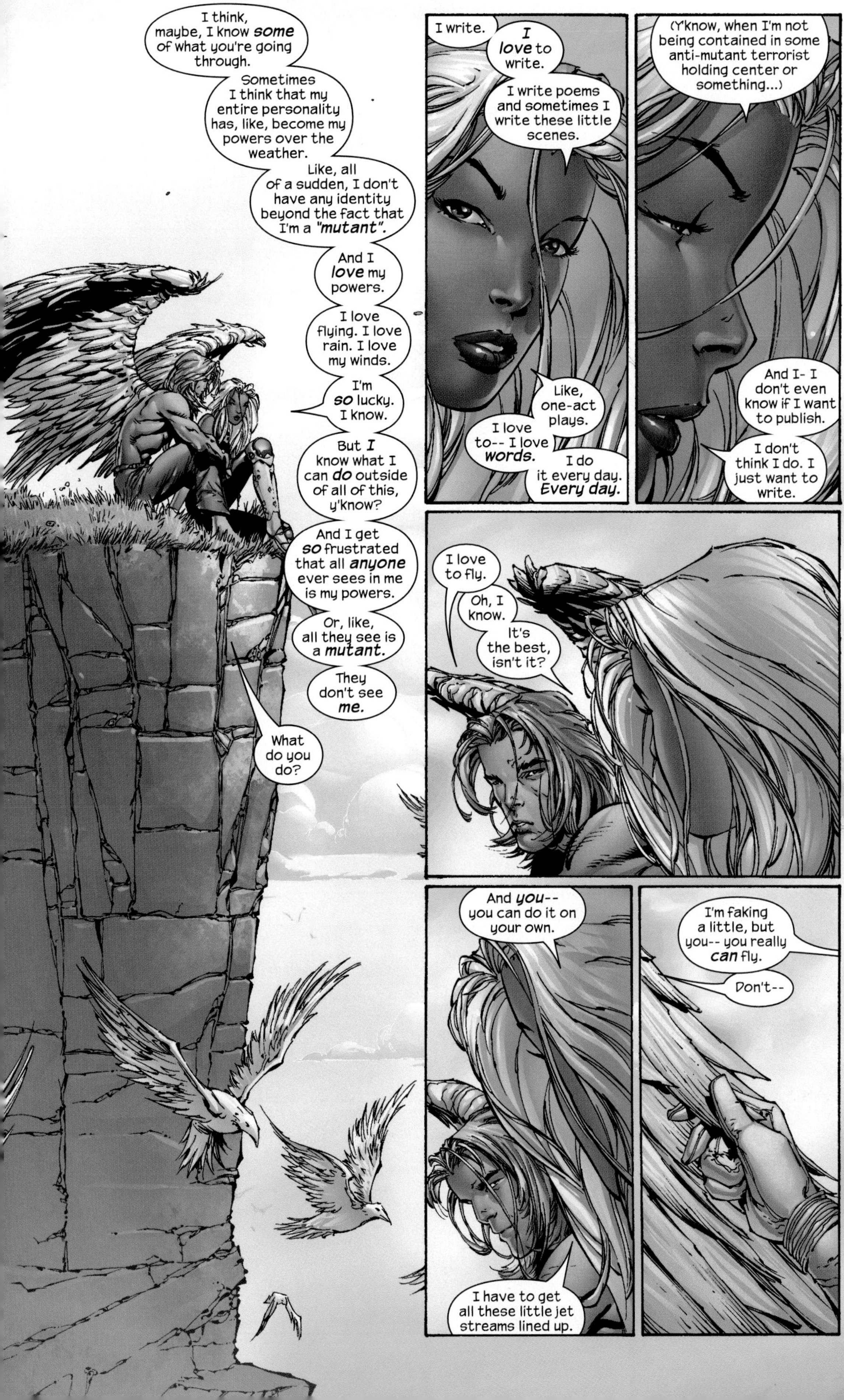

I think, maybe, I know *some* of what you're going through.
Sometimes I think that my entire personality has, like, become my powers over the weather.
Like, all of a sudden, I don't have any identity beyond the fact that I'm a *"mutant".*
And I *love* my powers.
I love flying. I love rain. I love my winds.
I'm *so* lucky. I know.
But *I* know what I can *do* outside of all of this, y'know?
And I get *so* frustrated that all *anyone* ever sees in me is my powers.
Or, like, all they see is a *mutant.*
They don't see *me.*
What do you do?
I write.
I love to write.
I write poems and sometimes I write these little scenes.
Like, one-act plays.
I love to-- I love *words.*
I do it every day. *Every day.*
(Y'know, when I'm not being contained in some anti-mutant terrorist holding center or something...)
And I- I don't even know if I want to publish.
I don't think I do. I just want to write.
I love to fly.
Oh, I know.
It's the best, isn't it?
And *you*-- you can do it on your own.
I have to get all these little jet streams lined up.
I'm faking a little, but you-- you really *can* fly.
Don't--

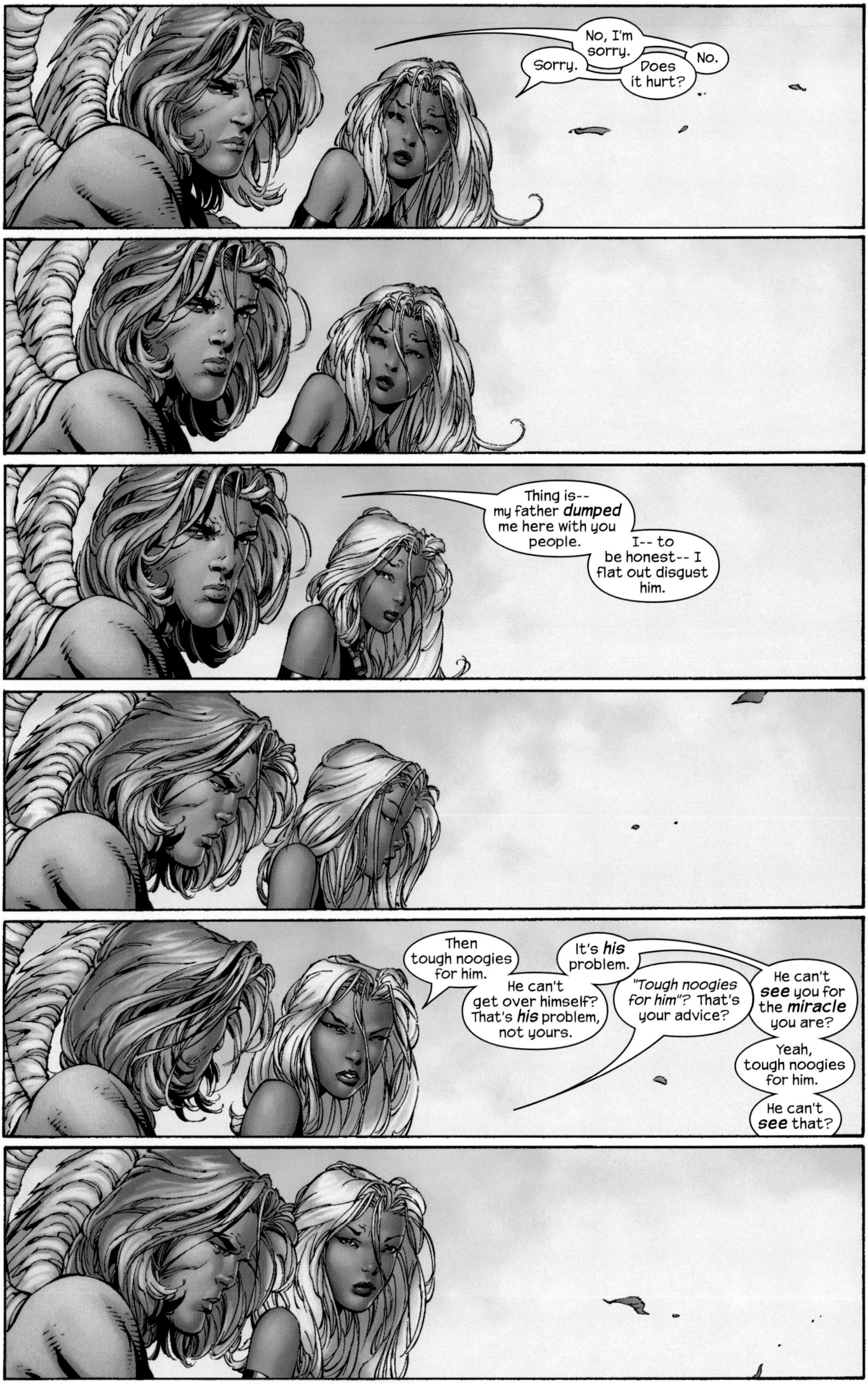
No, I'm sorry.
Sorry.
Does it hurt?
No.
Thing is-- my father *dumped* me here with you people.
I-- to be honest-- I flat out disgust him.
Then tough noogies for him.
He can't get over himself? That's *his* problem, not yours.
It's *his* problem.
"Tough noogies for him"? That's your advice?
He can't *see* you for the *miracle* you are?
Yeah, tough noogies for him.
He can't *see* that?

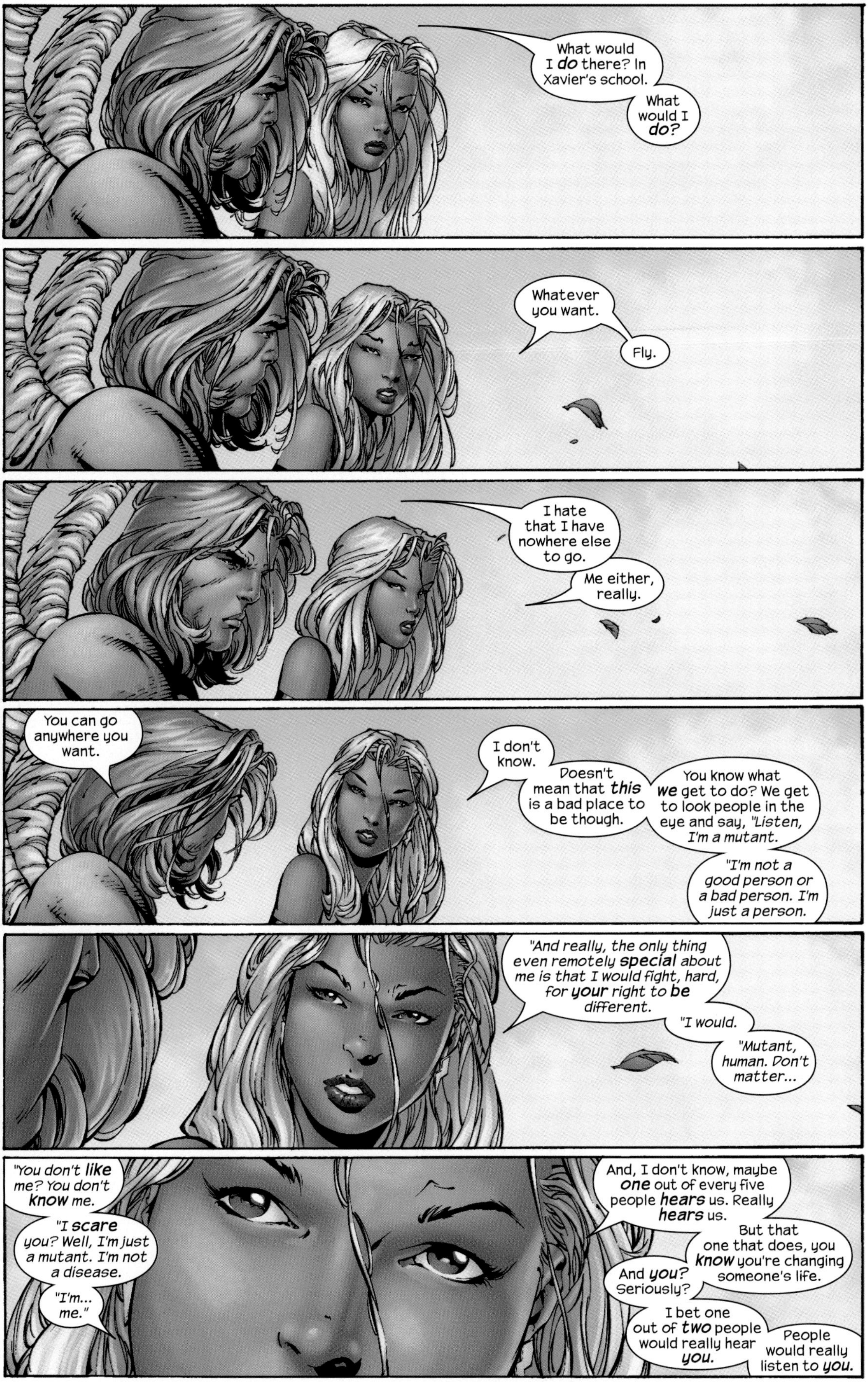
What would I *do* there? In Xavier's school.
What would I *do?*
Whatever you want.
Fly.
I hate that I have nowhere else to go.
Me either, really.
You can go anywhere you want.
I don't know.
Doesn't mean that *this* is a bad place to be though.
You know what *we* get to do? We get to look people in the eye and say, *"Listen, I'm a mutant.*
"I'm not a good person or a bad person. I'm just a person.
*"And really, the only thing even remotely **special** about me is that I would fight, hard, for **your** right to **be** different.*
"I would.
"Mutant, human. Don't matter...
*"You don't **like** me? You don't **know** me.*
*"I **scare** you? Well, I'm just a mutant. I'm not a disease.*
"I'm... me."
And, I don't know, maybe ***one*** out of every five people ***hears*** us. Really ***hears*** us.
But that one that does, you ***know*** you're changing someone's life.
And ***you?*** Seriously?
I bet one out of ***two*** people would really hear ***you.***
People would really listen to ***you.***

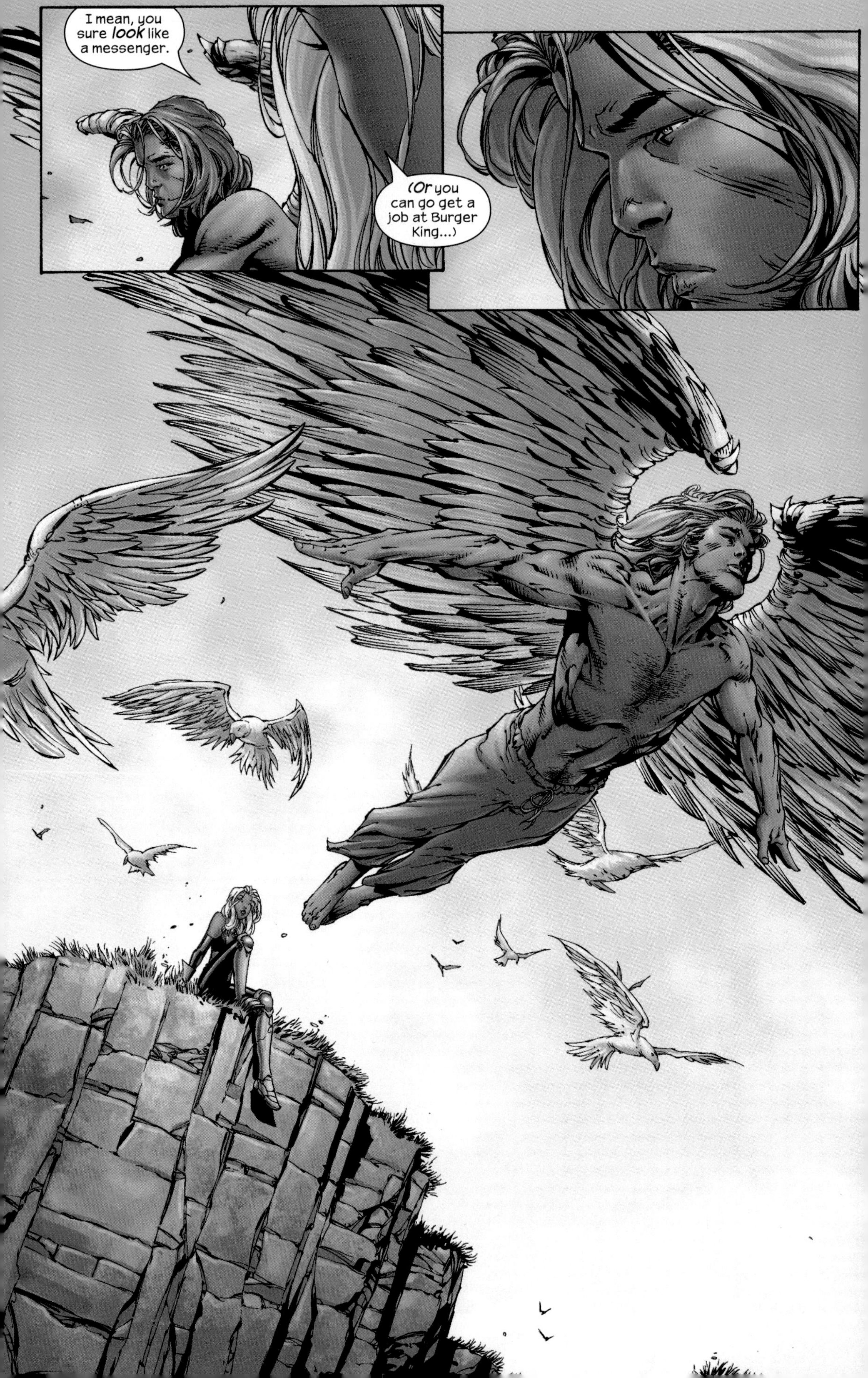
I mean, you sure *look* like a messenger.
(*Or* you can go get a job at Burger King...)

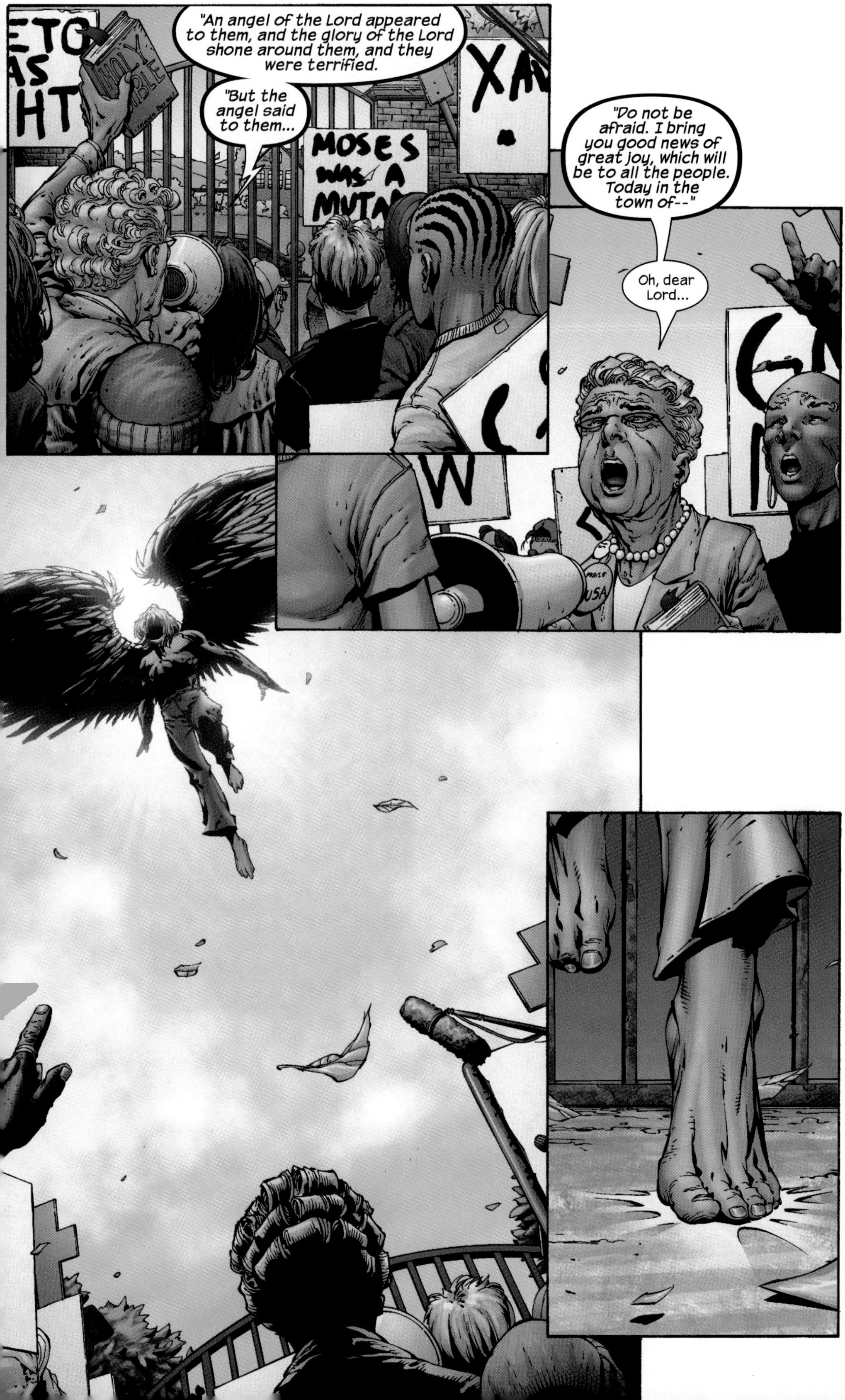
"An angel of the Lord appeared to them, and the glory of the Lord shone around them, and they were terrified.
"But the angel said to them...
"Do not be afraid. I bring you good news of great joy, which will be to all the people. Today in the town of--"
Oh, dear Lord...
MOSES WAS A MUTA
HOLY BIBLE

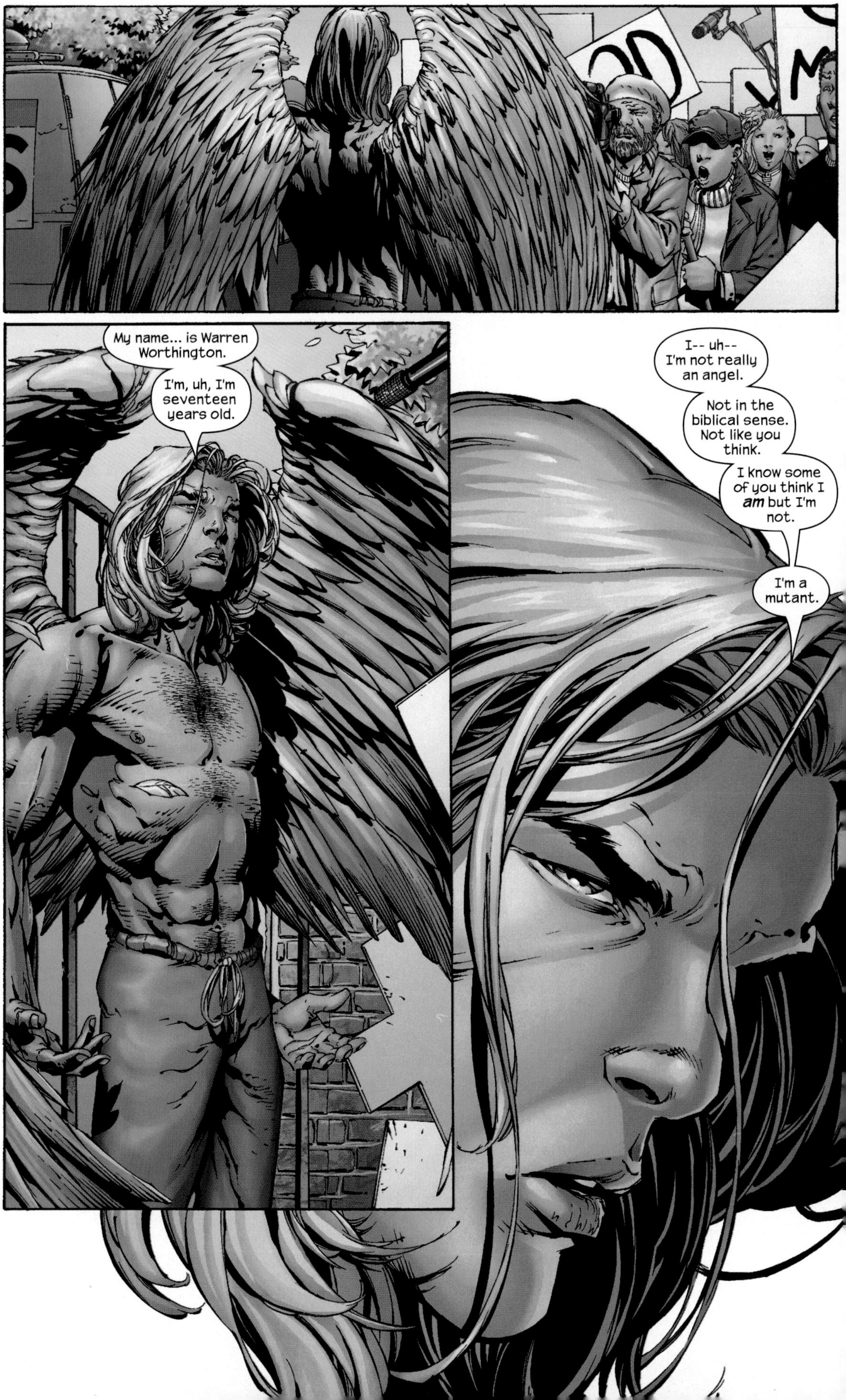
My name... is Warren Worthington.
I'm, uh, I'm seventeen years old.
I-- uh-- I'm not really an angel.
Not in the biblical sense. Not like you think.
I know some of you think I *am* but I'm not.
I'm a mutant.

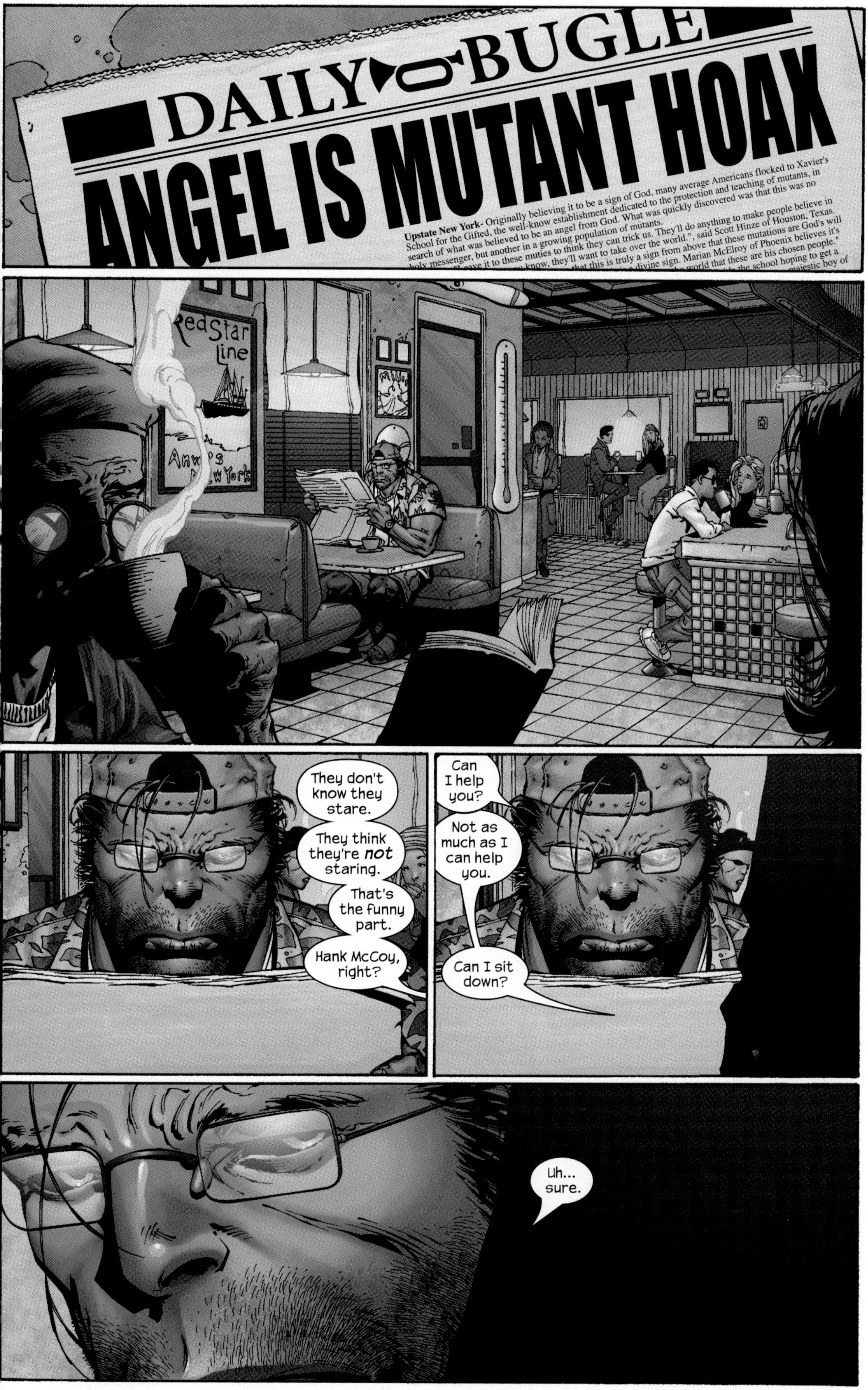
DAILY BUGLE
ANGEL IS MUTANT HOAX
Upstate New York- Originally believing it to be a sign of God, many average Americans flocked to Xavier's School for the Gifted, the well-know establishment dedicated to the protection and teaching of mutants, in search of what was believed to be an angel from God. What was quickly discovered was that this was no holy messenger, but another in a growing population of mutants.
Red Star Line
They don't know they stare.
They think they're *not* staring.
That's the funny part.
Hank McCoy, right?
Can I help you?
Not as much as I can help you.
Can I sit down?
Uh... sure.

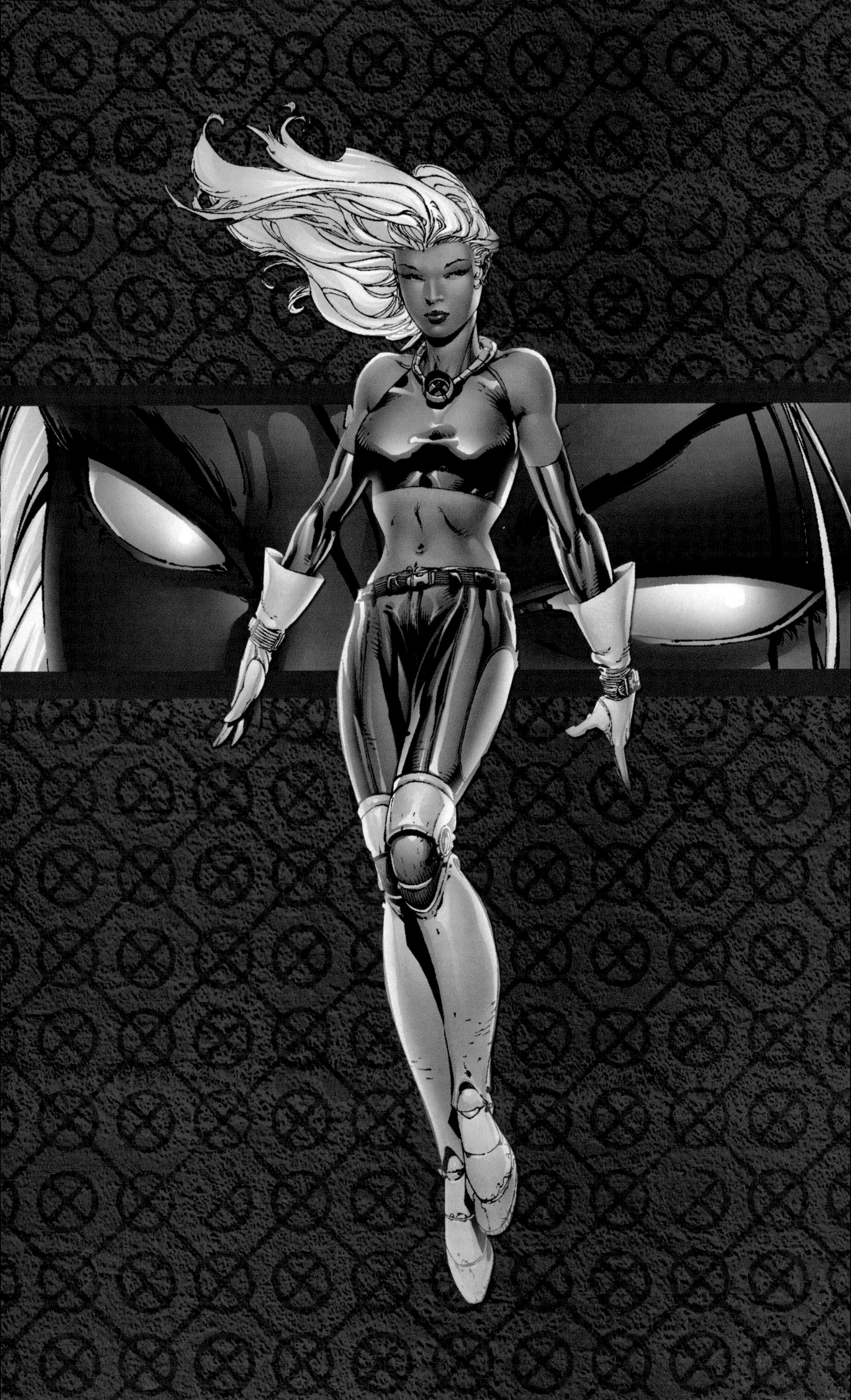

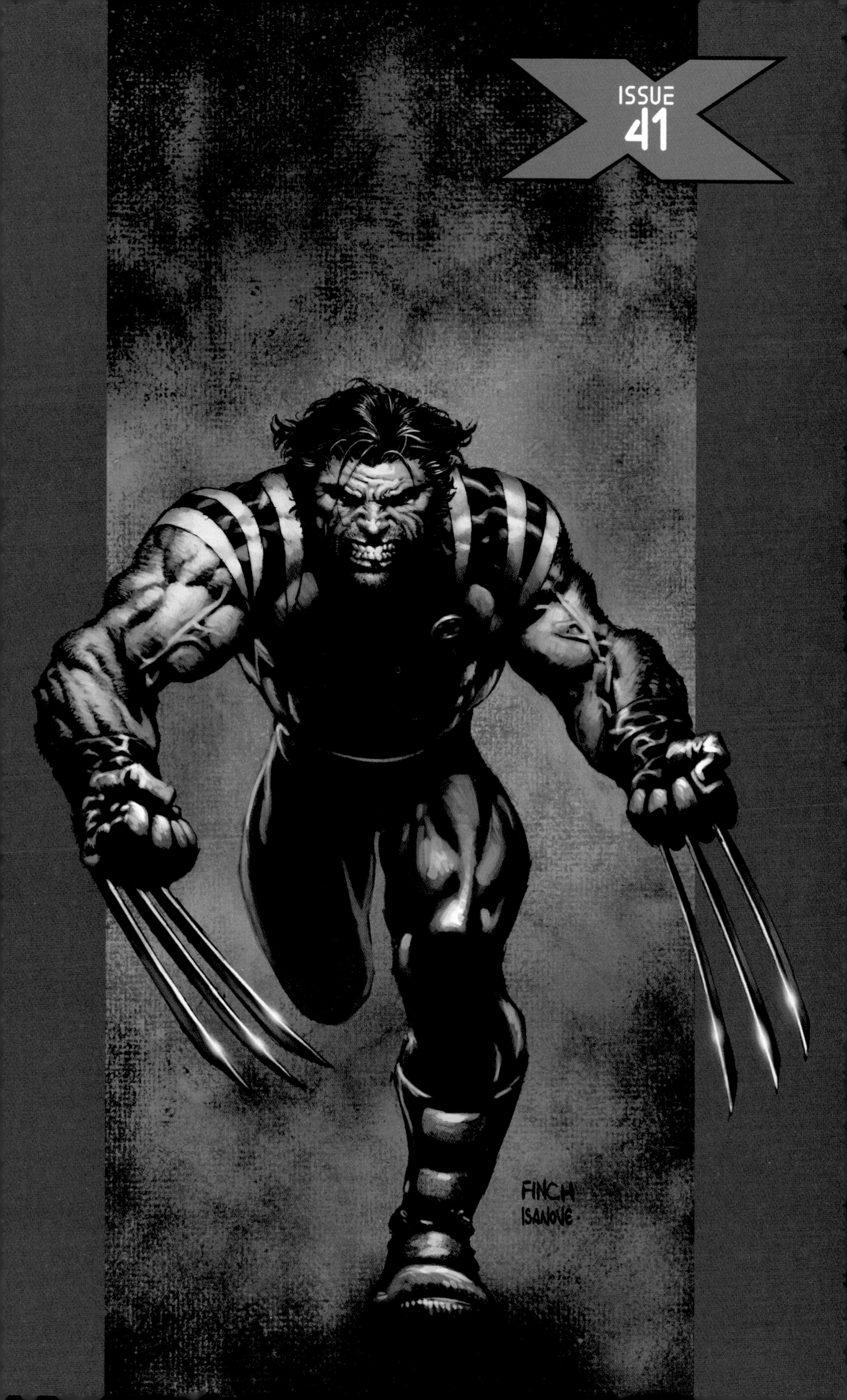
ISSUE
41
FINCH
ISANOVE

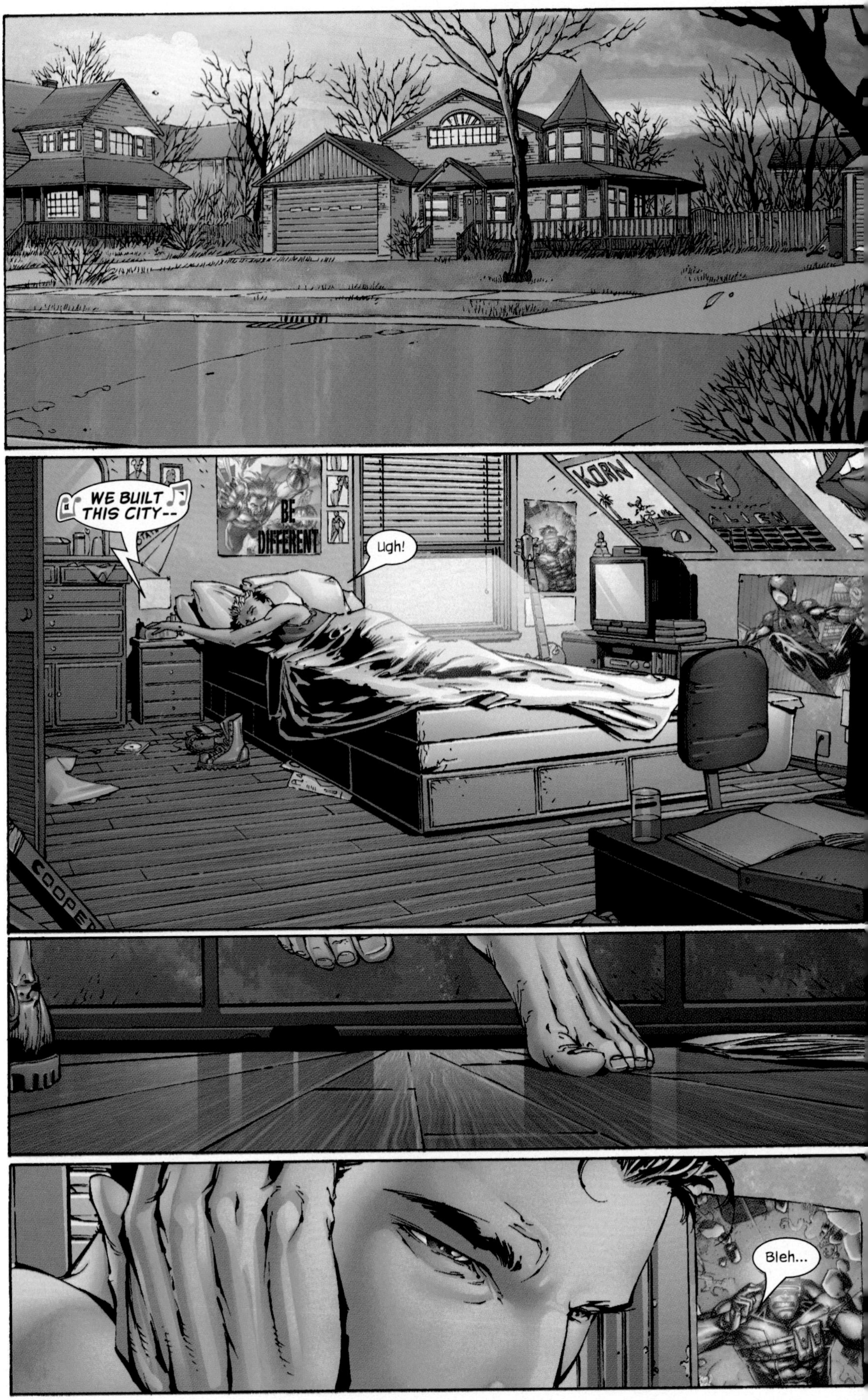
WE BUILT THIS CITY--
BE DIFFERENT
KORN
ALIEN
Ugh!
COOPER
Bleh...

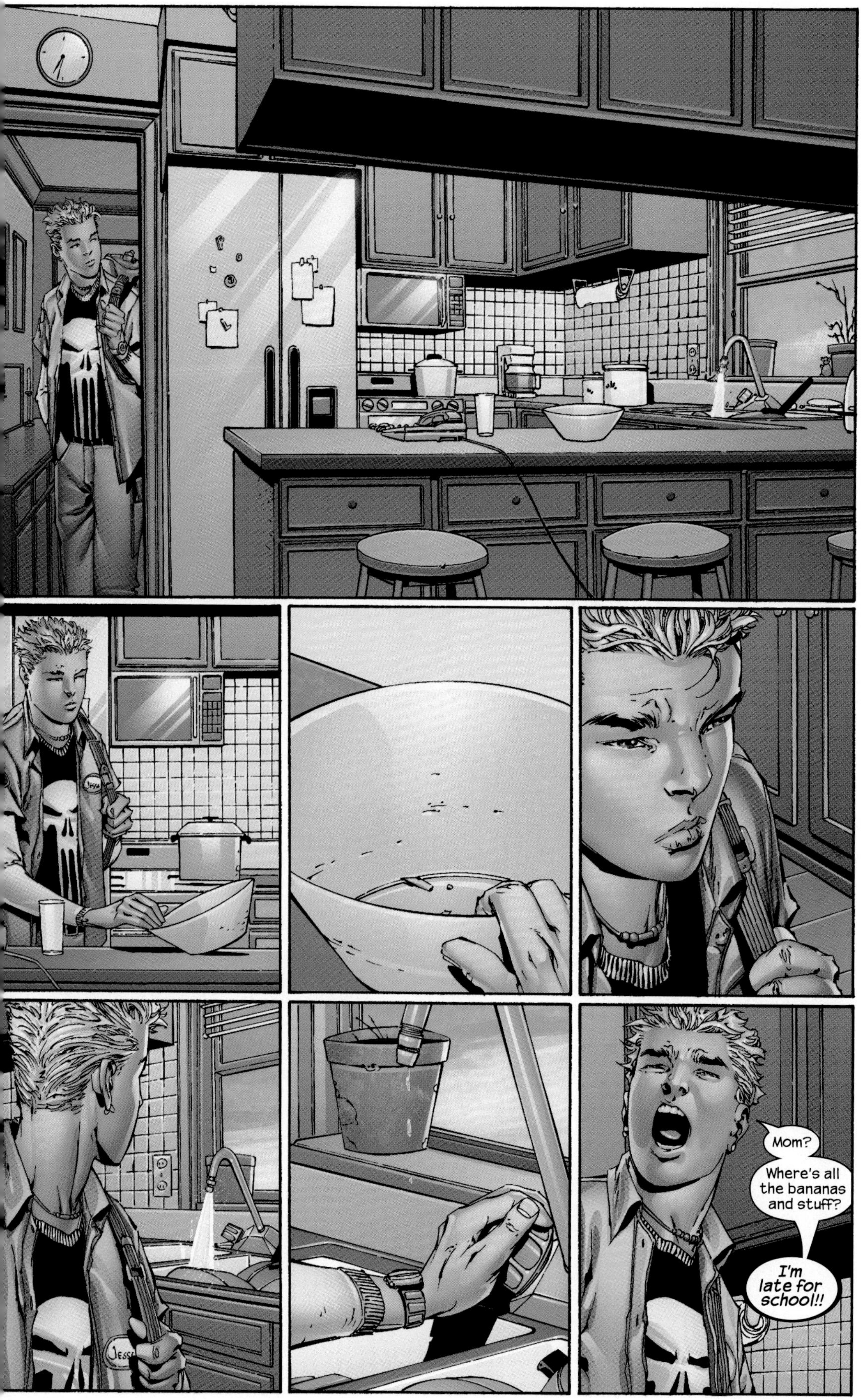
Mom?
Where's all the bananas and stuff?
I'm late for school!!

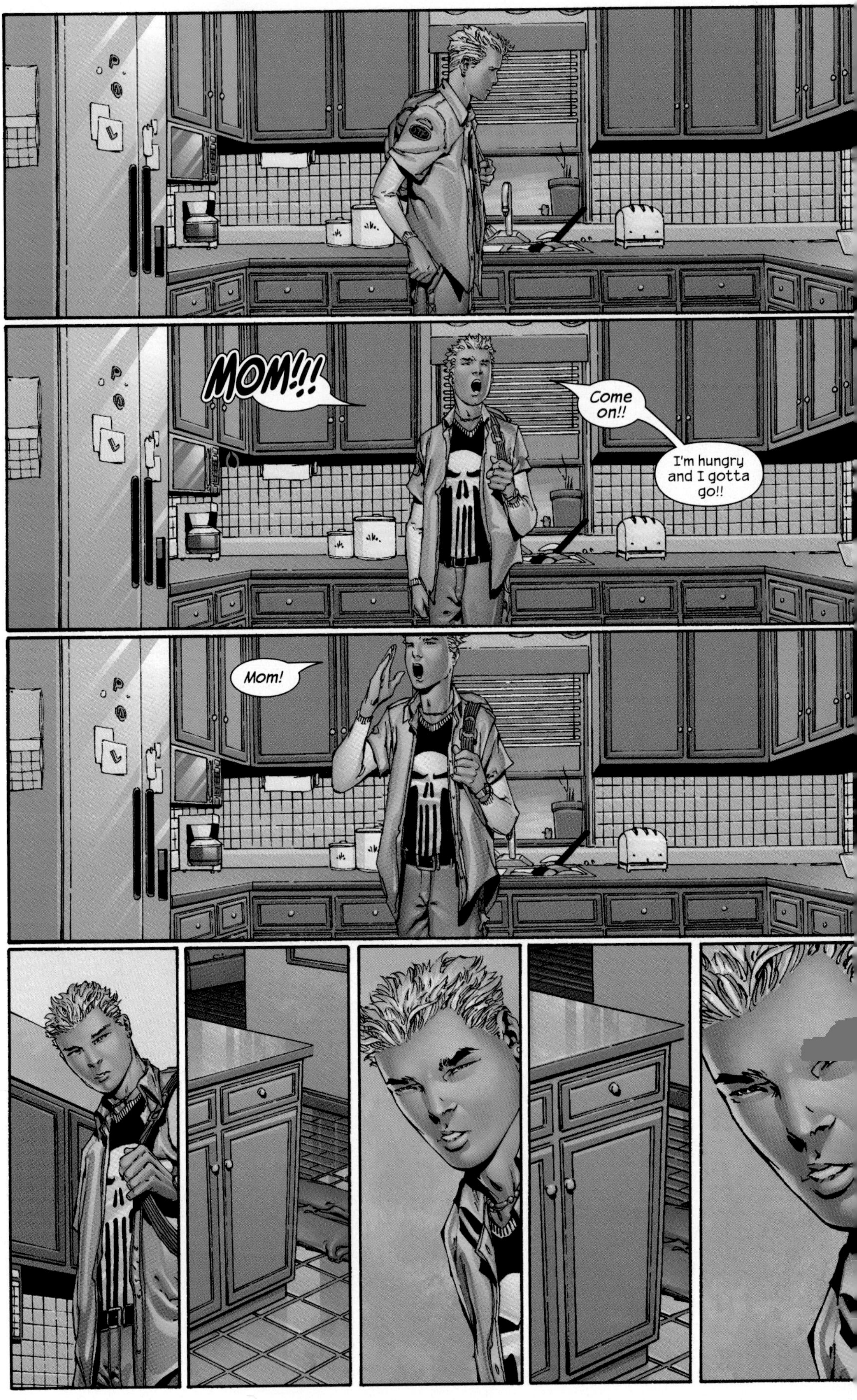
MOM!!!
Come on!!
I'm hungry and I gotta go!!
Mom!

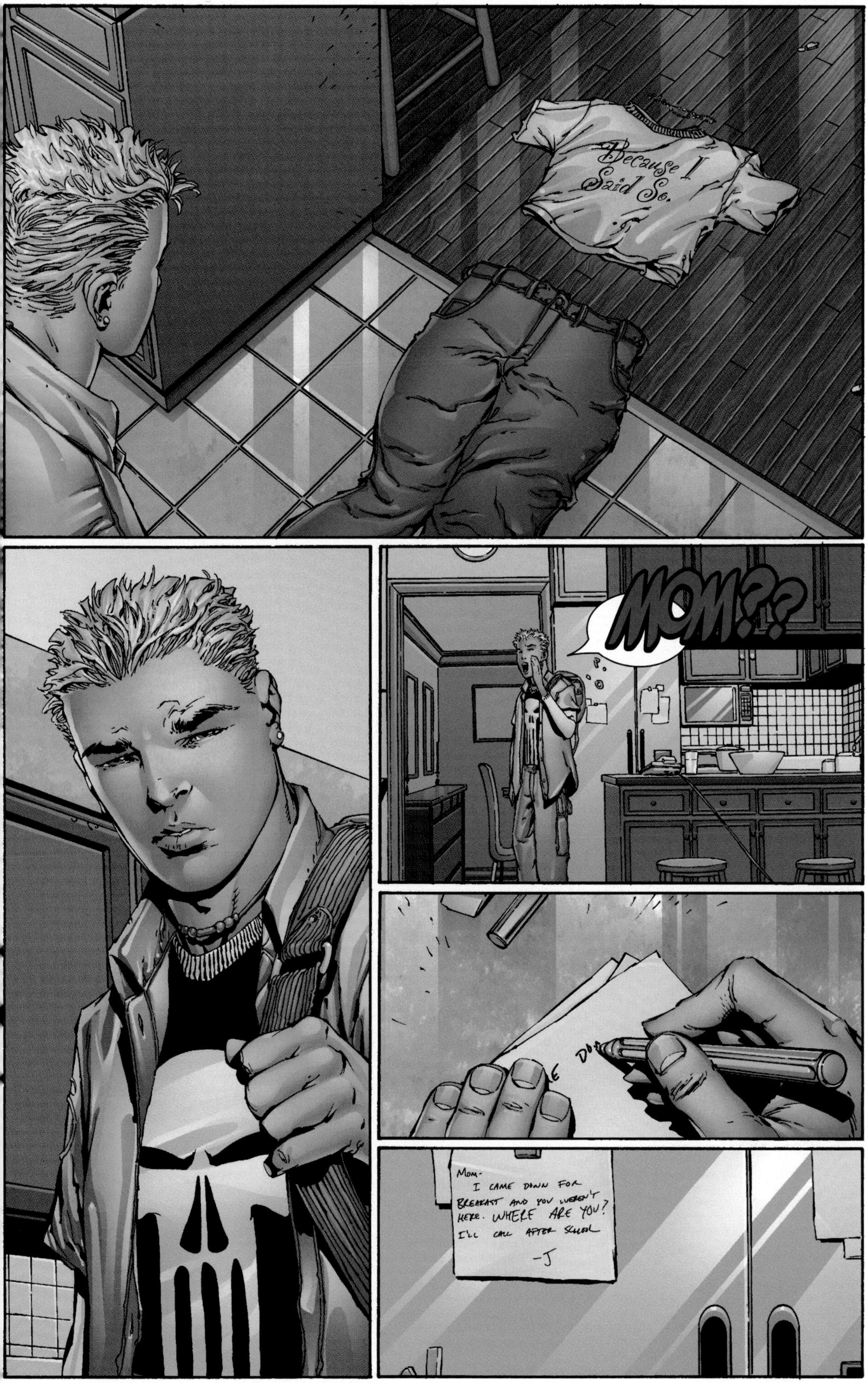
Because I Said So.
MOM??
Mom-
I CAME DOWN FOR BREAKFAST AND YOU WEREN'T HERE. WHERE ARE YOU? I'LL CALL AFTER SCHOOL
-J

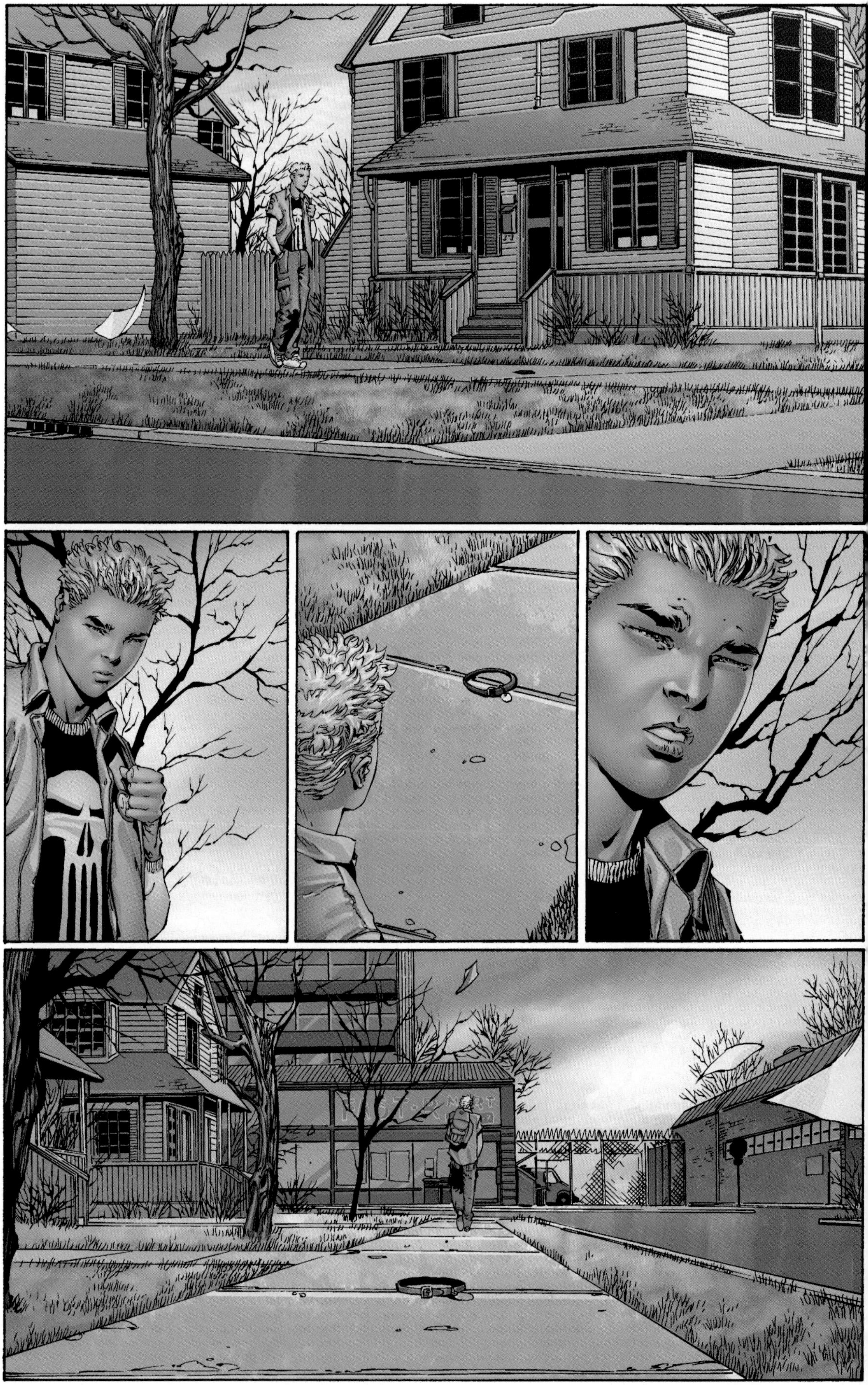

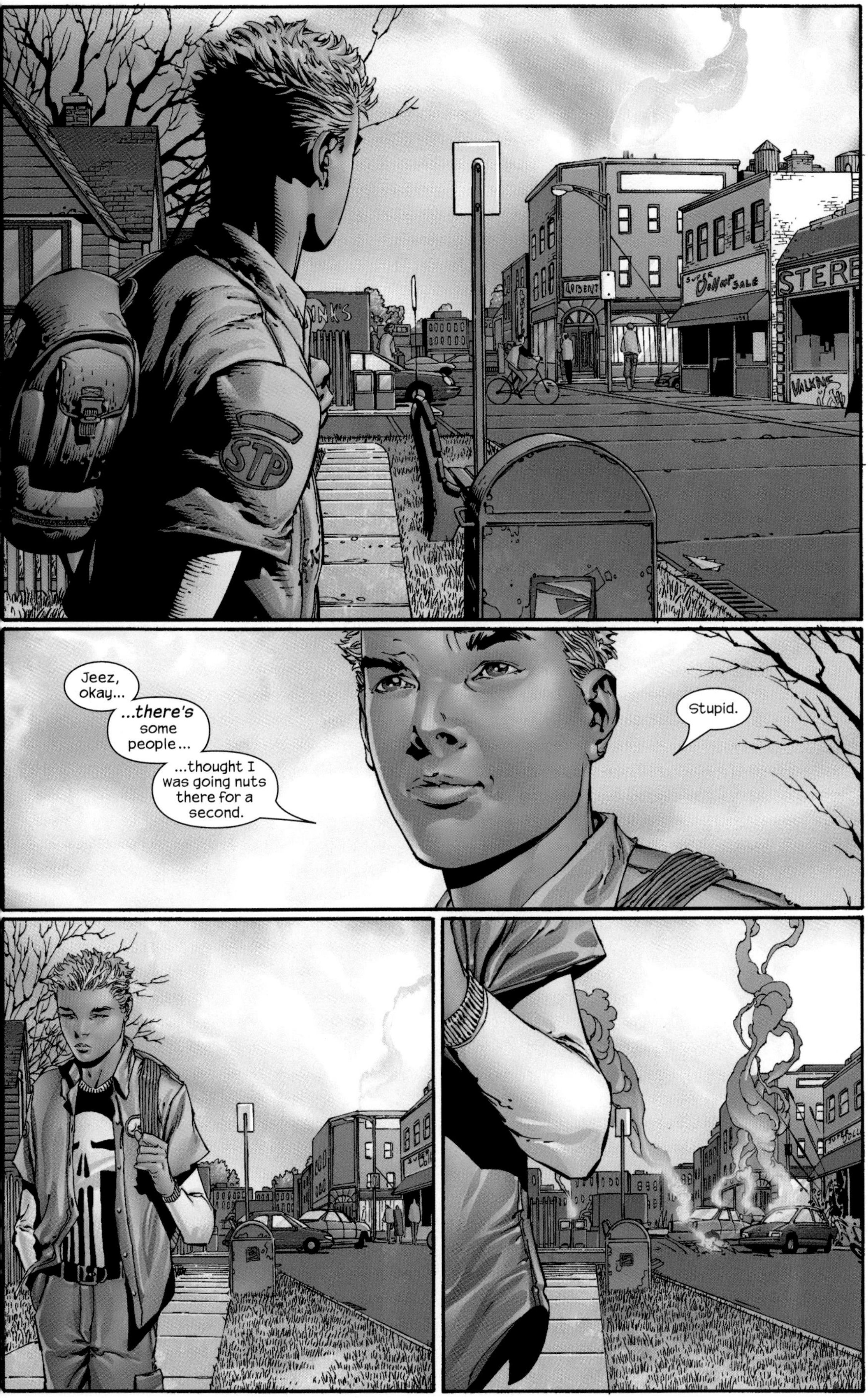
Jeez, okay...
...*there's* some people...
...thought I was going nuts there for a second.
Stupid.

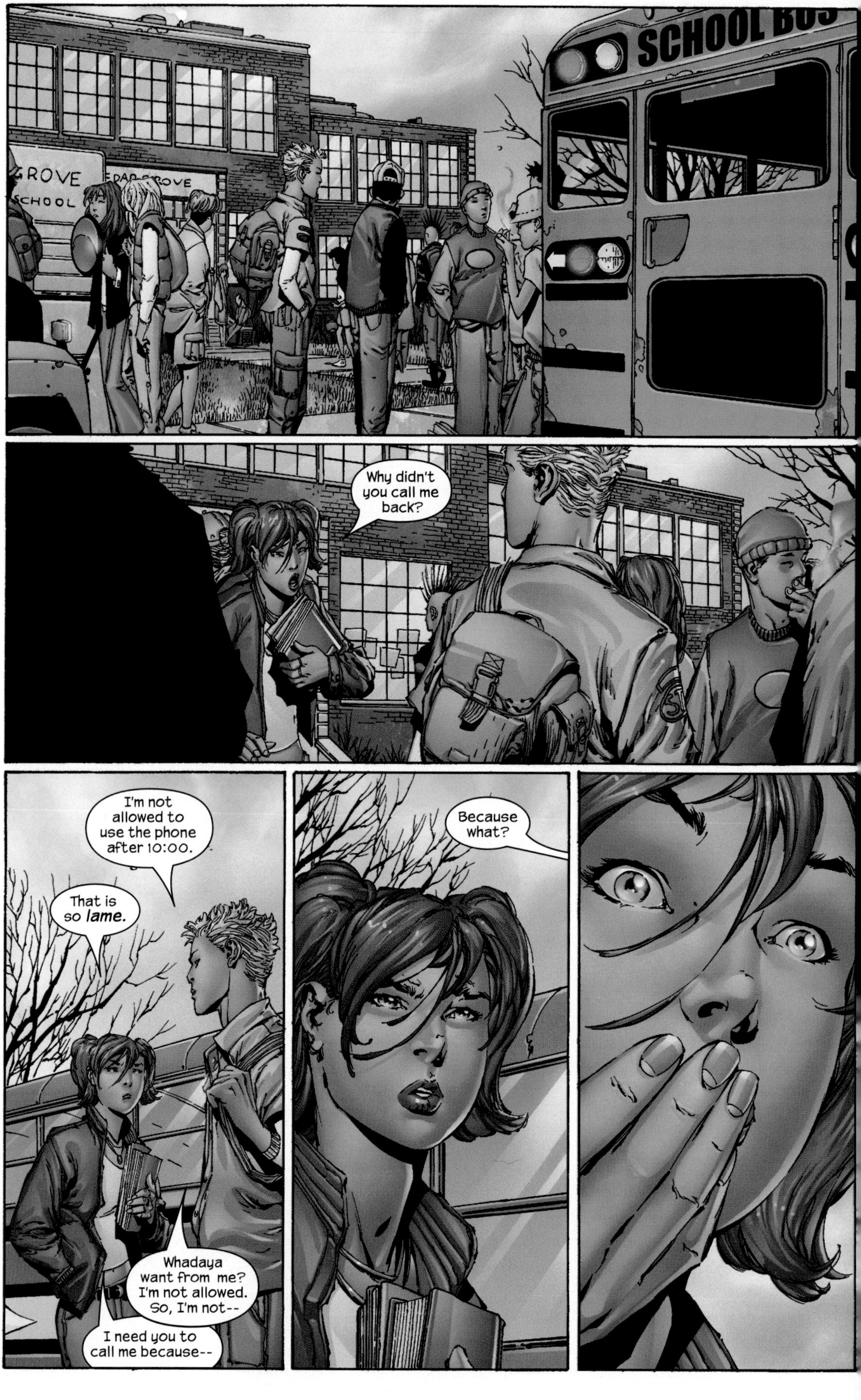
SCHOOL BUS
CEDAR GROVE SCHOOL
Why didn't you call me back?
I'm not allowed to use the phone after 10:00.
That is so *lame.*
Whadaya want from me? I'm not allowed. So, I'm not--
I need you to call me because--
Because what?

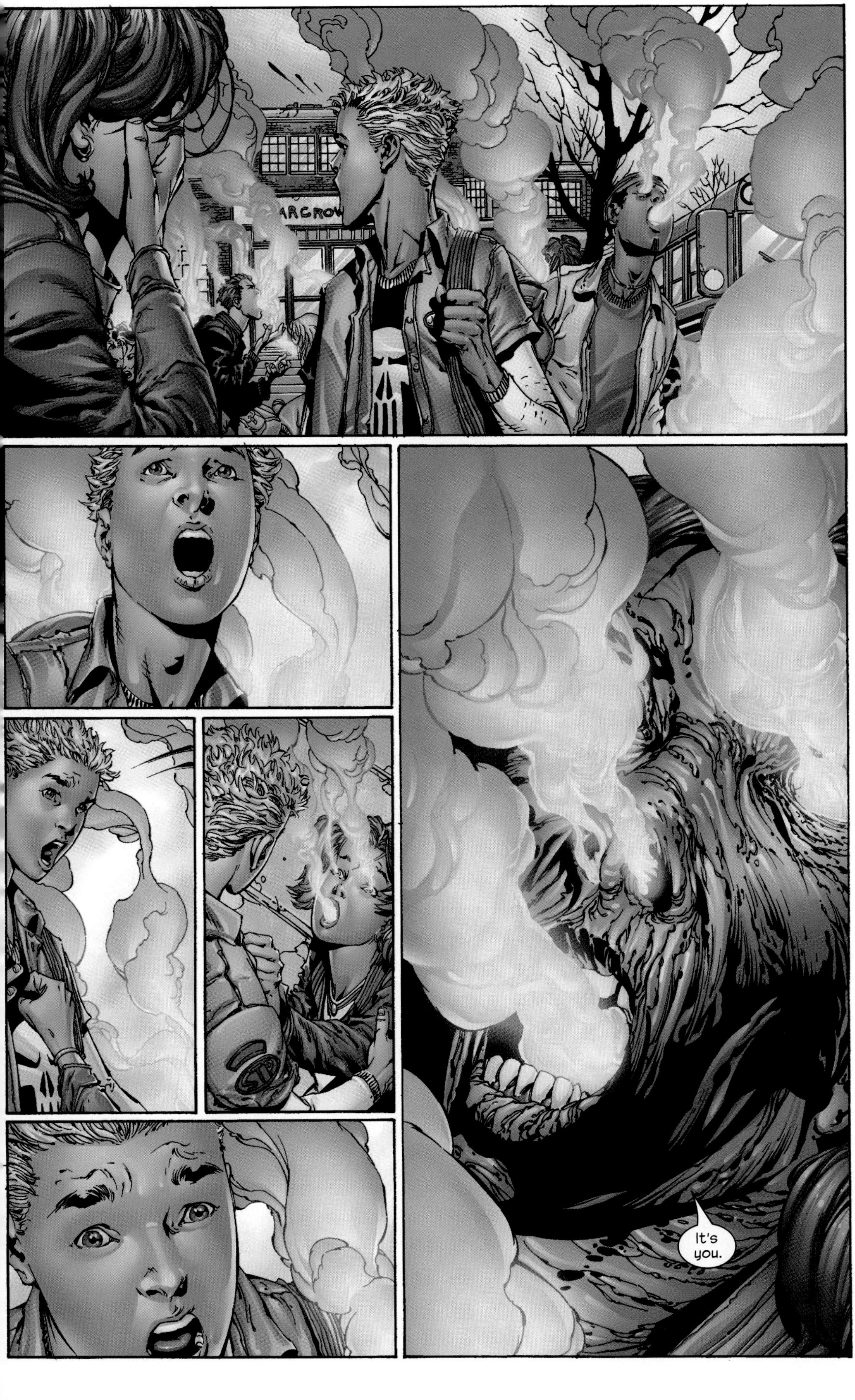
It's you.

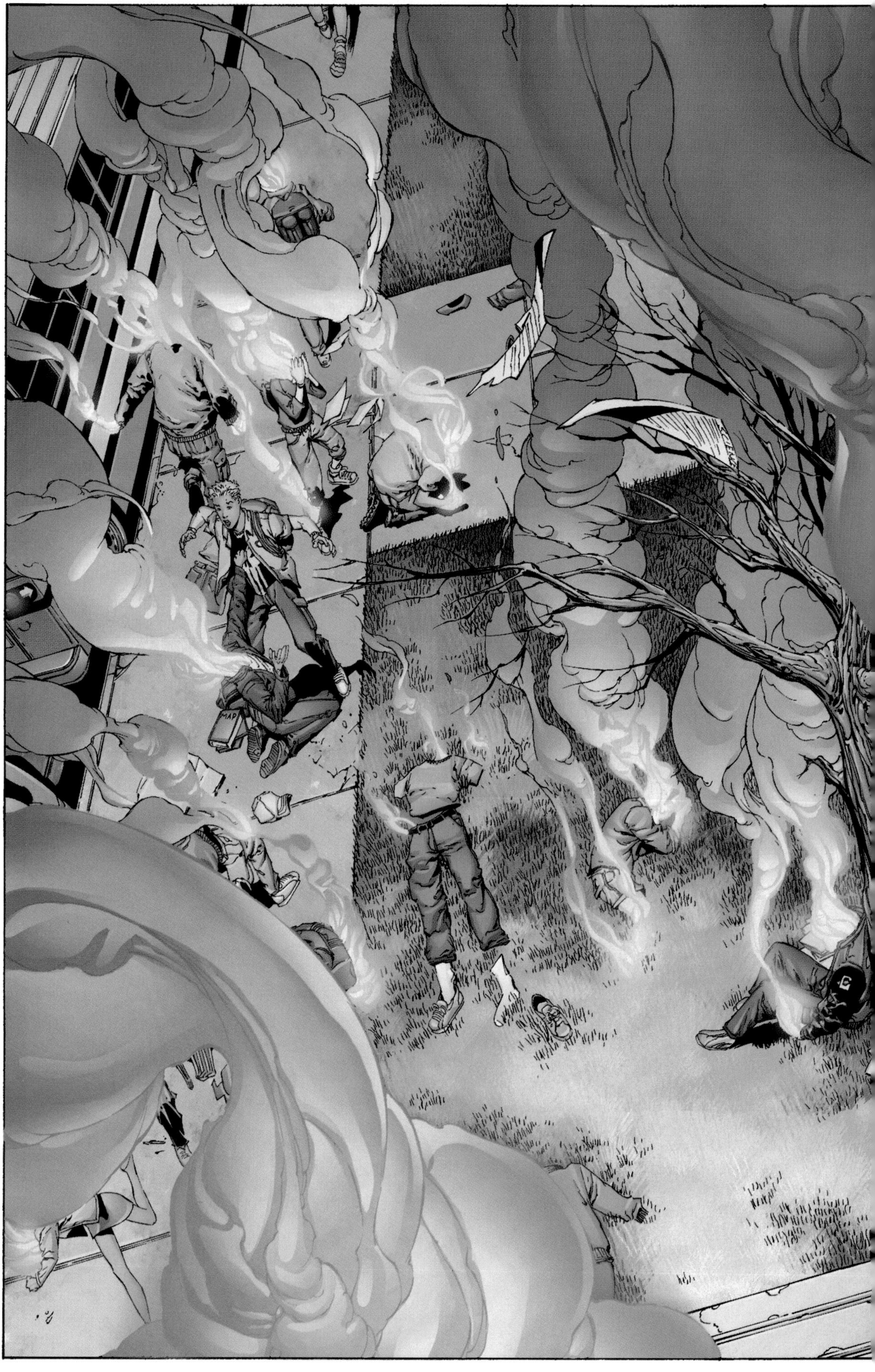
MAP

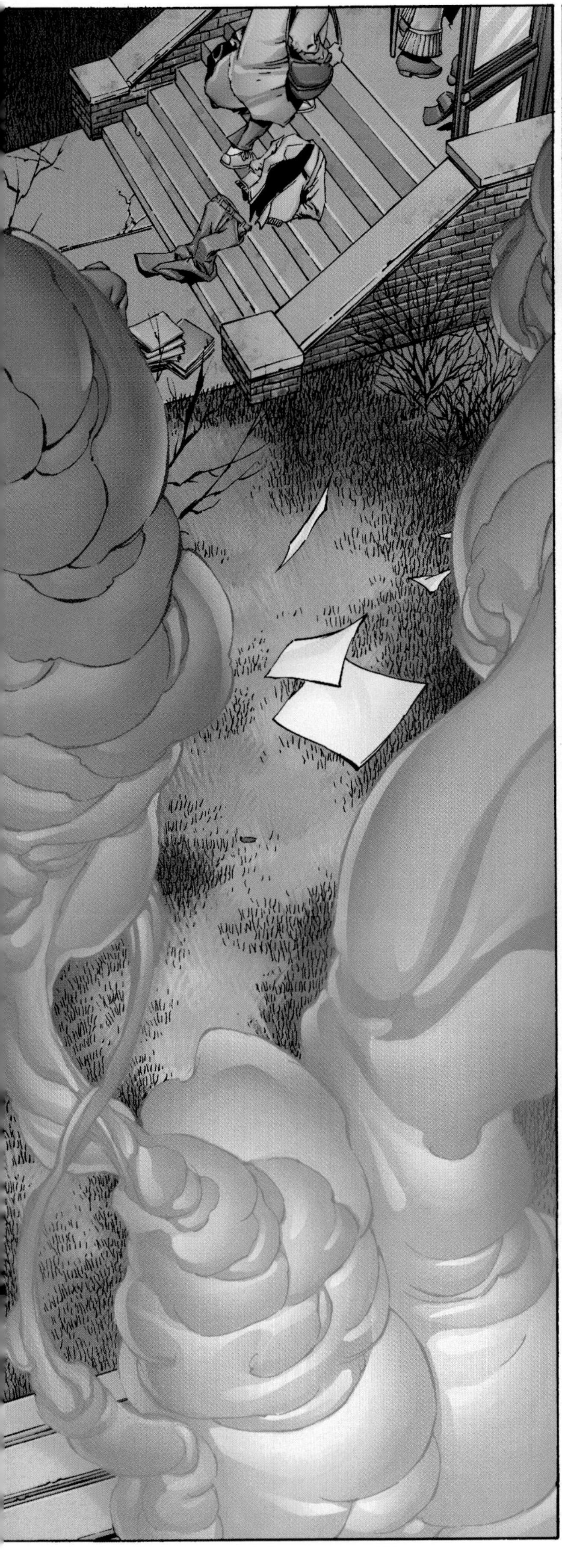
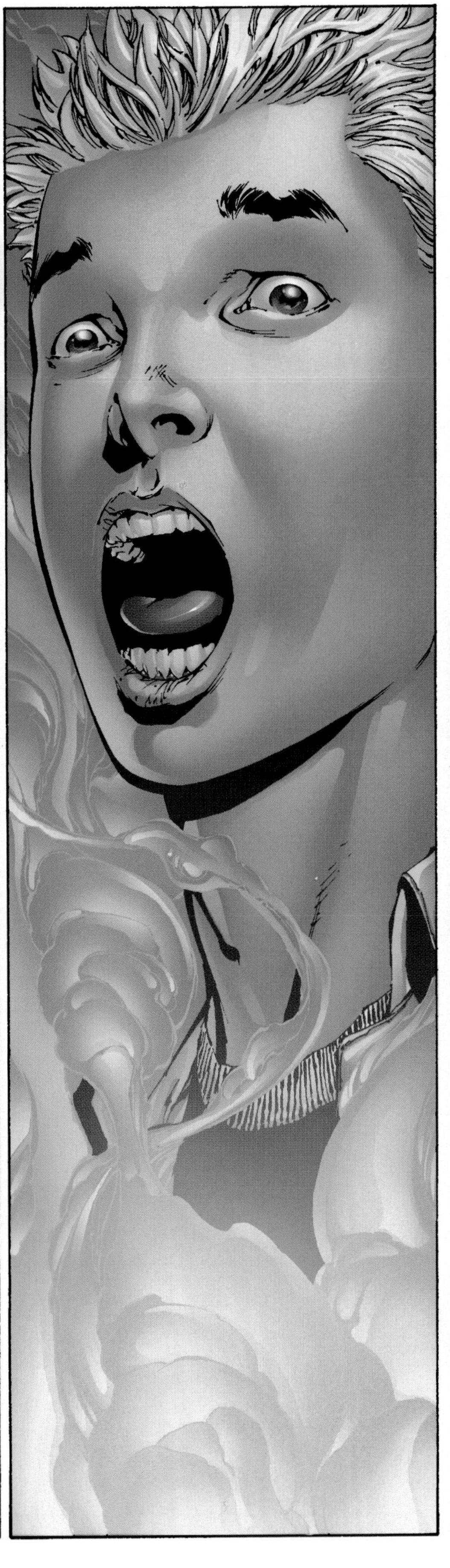

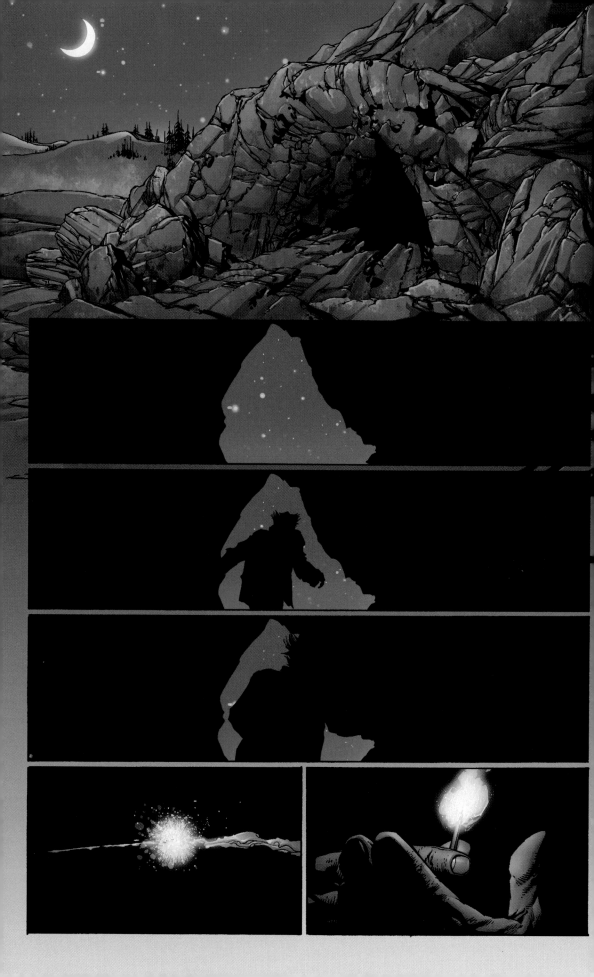

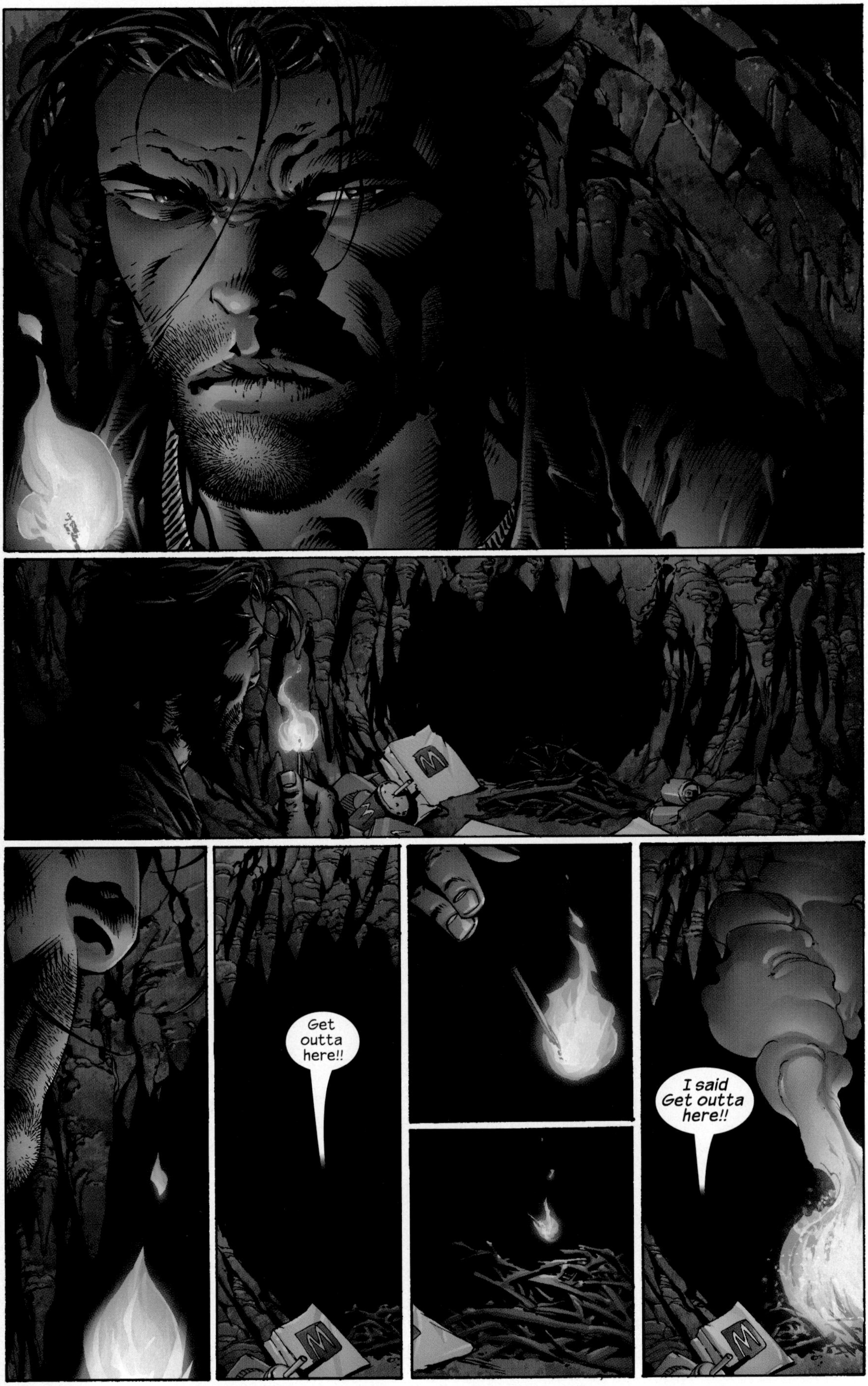
Get outta here!!
I said Get outta here!!

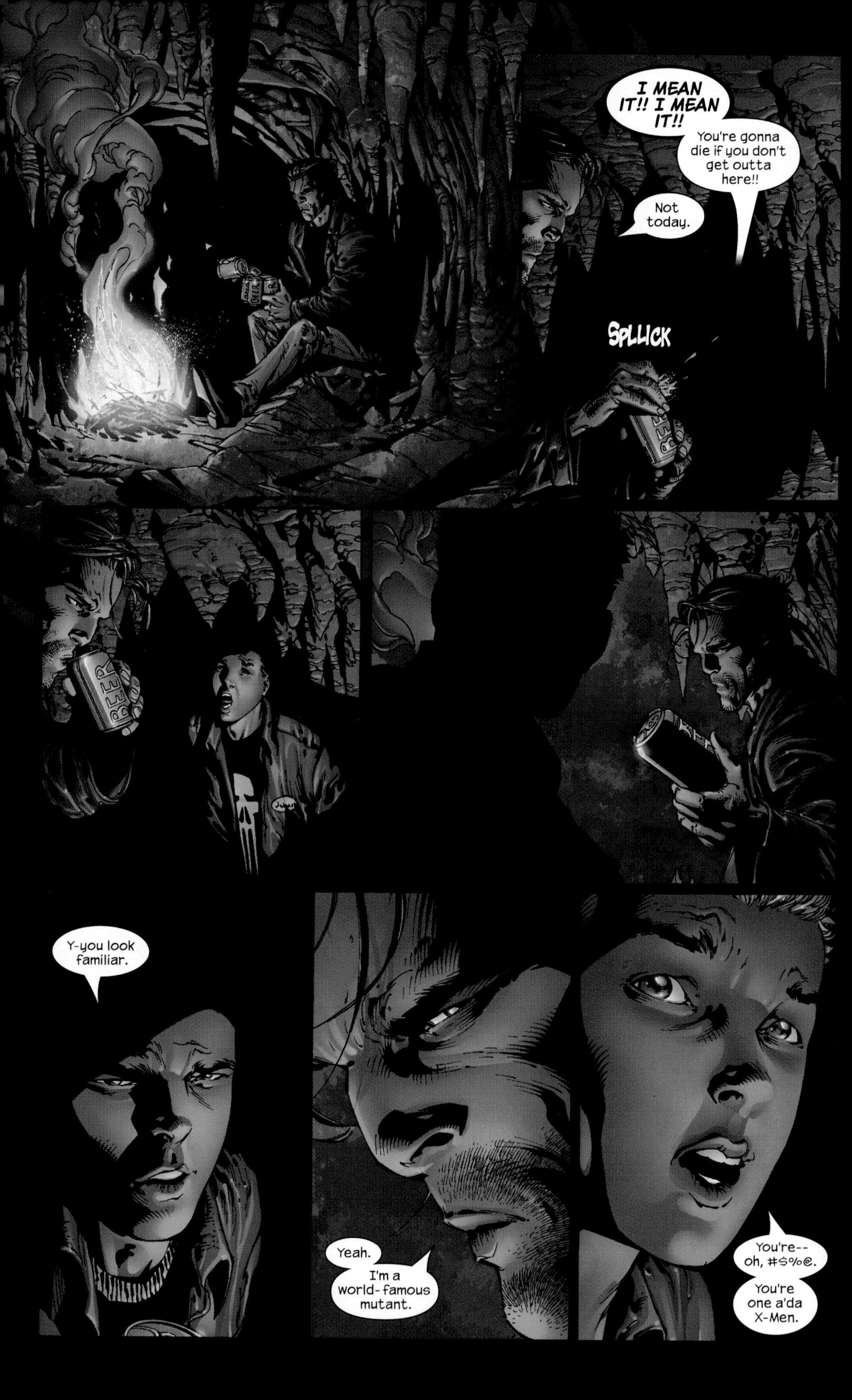

I MEAN IT!! I MEAN IT!!
You're gonna die if you don't get outta here!!
Not today.
SPLLICK
BEER
Y-you look familiar.
Yeah.
I'm a world-famous mutant.
You're-- oh, #$%@.
You're one a'da X-Men.

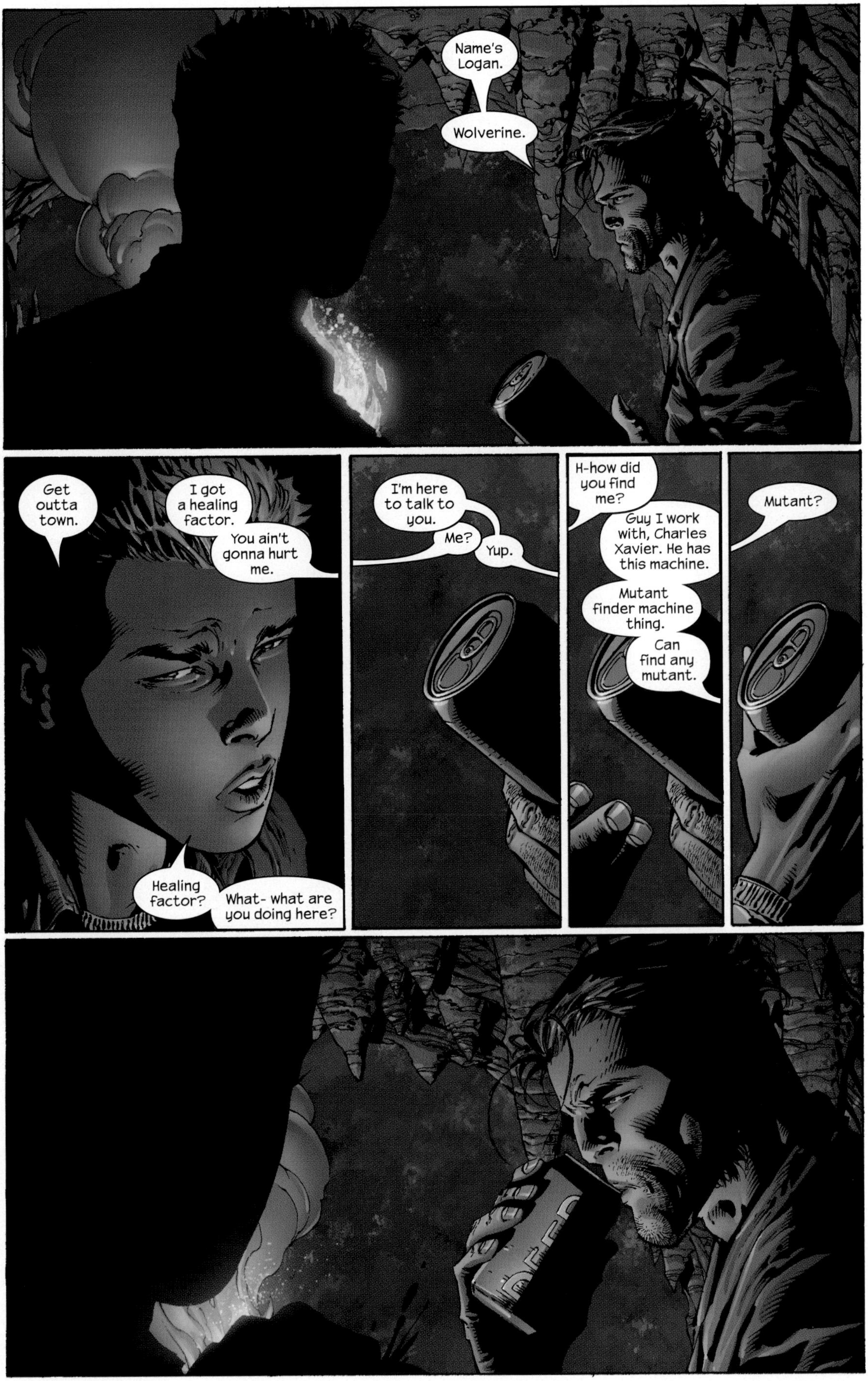
Name's Logan.
Wolverine.
Get outta town.
I got a healing factor.
You ain't gonna hurt me.
Healing factor?
What- what are you doing here?
I'm here to talk to you.
Me?
Yup.
H-how did you find me?
Guy I work with, Charles Xavier. He has this machine.
Mutant finder machine thing.
Can find any mutant.
Mutant?

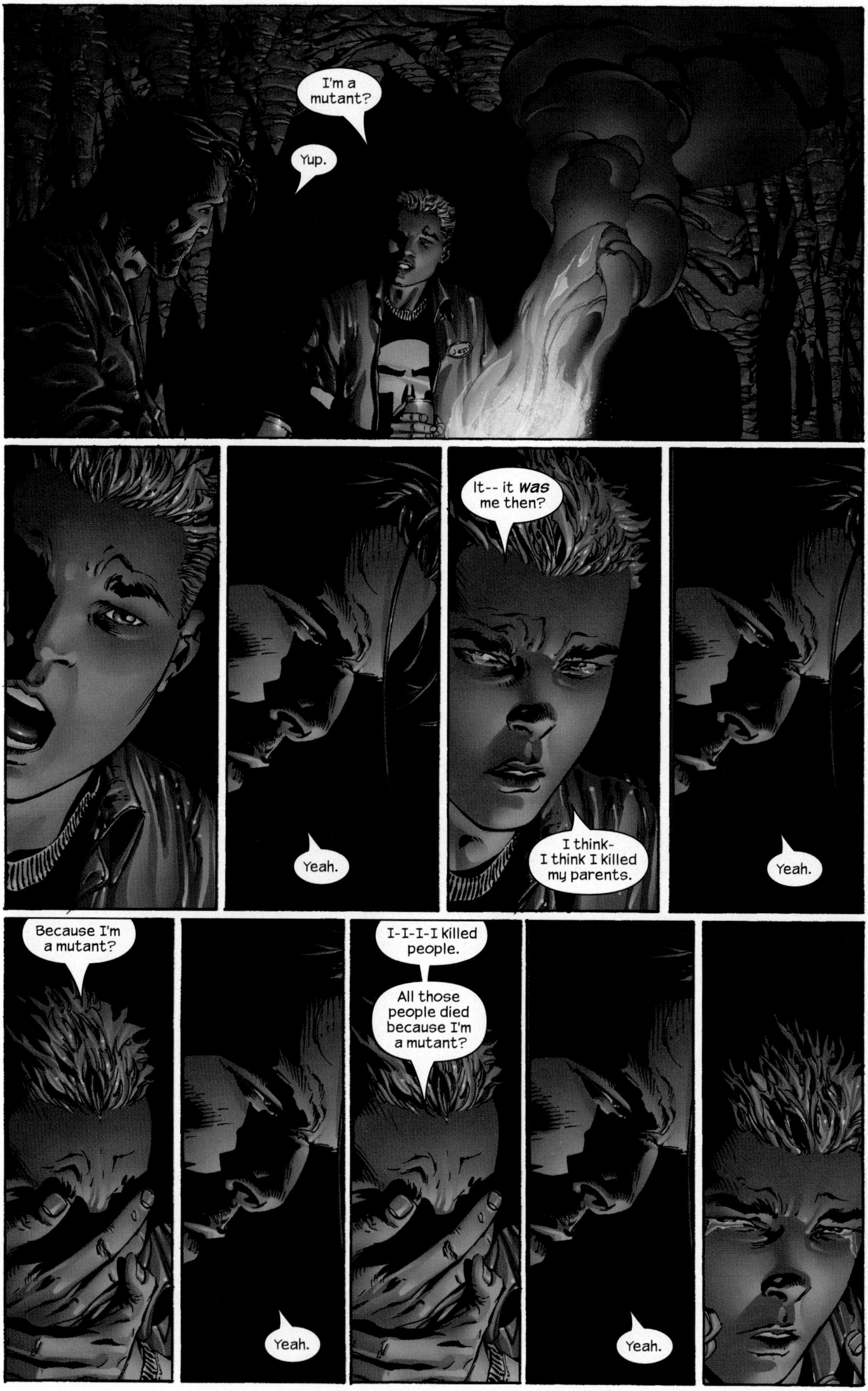
I'm a mutant?
Yup.
Yeah.
It-- it *was* me then?
I think- I think I killed my parents.
Yeah.
Because I'm a mutant?
Yeah.
I-I-I-I killed people.
All those people died because I'm a mutant?
Yeah.

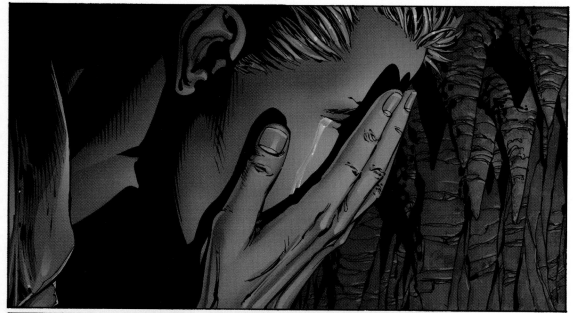

Sniff...

How many people did I *kill*?

You really don't want to know.

No. Yes.

Please.

They say 265.

Maybe more.

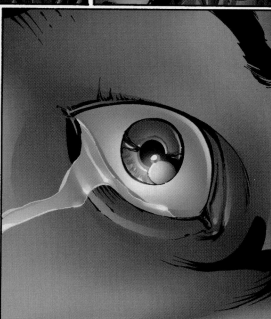

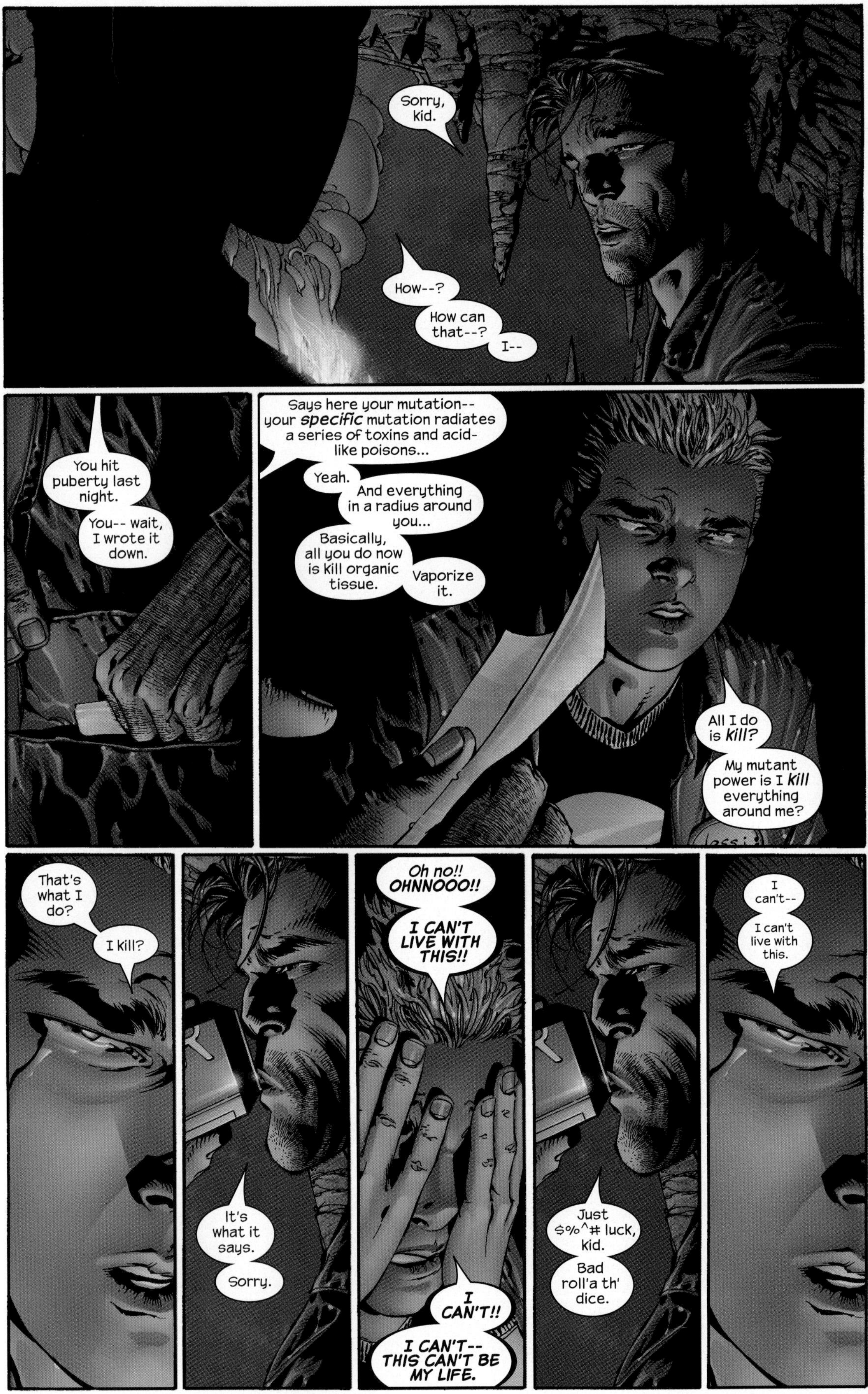
Sorry, kid.
How--?
How can that--?
I--
You hit puberty last night.
You-- wait, I wrote it down.
Says here your mutation-- your *specific* mutation radiates a series of toxins and acid-like poisons...
Yeah.
And everything in a radius around you...
Basically, all you do now is kill organic tissue.
Vaporize it.
All I do is *kill?*
My mutant power is I *kill* everything around me?
That's what I do?
I kill?
It's what it says.
Sorry.
Oh no!! OHNNOOO!!
I CAN'T LIVE WITH THIS!!
I CAN'T!!
I CAN'T-- THIS CAN'T BE MY LIFE.
Just $%^# luck, kid.
Bad roll'a th' dice.
I can't--
I can't live with this.

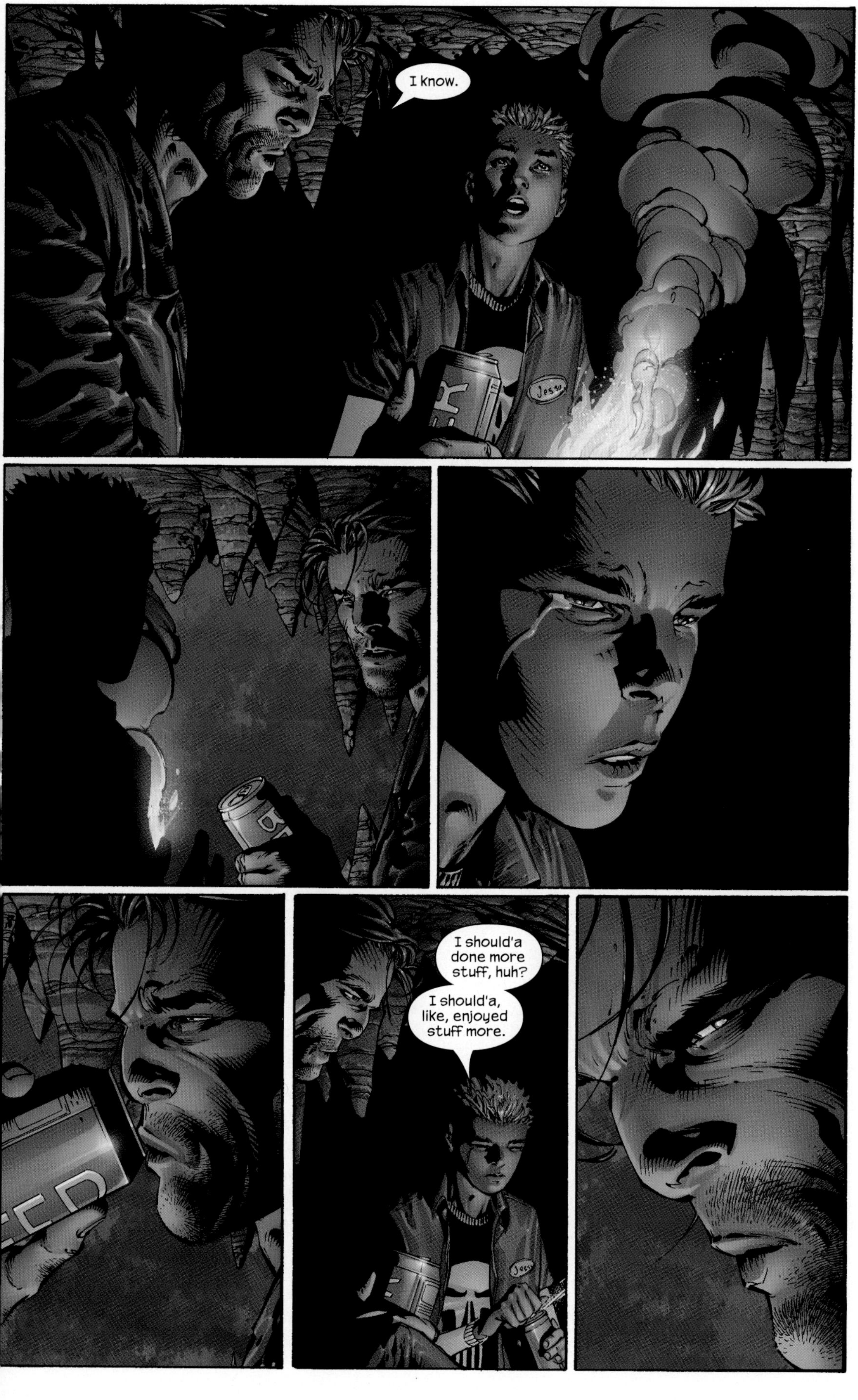
I know.
I should'a done more stuff, huh?
I should'a, like, enjoyed stuff more.

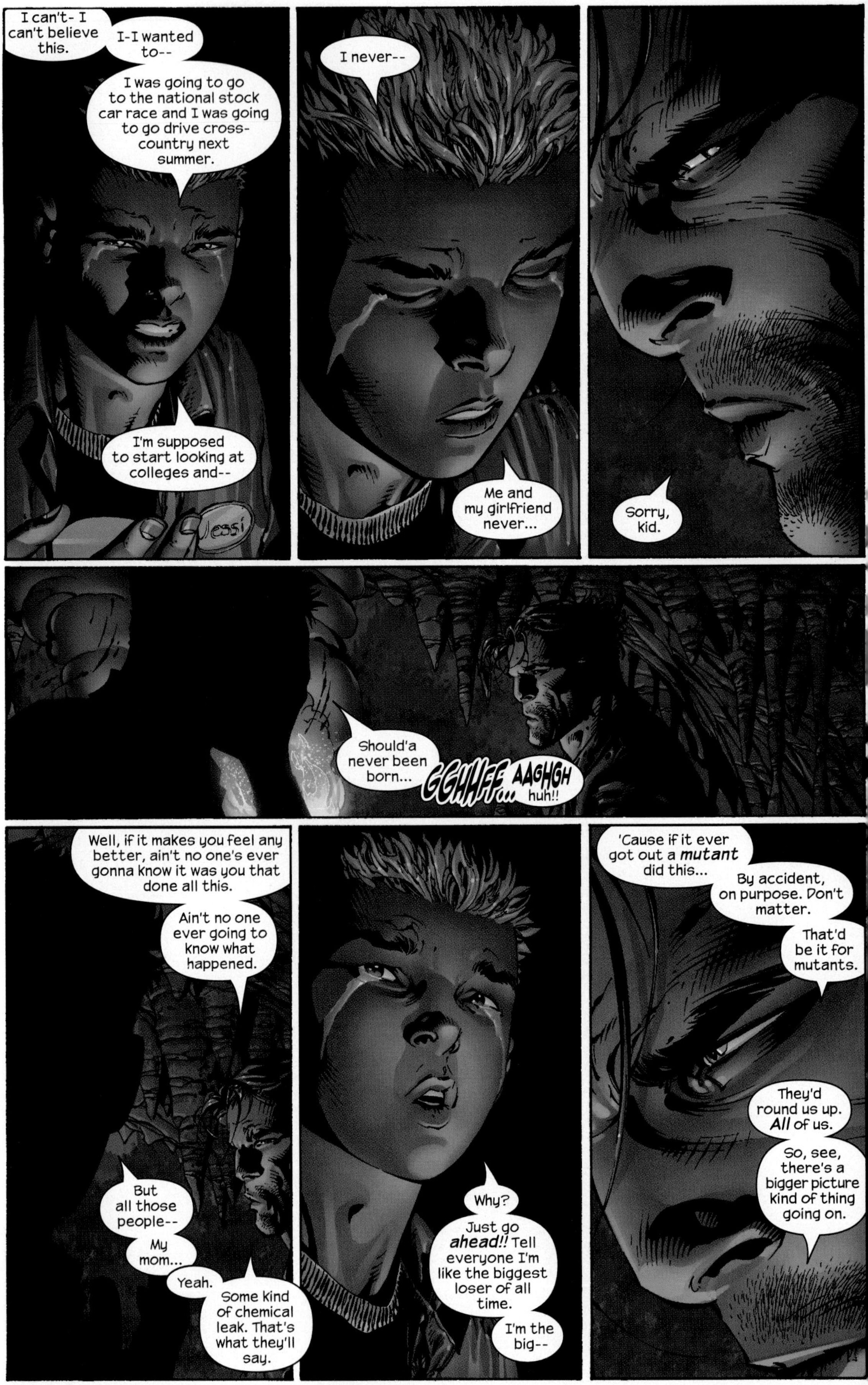
I can't- I can't believe this.
I-I wanted to--
I was going to go to the national stock car race and I was going to go drive cross-country next summer.
I'm supposed to start looking at colleges and--
Jessi
I never--
Me and my girlfriend never...
Sorry, kid.
Should'a never been born...
GGHHFF... AAGHGH huh!!
Well, if it makes you feel any better, ain't no one's ever gonna know it was you that done all this.
Ain't no one ever going to know what happened.
But all those people--
My mom...
Yeah.
Some kind of chemical leak. That's what they'll say.
Why?
Just go *ahead!!* Tell everyone I'm like the biggest loser of all time.
I'm the big--
'Cause if it ever got out a *mutant* did this...
By accident, on purpose. Don't matter.
That'd be it for mutants.
They'd round us up. *All* of us.
So, see, there's a bigger picture kind of thing going on.

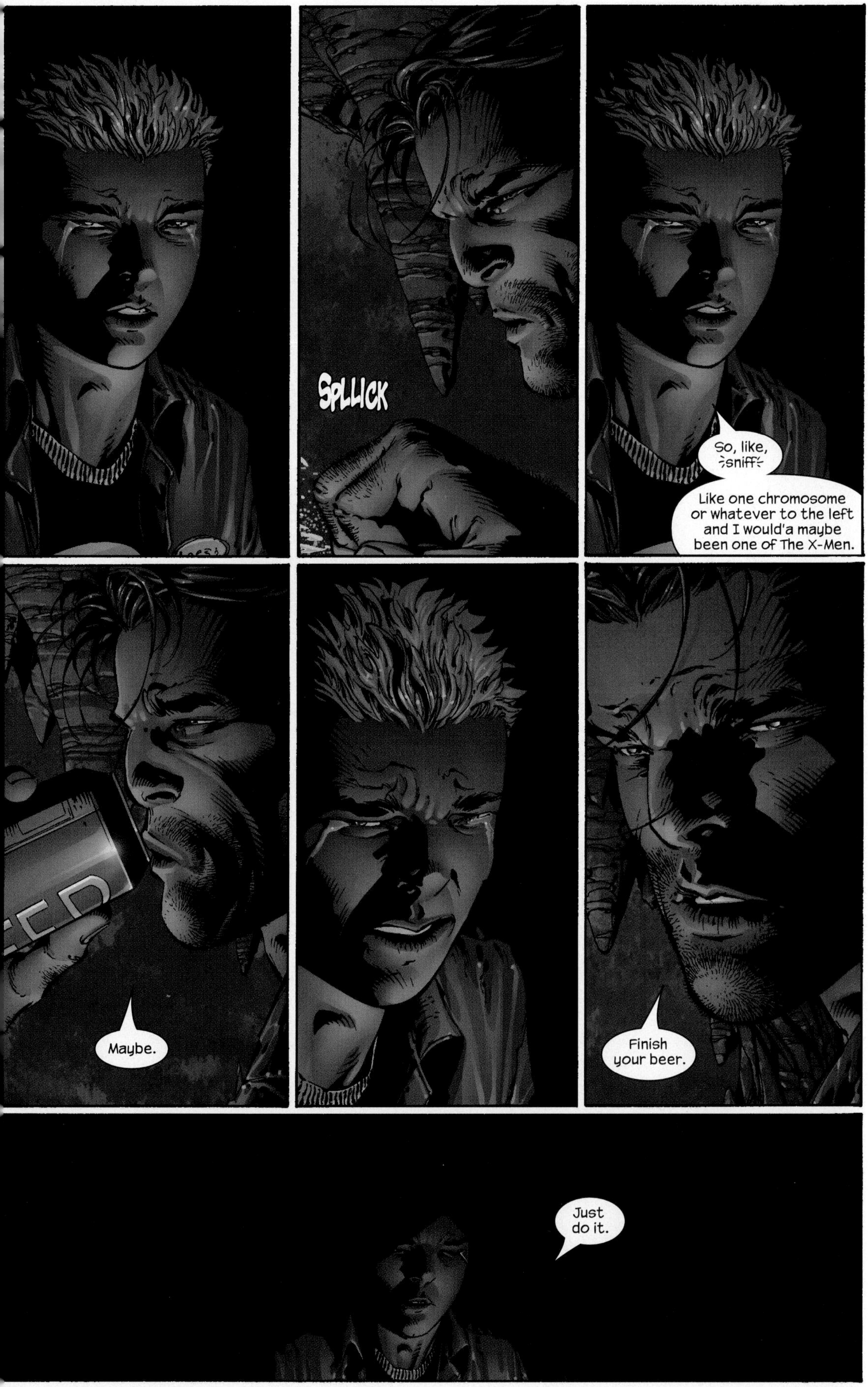
SPLLICK
So, like, ~sniff~
Like one chromosome or whatever to the left and I would'a maybe been one of The X-Men.
Maybe.
Finish your beer.
Just do it.

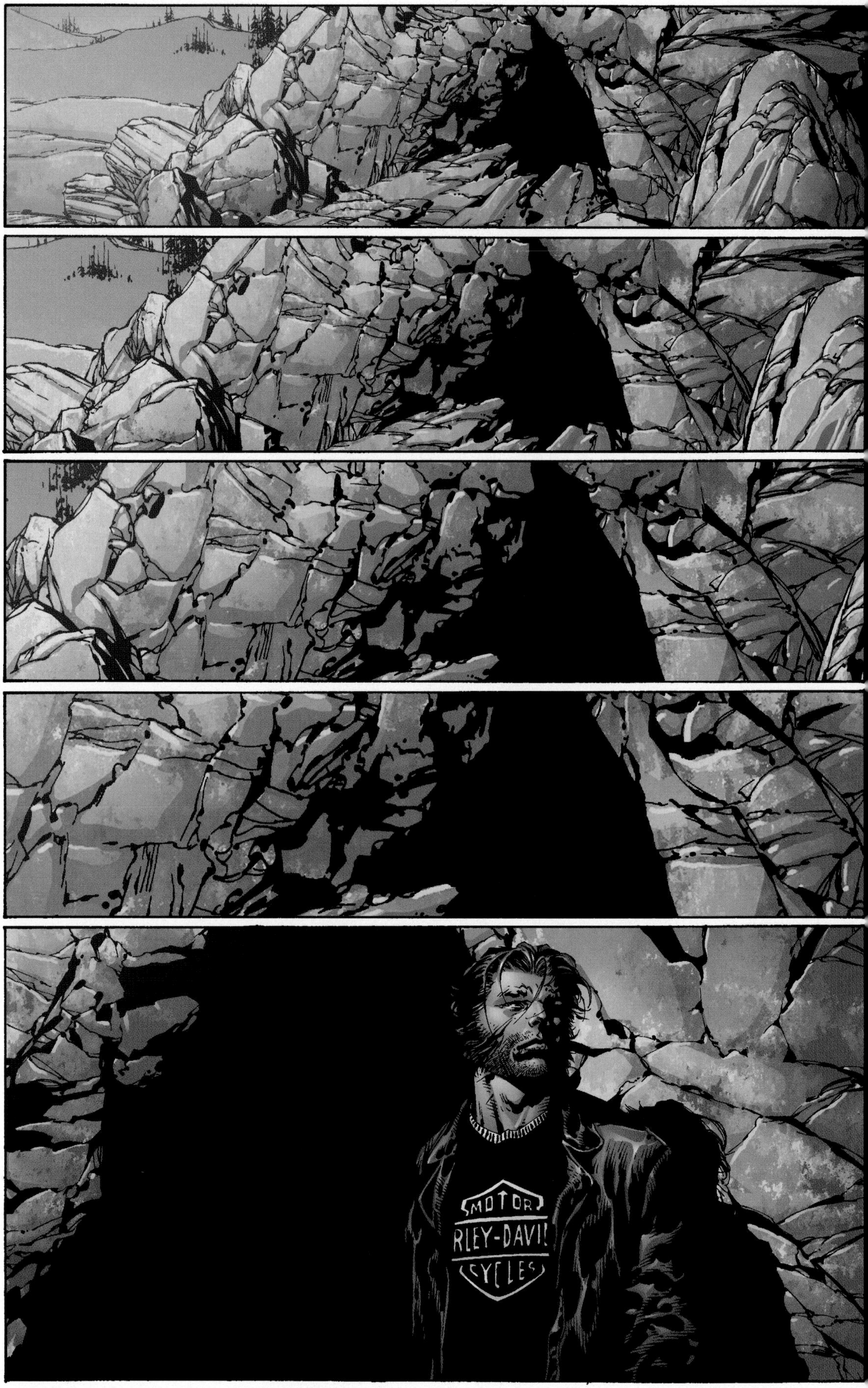
MOTOR
RLEY-DAVI
CYCLES

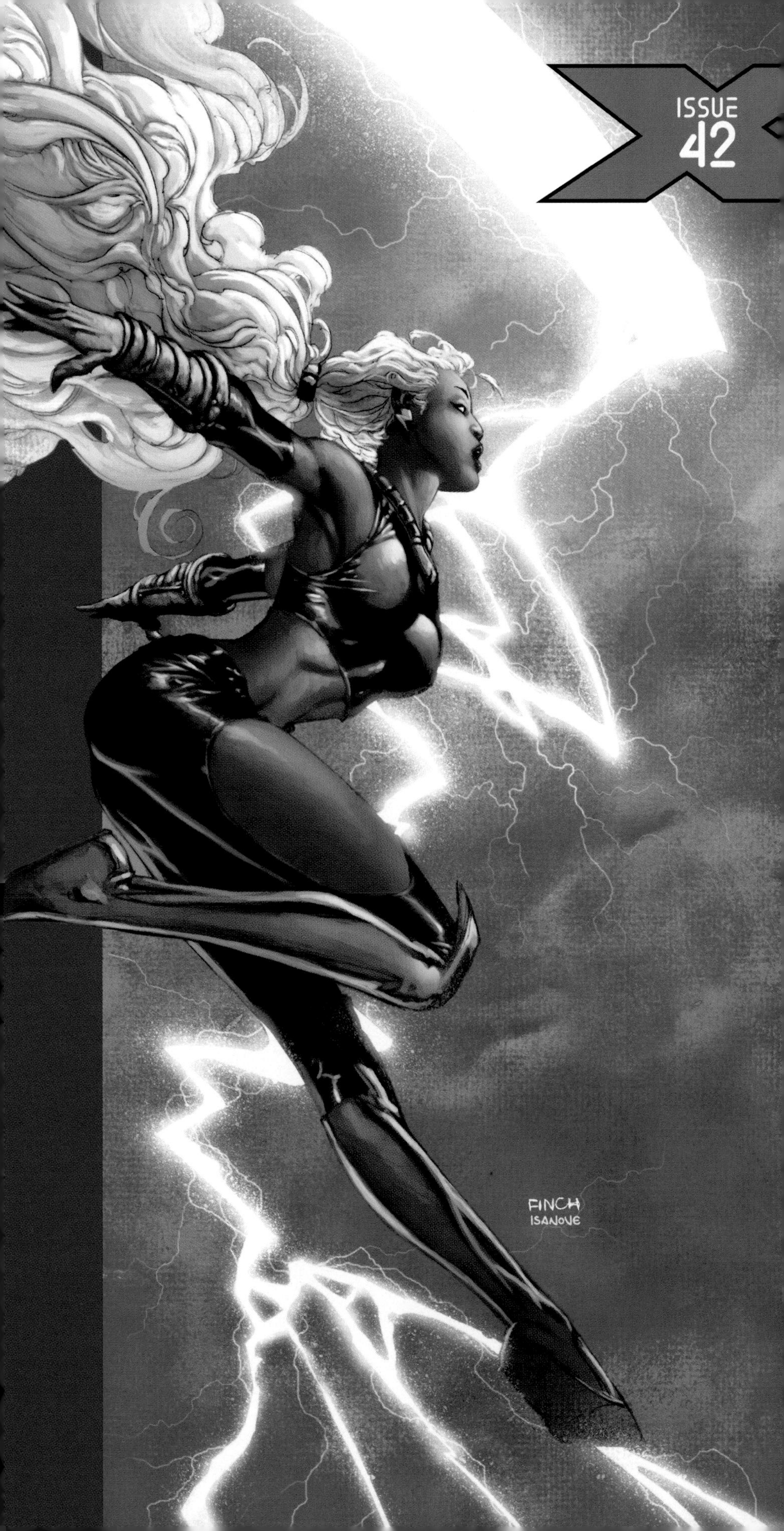
ISSUE
42
FINCH
ISANOVE

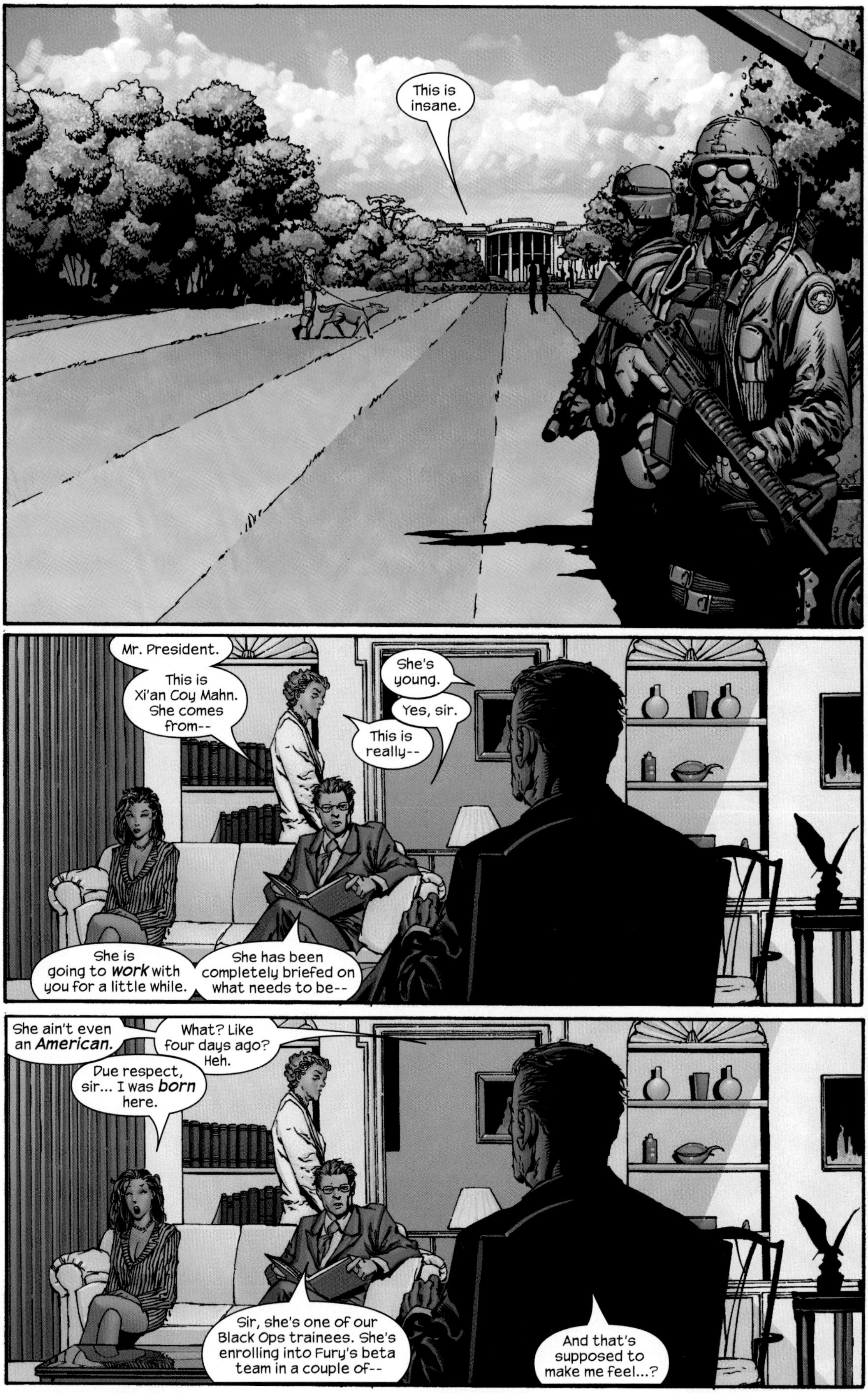
This is insane.
Mr. President.
This is Xi'an Coy Mahn. She comes from--
She's young.
Yes, sir.
This is really--
She is going to *work* with you for a little while.
She has been completely briefed on what needs to be--
She ain't even an *American.*
What? Like four days ago? Heh.
Due respect, sir... I was *born* here.
Sir, she's one of our Black Ops trainees. She's enrolling into Fury's beta team in a couple of--
And that's supposed to make me feel...?

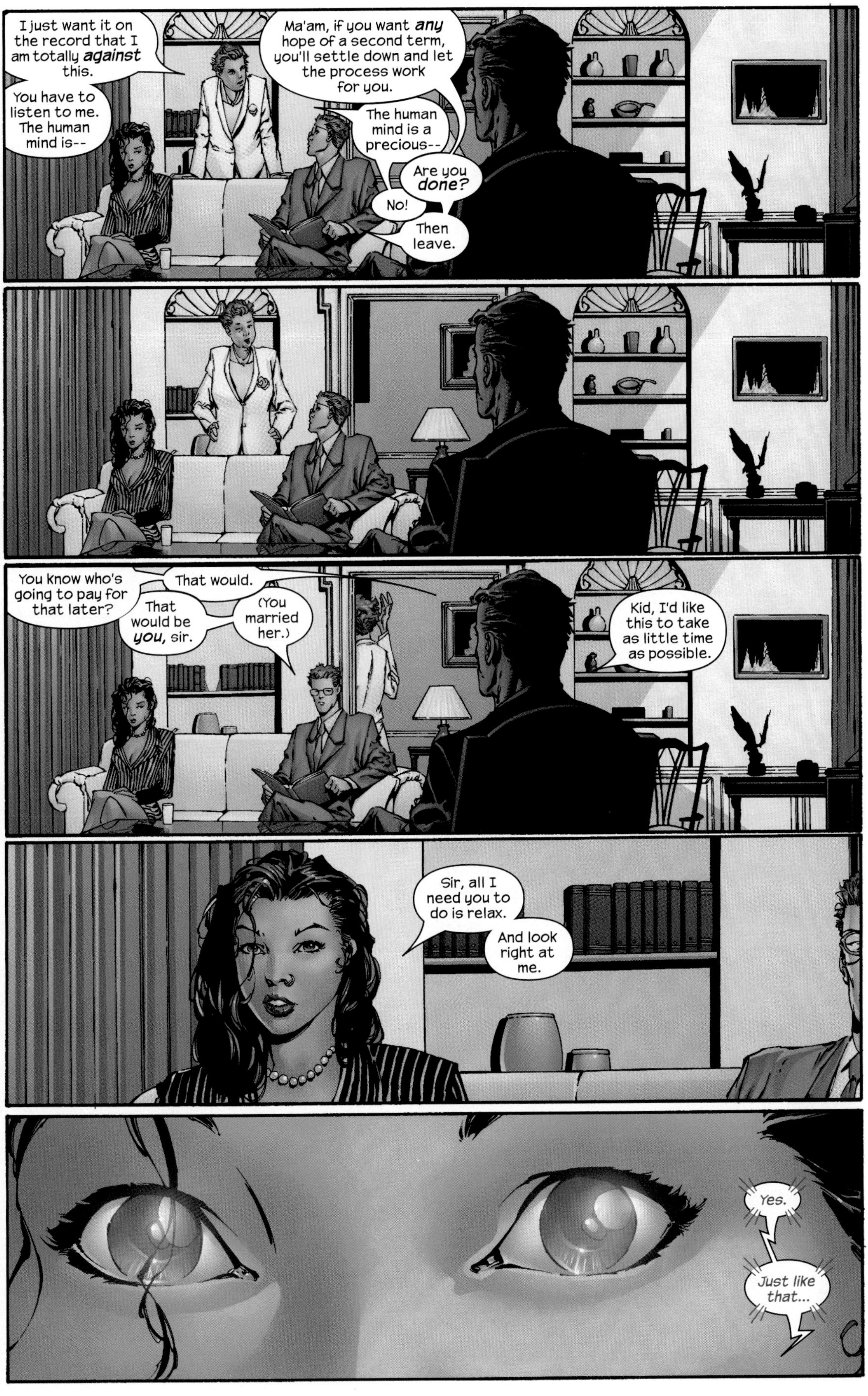
I just want it on the record that I am totally *against* this.
You have to listen to me. The human mind is--
Ma'am, if you want *any* hope of a second term, you'll settle down and let the process work for you.
The human mind is a precious--
Are you *done?*
No!
Then leave.
You know who's going to pay for that later?
That would.
That would be *you,* sir.
(You married her.)
Kid, I'd like this to take as little time as possible.
Sir, all I need you to do is relax.
And look right at me.
Yes.
Just like that...

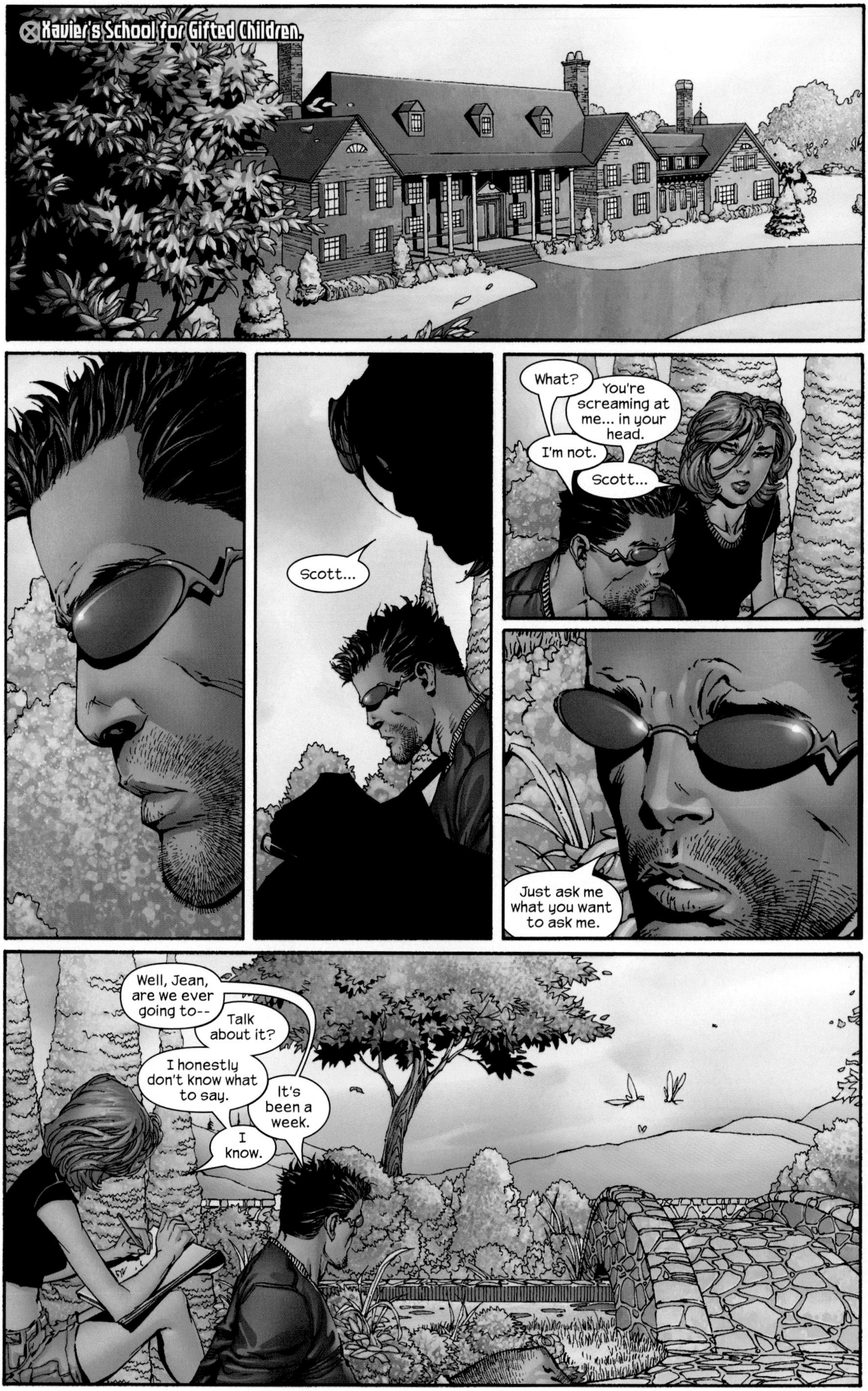
Xavier's School for Gifted Children.
Scott...
What?
You're screaming at me... in your head.
I'm not.
Scott...
Just ask me what you want to ask me.
Well, Jean, are we ever going to--
Talk about it?
I honestly don't know what to say.
It's been a week.
I know.

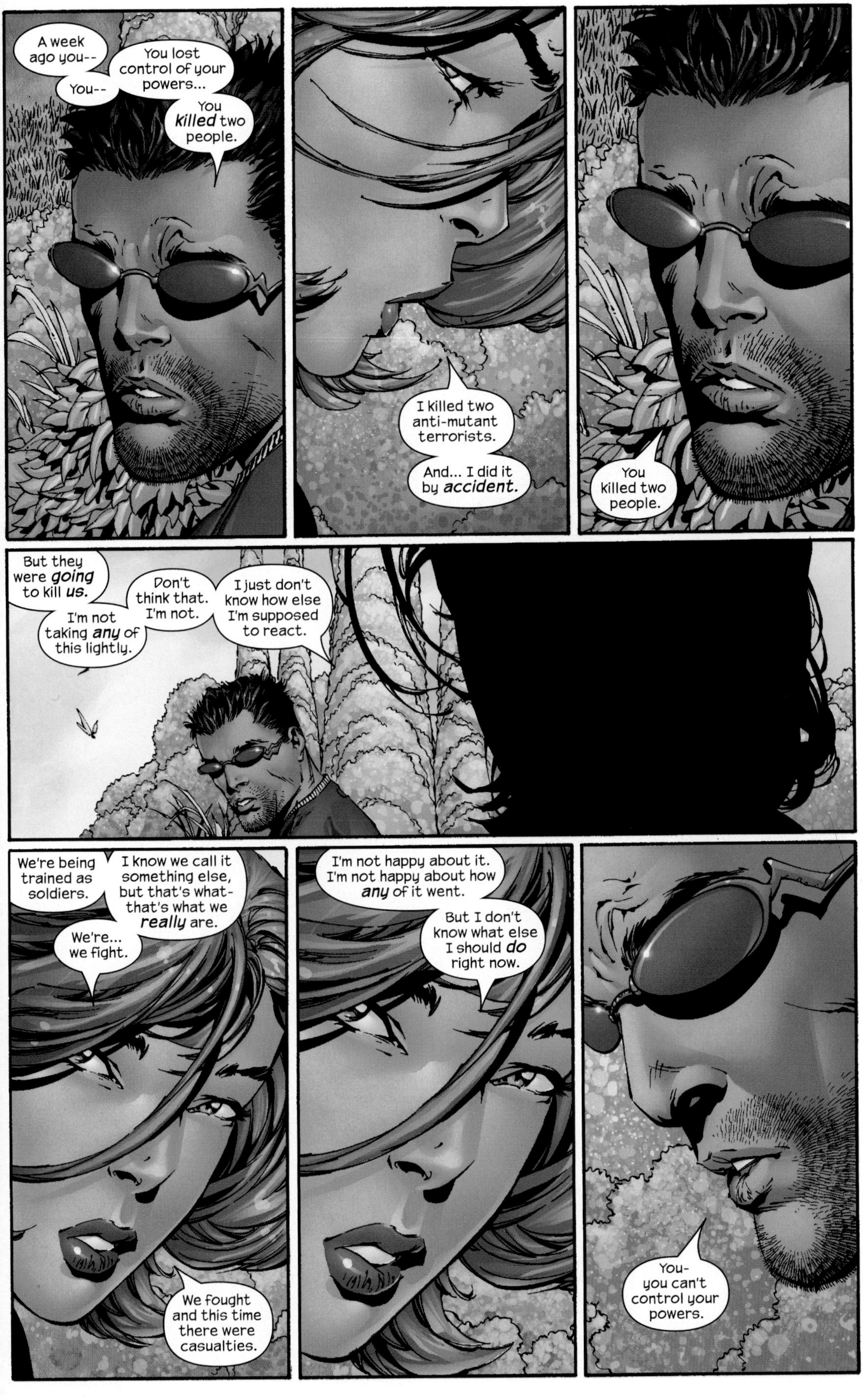
A week ago you--
You--
You lost control of your powers...
You *killed* two people.
I killed two anti-mutant terrorists.
And... I did it by *accident.*
You killed two people.
But they were *going* to kill *us.*
I'm not taking *any* of this lightly.
Don't think that. I'm not.
I just don't know how else I'm supposed to react.
We're being trained as soldiers.
I know we call it something else, but that's what- that's what we *really* are.
We're... we fight.
We fought and this time there were casualties.
I'm not happy about it. I'm not happy about how *any* of it went.
But I don't know what else I should *do* right now.
You- you can't control your powers.

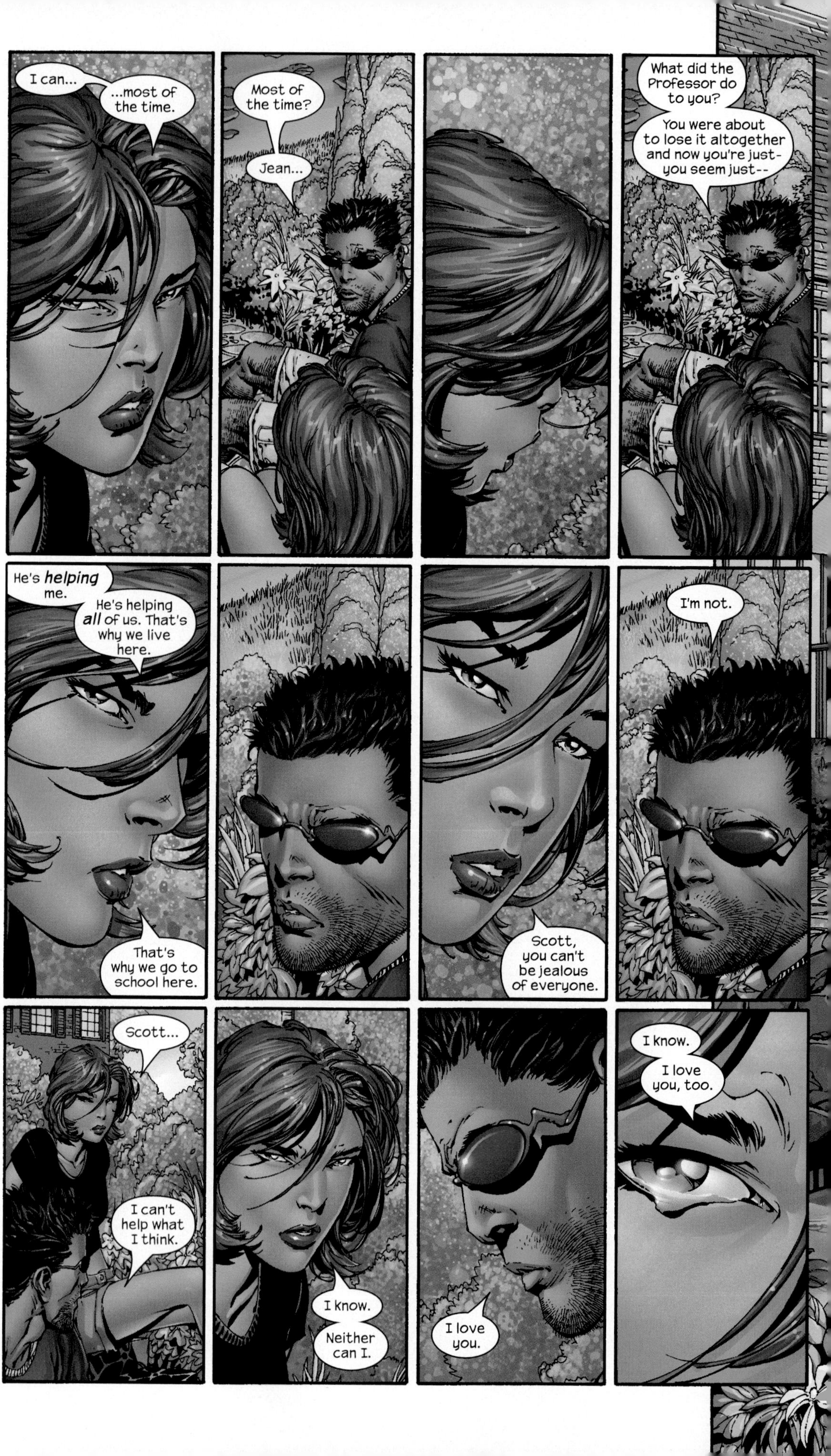
I can...
...most of the time.
Most of the time?
Jean...
What did the Professor do to you?
You were about to lose it altogether and now you're just- you seem just--
He's **helping** me.
He's helping ***all*** of us. That's why we live here.
That's why we go to school here.
Scott, you can't be jealous of everyone.
I'm not.
Scott...
I can't help what I think.
I know.
Neither can I.
I love you.
I know.
I love you, too.

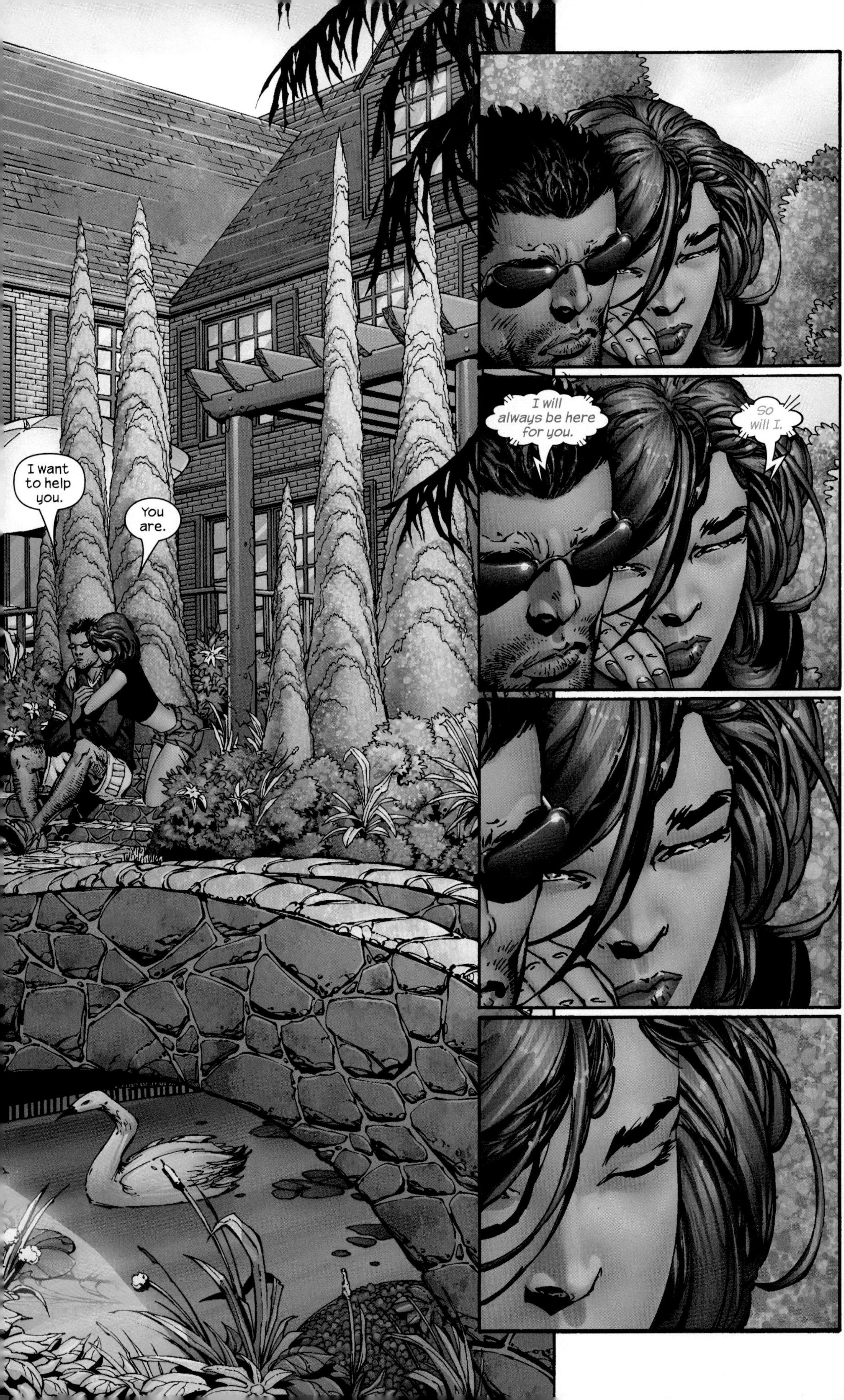
I want to help you.
You are.
I will always be here for you.
So will I.

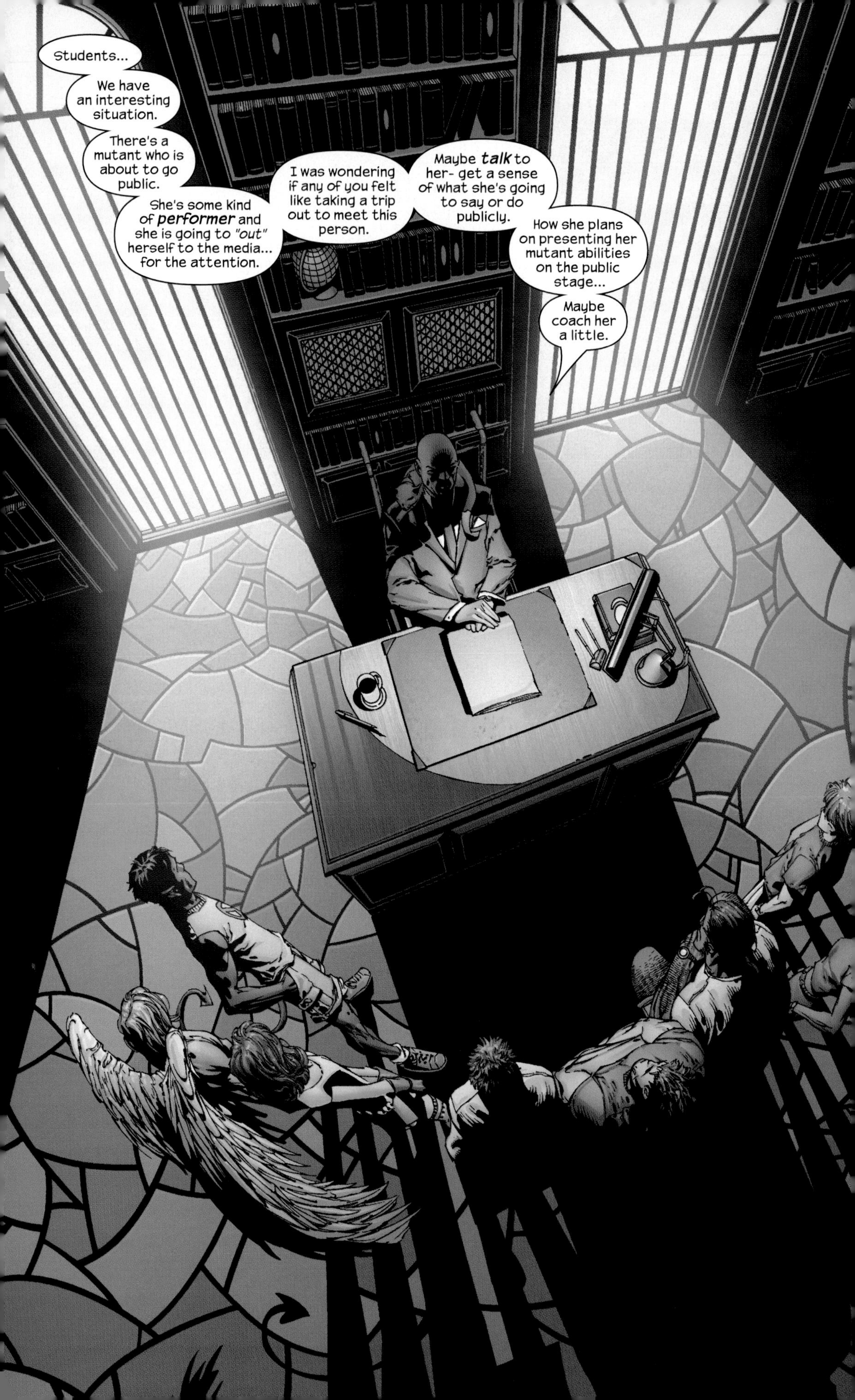
Students...
We have an interesting situation.
There's a mutant who is about to go public.
She's some kind of *performer* and she is going to *"out"* herself to the media... for the attention.
I was wondering if any of you felt like taking a trip out to meet this person.
Maybe ***talk*** to her- get a sense of what she's going to say or do publicly.
How she plans on presenting her mutant abilities on the public stage...
Maybe coach her a little.

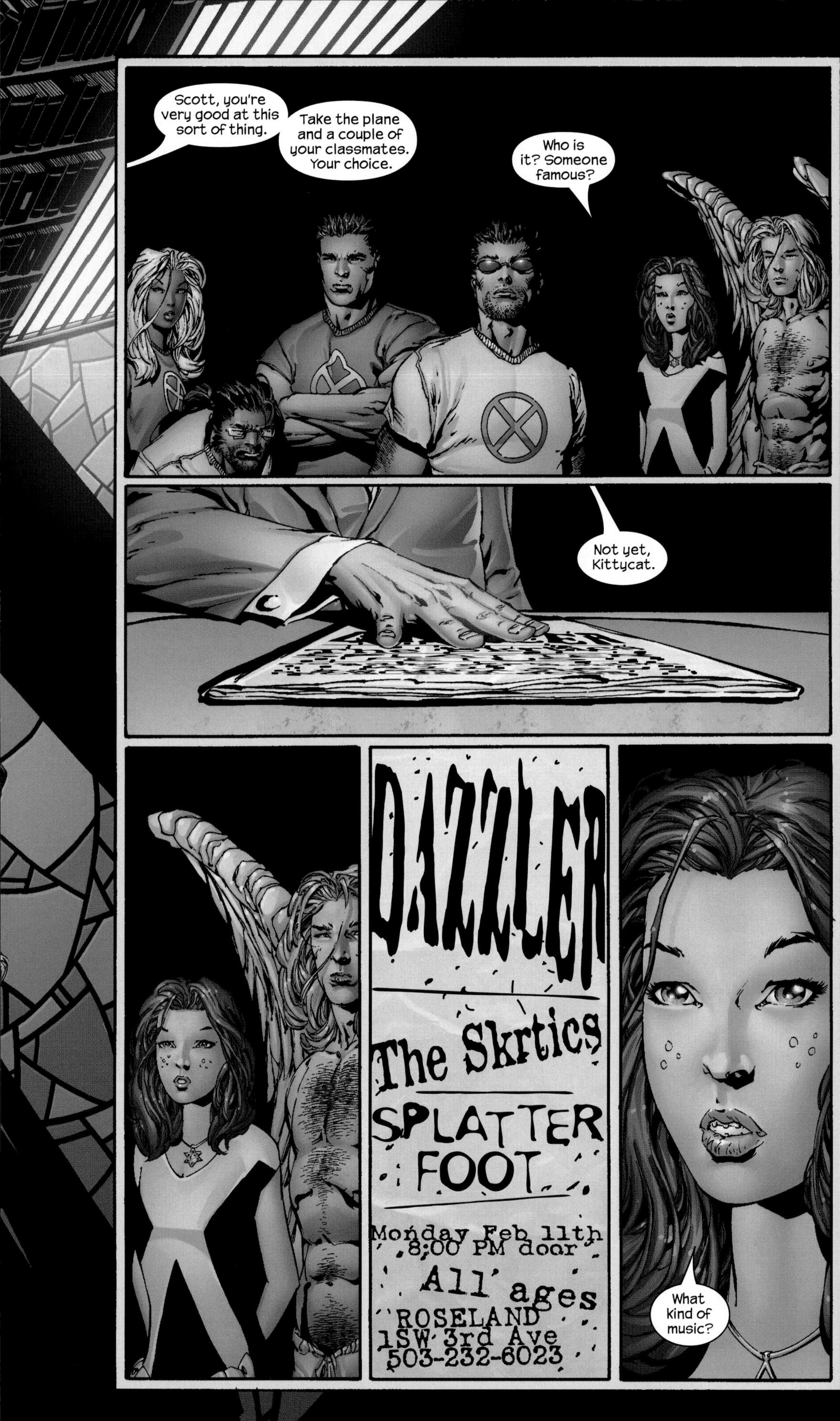
Scott, you're very good at this sort of thing.
Take the plane and a couple of your classmates. Your choice.
Who is it? Someone famous?
Not yet, Kittycat.
DAZZLER
The Skrtics
SPLATTER FOOT
Monday Feb 11th 8:00 PM door
All ages
ROSELAND
1SW 3rd Ave
503-232-6023
What kind of music?

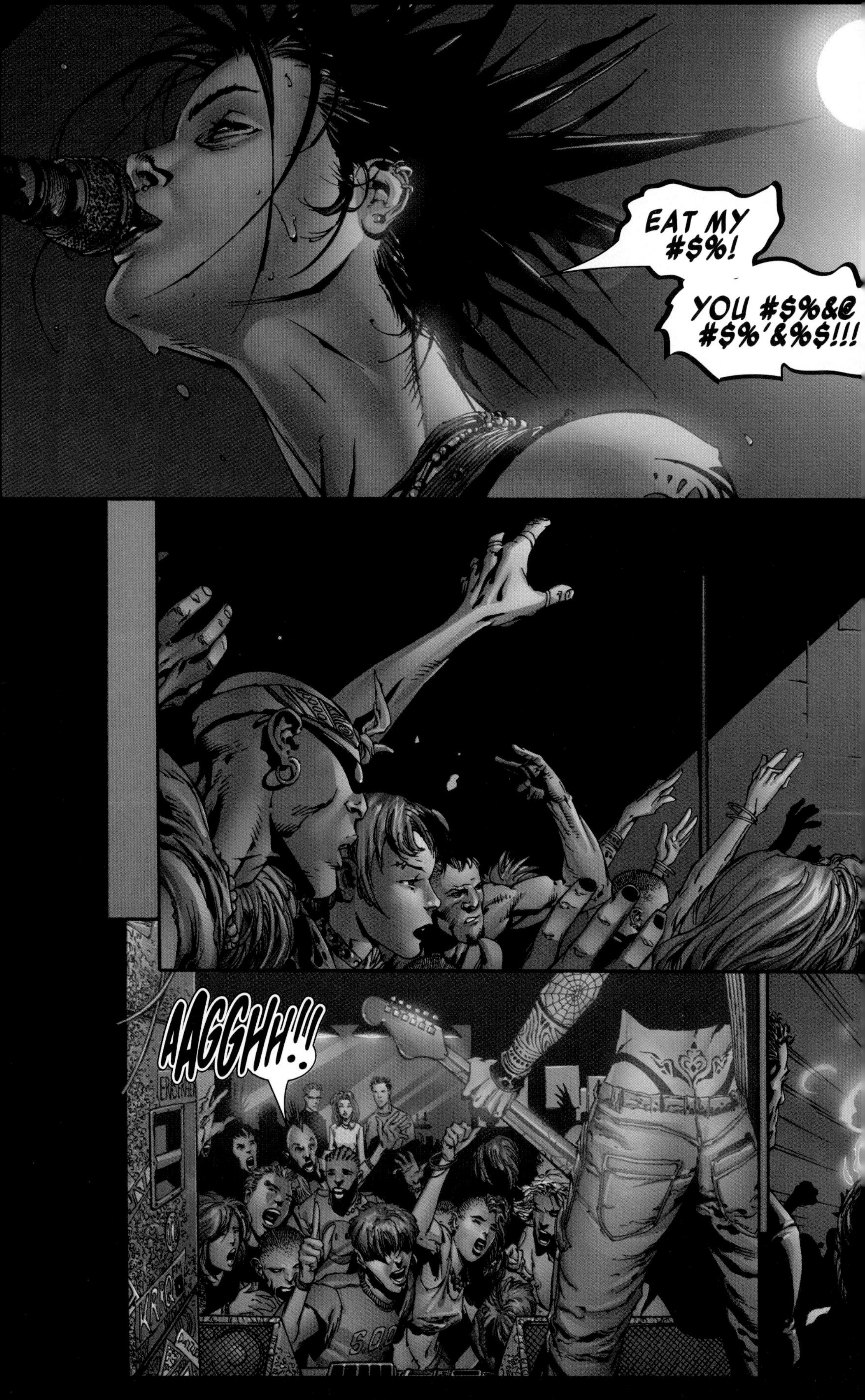
EAT MY #$%!
YOU #$%&@ #$%'&%$!!!
AAGGHH!!!
KROQ

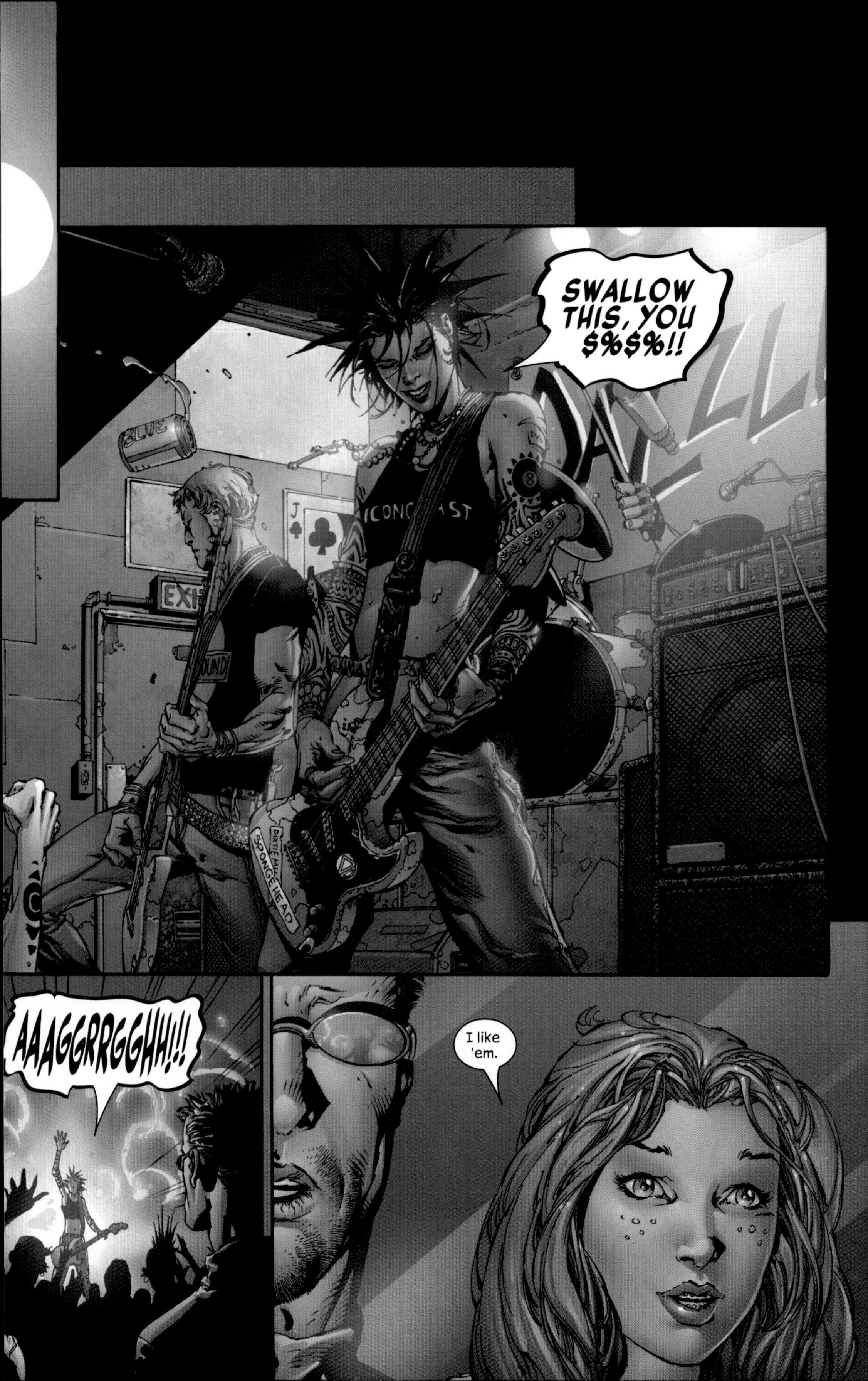
SWALLOW THIS, YOU $%$%!!
ICONOCLAST
EXIT
SPONGEHEAD
AAAGGRRGGHH!!!
I like 'em.

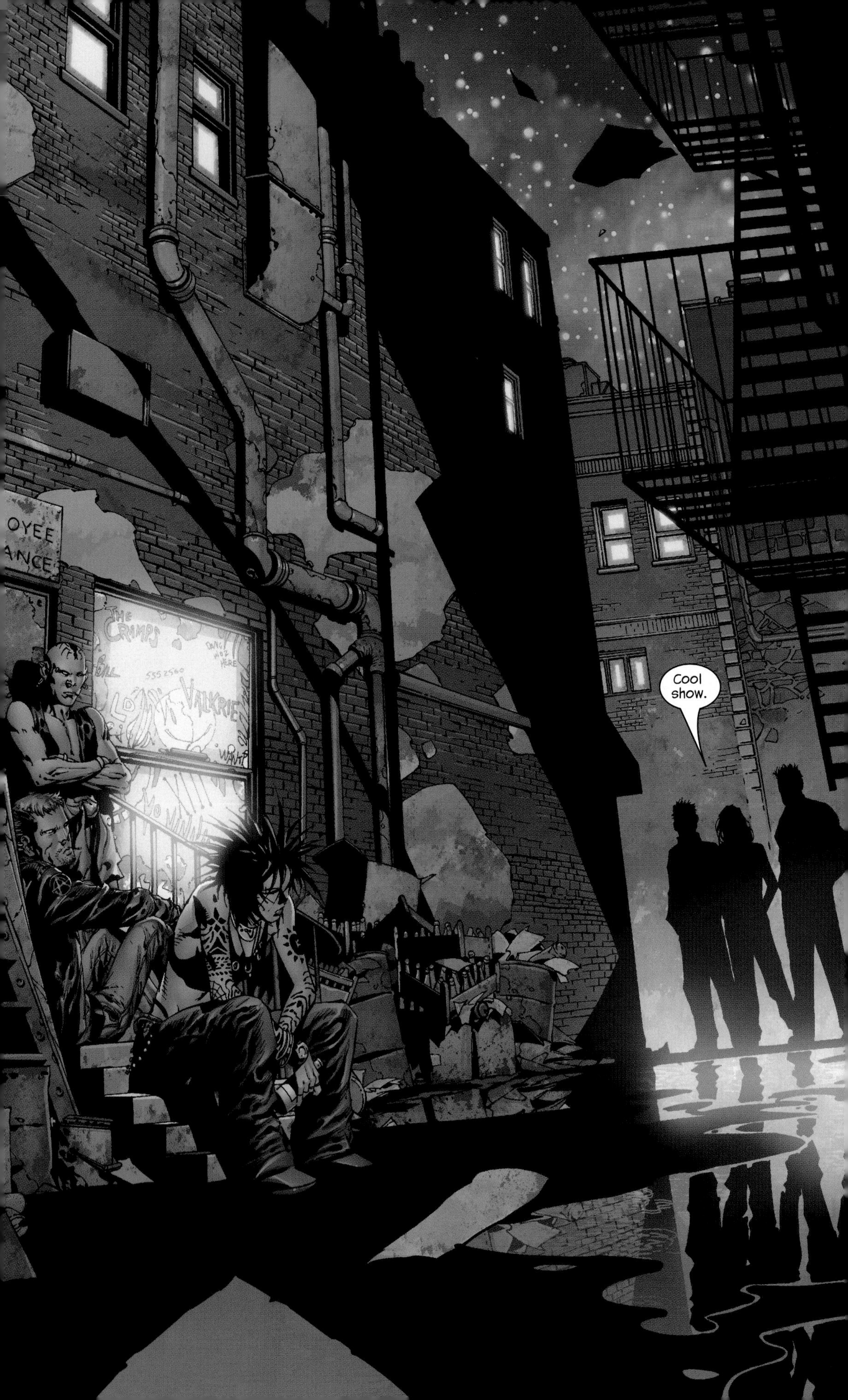
THE CRAMPS
DANG WOZ HERE
5552560
VALKRIE
Cool show.

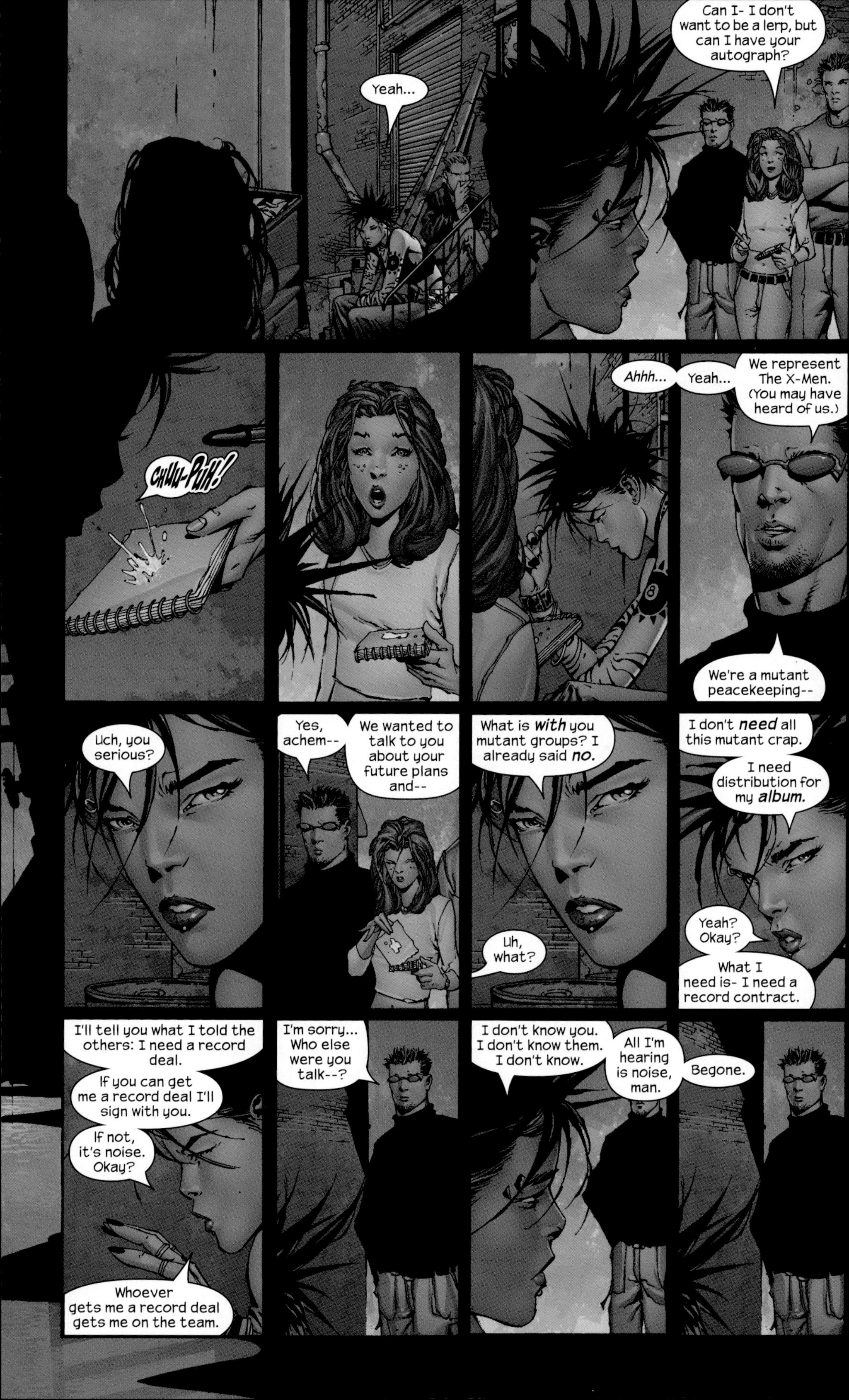
Yeah...
Can I- I don't want to be a lerp, but can I have your autograph?
CHUU-PUH!
Ahhh...
Yeah...
We represent The X-Men. (You may have heard of us.)
We're a mutant peacekeeping--
Uch, you serious?
Yes, achem--
We wanted to talk to you about your future plans and--
What is with you mutant groups? I already said no.
Uh, what?
I don't need all this mutant crap.
I need distribution for my album.
Yeah? Okay?
What I need is- I need a record contract.
I'll tell you what I told the others: I need a record deal.
If you can get me a record deal I'll sign with you.
If not, it's noise. Okay?
Whoever gets me a record deal gets me on the team.
I'm sorry... Who else were you talk--?
I don't know you. I don't know them. I don't know.
All I'm hearing is noise, man.
Begone.

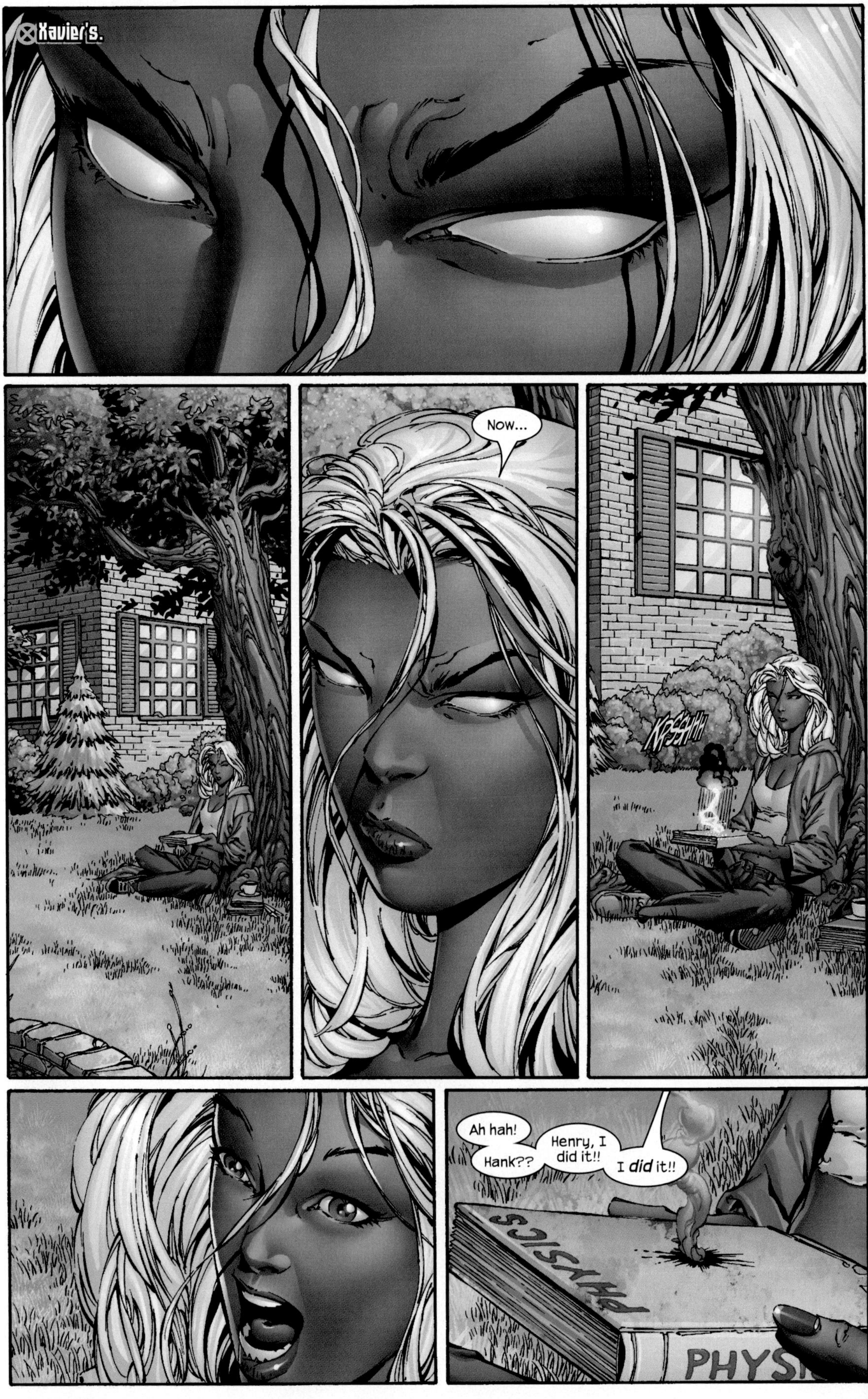
Xavier's.
Now...
KRSSHHH
Ah hah!
Hank??
Henry, I did it!!
I *did* it!!
PHYSICS
PHYSI

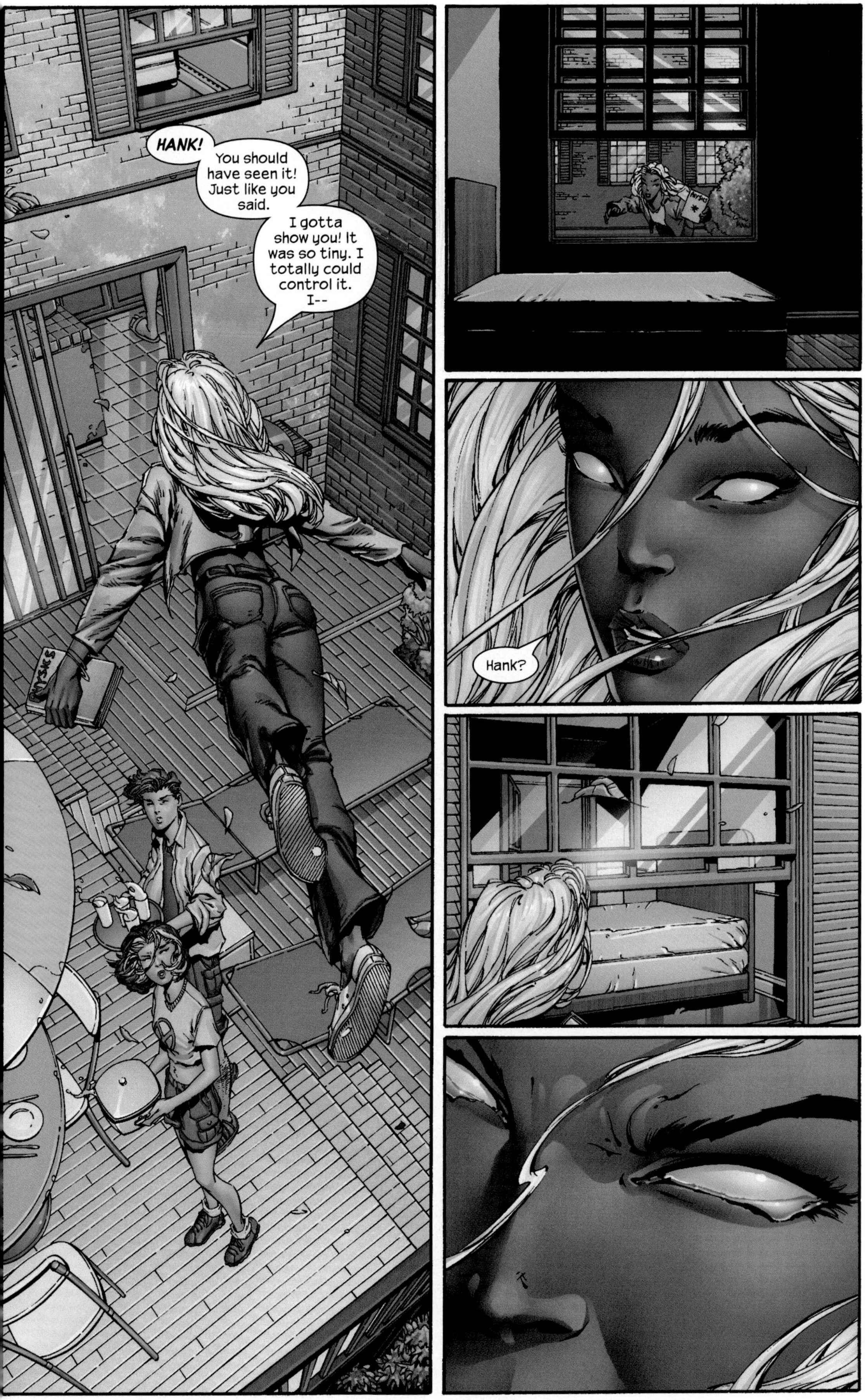
HANK!
You should have seen it! Just like you said.
I gotta show you! It was so tiny. I totally could control it. I--
Hank?

RRRUUUMMBBBLLEEE

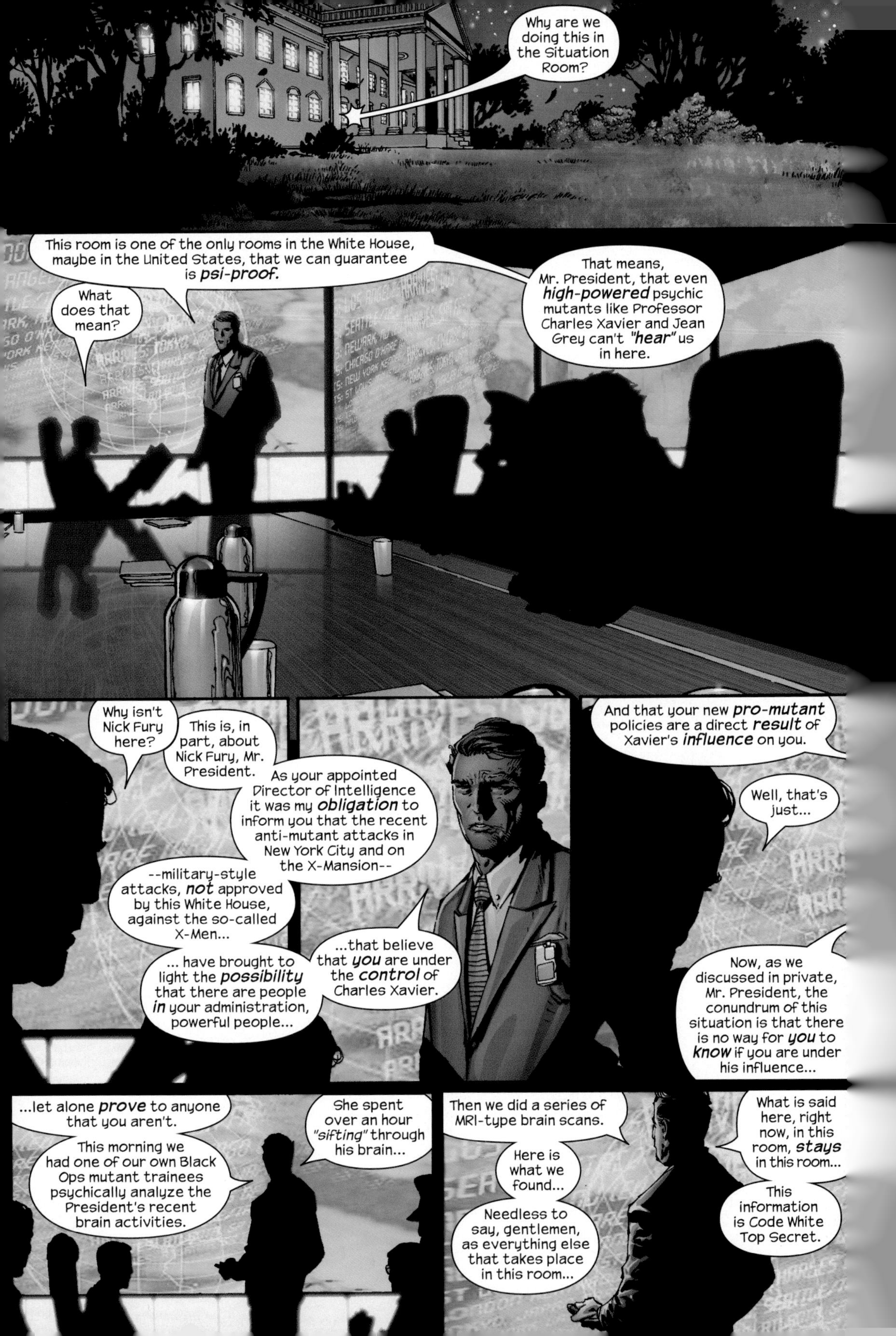
Why are we doing this in the Situation Room?
This room is one of the only rooms in the White House, maybe in the United States, that we can guarantee is psi-proof.
What does that mean?
That means, Mr. President, that even high-powered psychic mutants like Professor Charles Xavier and Jean Grey can't "hear" us in here.
Why isn't Nick Fury here?
This is, in part, about Nick Fury, Mr. President.
As your appointed Director of Intelligence it was my obligation to inform you that the recent anti-mutant attacks in New York City and on the X-Mansion--
--military-style attacks, not approved by this White House, against the so-called X-Men...
... have brought to light the possibility that there are people in your administration, powerful people...
...that believe that you are under the control of Charles Xavier.
And that your new pro-mutant policies are a direct result of Xavier's influence on you.
Well, that's just...
Now, as we discussed in private, Mr. President, the conundrum of this situation is that there is no way for you to know if you are under his influence...
...let alone prove to anyone that you aren't.
This morning we had one of our own Black Ops mutant trainees psychically analyze the President's recent brain activities.
She spent over an hour "sifting" through his brain...
Then we did a series of MRI-type brain scans.
Here is what we found...
Needless to say, gentlemen, as everything else that takes place in this room...
What is said here, right now, in this room, stays in this room...
This information is Code White Top Secret.

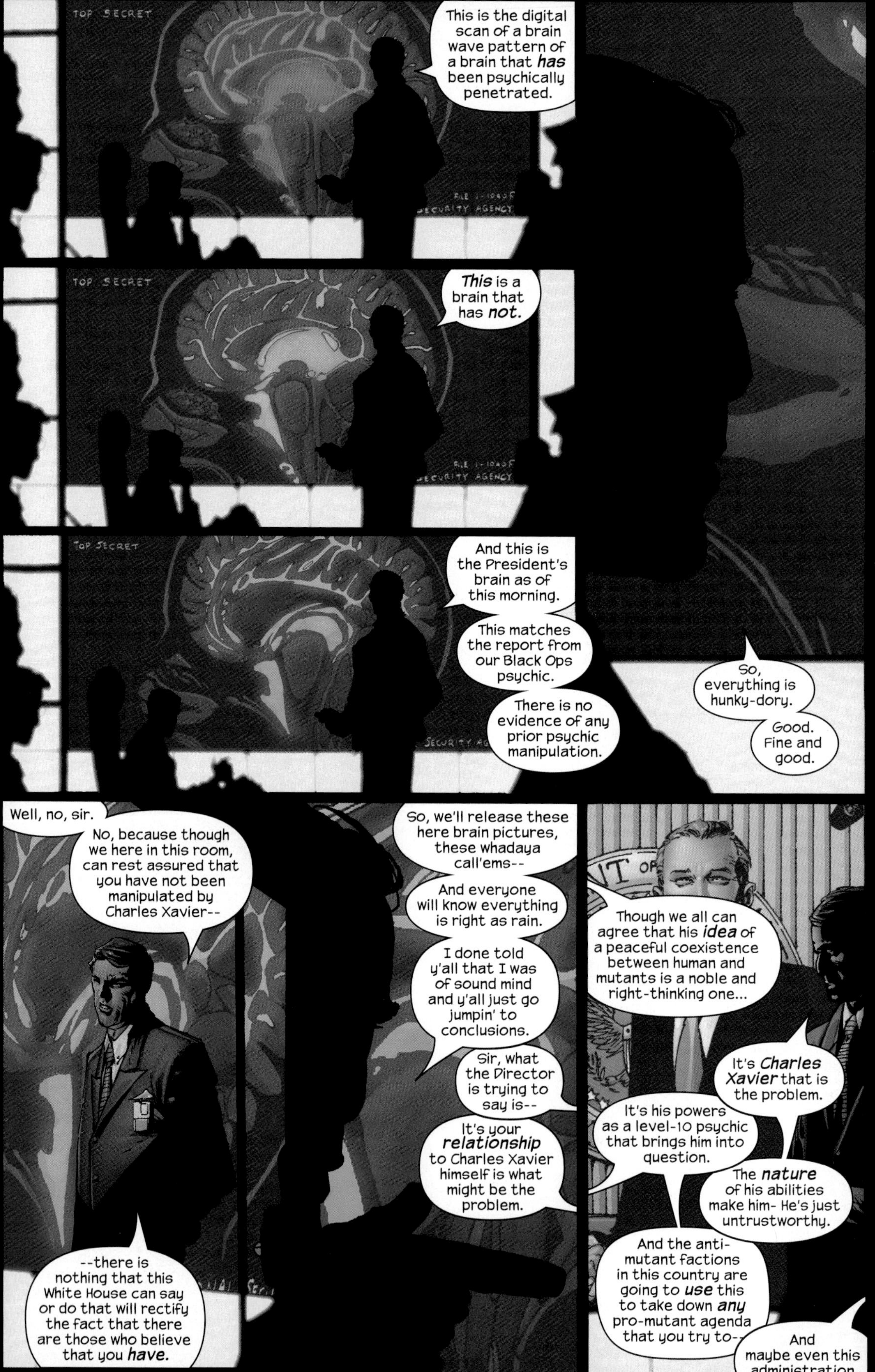
TOP SECRET
This is the digital scan of a brain wave pattern of a brain that *has* been psychically penetrated.
TOP SECRET
This is a brain that has *not.*
TOP SECRET
And this is the President's brain as of this morning.
This matches the report from our Black Ops psychic.
There is no evidence of any prior psychic manipulation.
So, everything is hunky-dory.
Good. Fine and good.
Well, no, sir.
No, because though we here in this room, can rest assured that you have not been manipulated by Charles Xavier--
--there is nothing that this White House can say or do that will rectify the fact that there are those who believe that you *have.*
So, we'll release these here brain pictures, these whadaya call'ems--
And everyone will know everything is right as rain.
I done told y'all that I was of sound mind and y'all just go jumpin' to conclusions.
Sir, what the Director is trying to say is--
It's your *relationship* to Charles Xavier himself is what might be the problem.
Though we all can agree that his *idea* of a peaceful coexistence between human and mutants is a noble and right-thinking one...
It's *Charles Xavier* that is the problem.
It's his powers as a level-10 psychic that brings him into question.
The *nature* of his abilities make him- He's just untrustworthy.
And the anti-mutant factions in this country are going to *use* this to take down *any* pro-mutant agenda that you try to--
And maybe even this

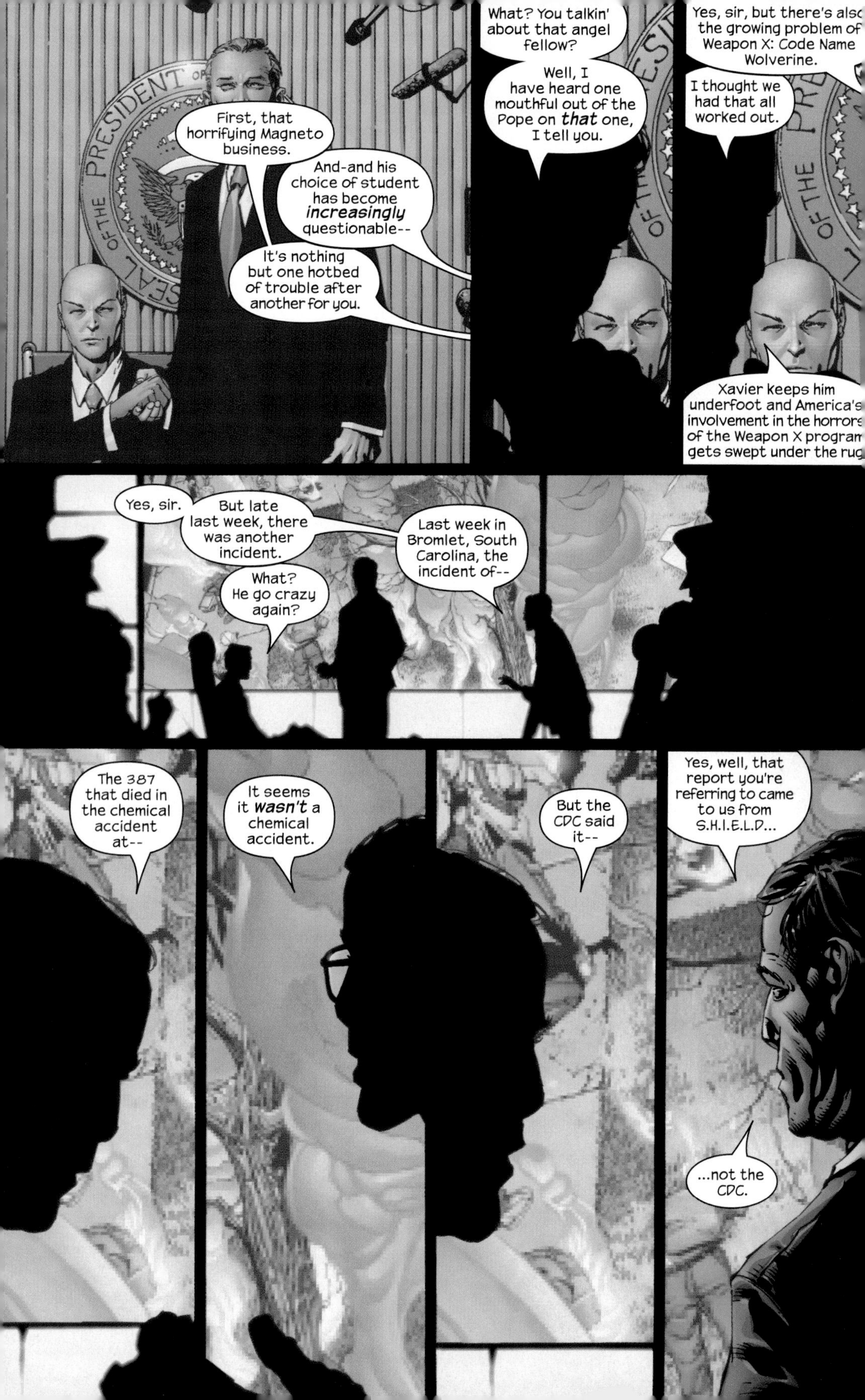
First, that horrifying Magneto business.
And-and his choice of student has become *increasingly* questionable--
It's nothing but one hotbed of trouble after another for you.
What? You talkin' about that angel fellow?
Well, I have heard one mouthful out of the Pope on *that* one, I tell you.
Yes, sir, but there's also the growing problem of Weapon X: Code Name Wolverine.
I thought we had that all worked out.
Xavier keeps him underfoot and America's involvement in the horrors of the Weapon X program gets swept under the rug.
Yes, sir.
But late last week, there was another incident.
What? He go crazy again?
Last week in Bromlet, South Carolina, the incident of--
The 387 that died in the chemical accident at--
It seems it *wasn't* a chemical accident.
But the CDC said it--
Yes, well, that report you're referring to came to us from S.H.I.E.L.D...
...not the CDC.

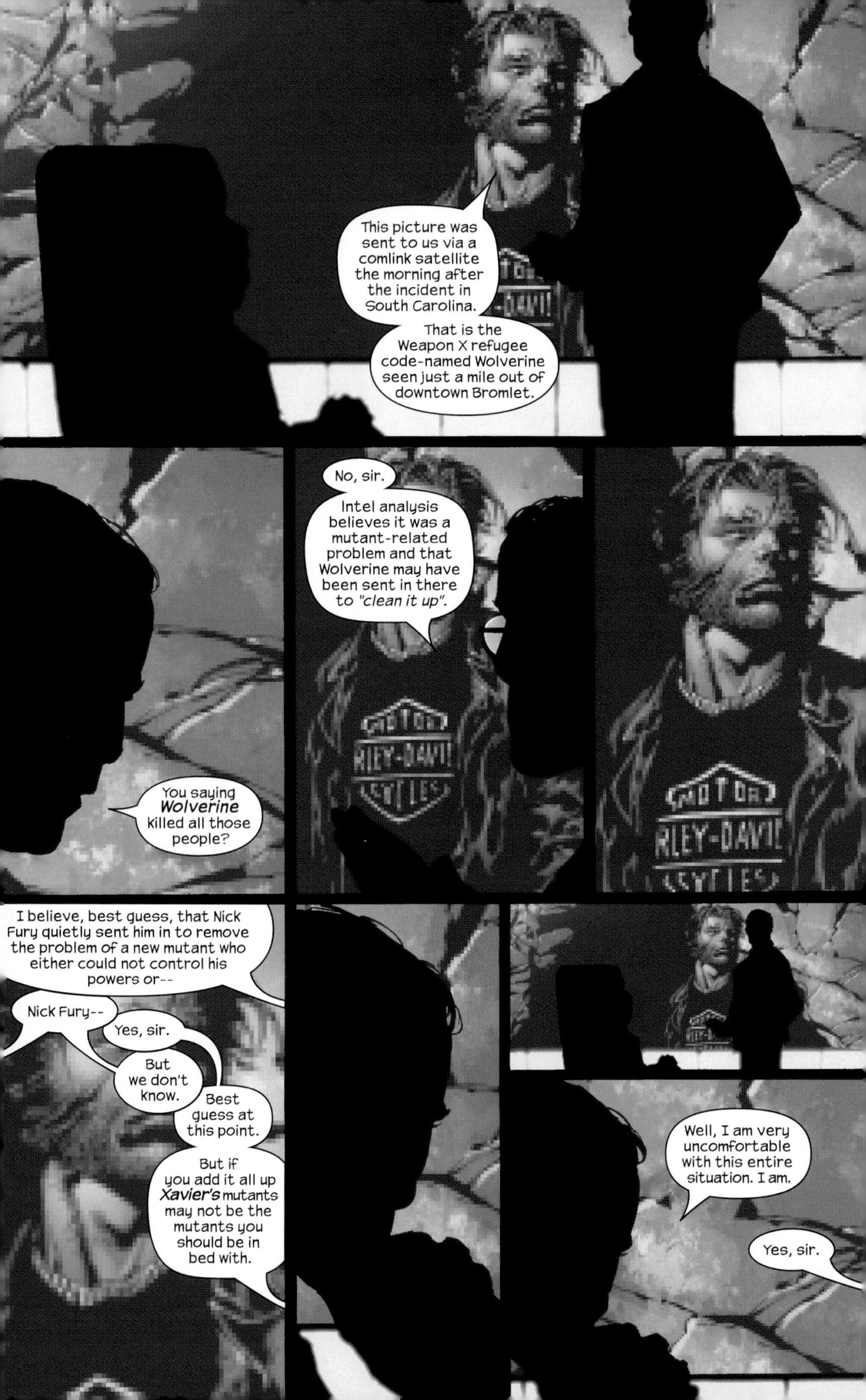
This picture was sent to us via a comlink satellite the morning after the incident in South Carolina.
That is the Weapon X refugee code-named Wolverine seen just a mile out of downtown Bromlet.
You saying *Wolverine* killed all those people?
No, sir.
Intel analysis believes it was a mutant-related problem and that Wolverine may have been sent in there to *"clean it up"*.
I believe, best guess, that Nick Fury quietly sent him in to remove the problem of a new mutant who either could not control his powers or--
Nick Fury--
Yes, sir.
But we don't know.
Best guess at this point.
But if you add it all up *Xavier's* mutants may not be the mutants you should be in bed with.
Well, I am very uncomfortable with this entire situation. I am.
Yes, sir.

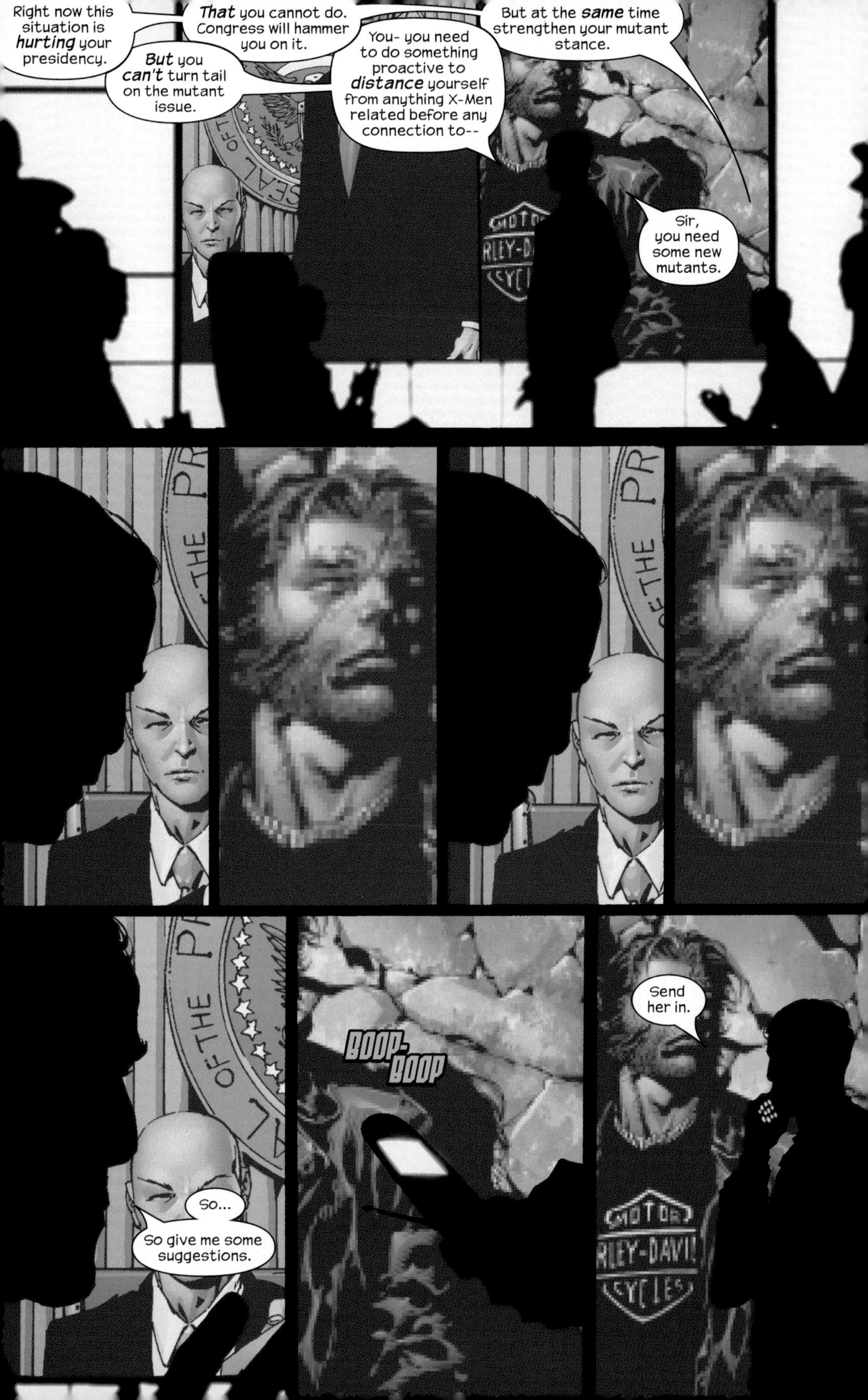

Right now this situation is *hurting* your presidency.
That you cannot do. Congress will hammer you on it.
But you *can't* turn tail on the mutant issue.
You- you need to do something proactive to *distance* yourself from anything X-Men related before any connection to--
But at the *same* time strengthen your mutant stance.
Sir, you need some new mutants.
So...
So give me some suggestions.
BOOP-BOOP
Send her in.

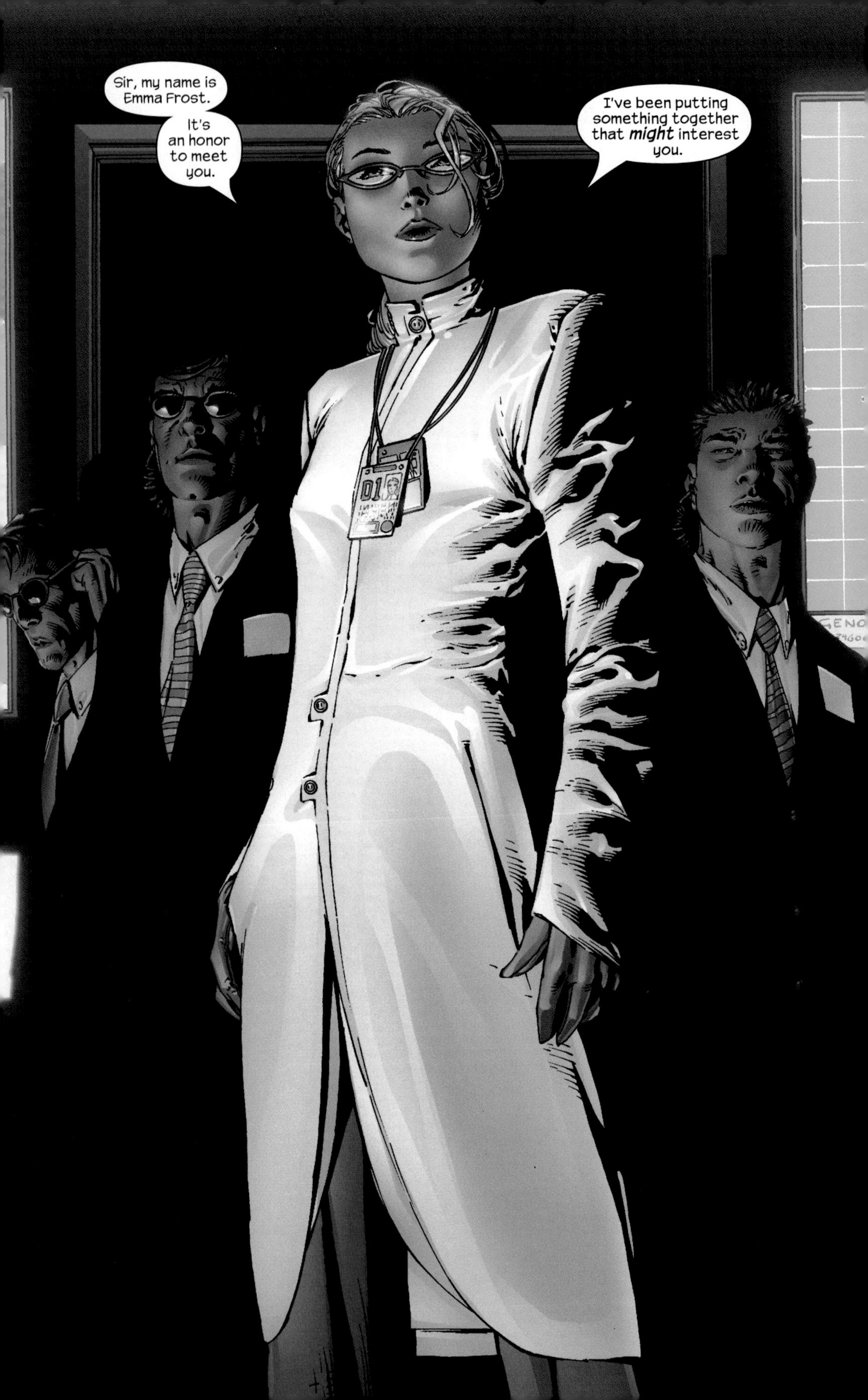
Sir, my name is Emma Frost.
It's an honor to meet you.
I've been putting something together that *might* interest you.

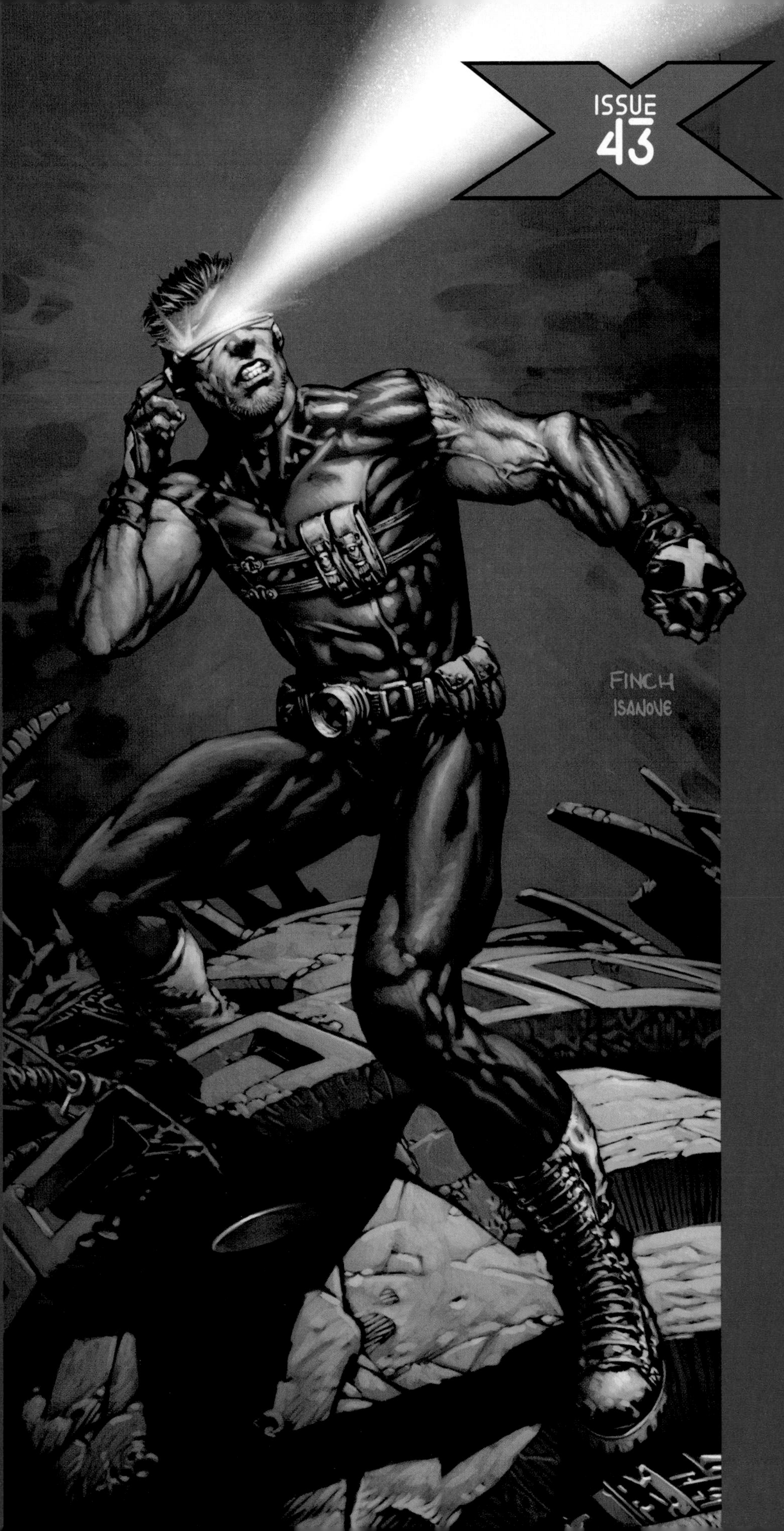
ISSUE
43
FINCH
ISANOVE

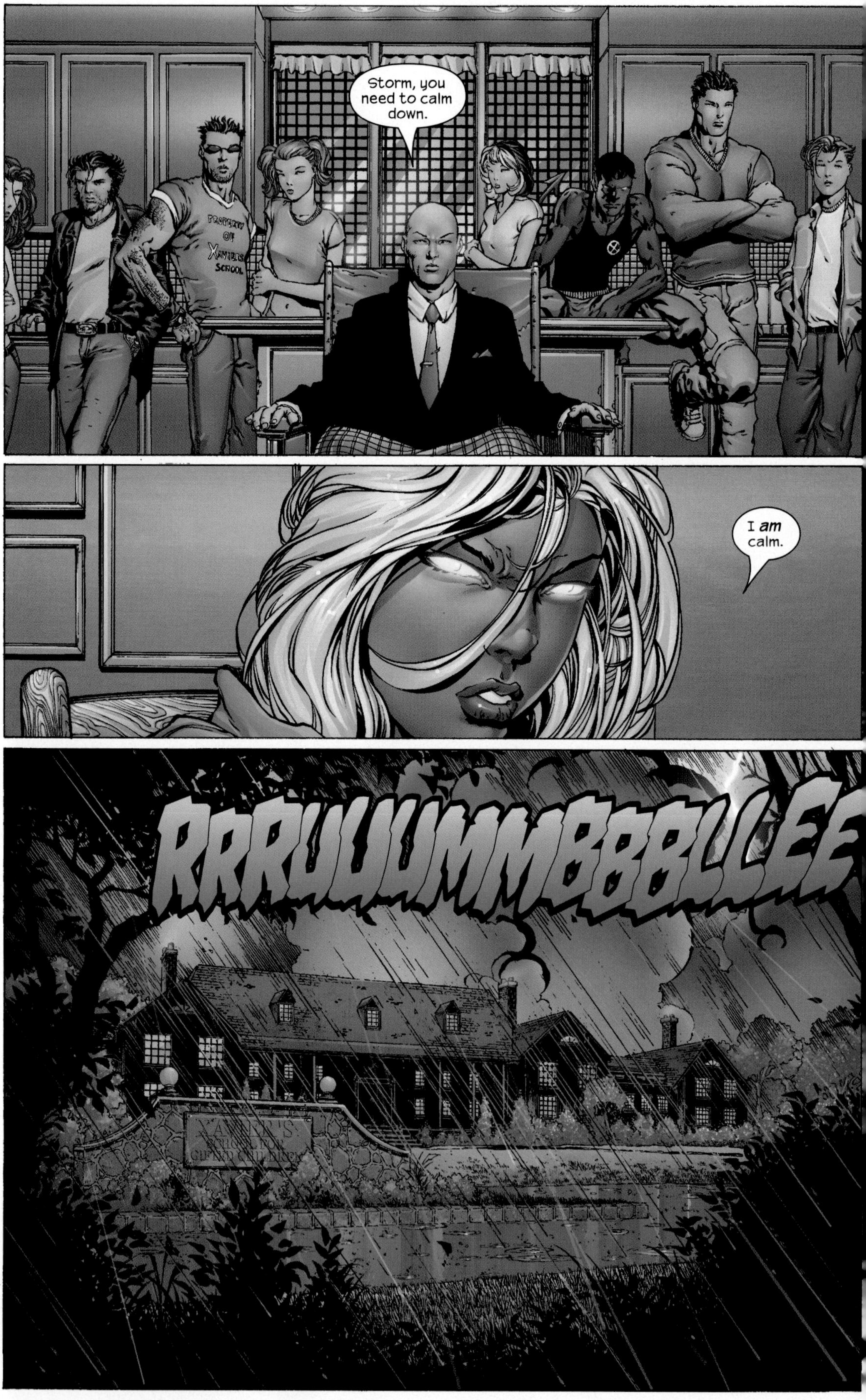
Storm, you need to calm down.
PROPERTY OF XAVIERS SCHOOL
I *am* calm.
RRRUUUMMBBBLLEE

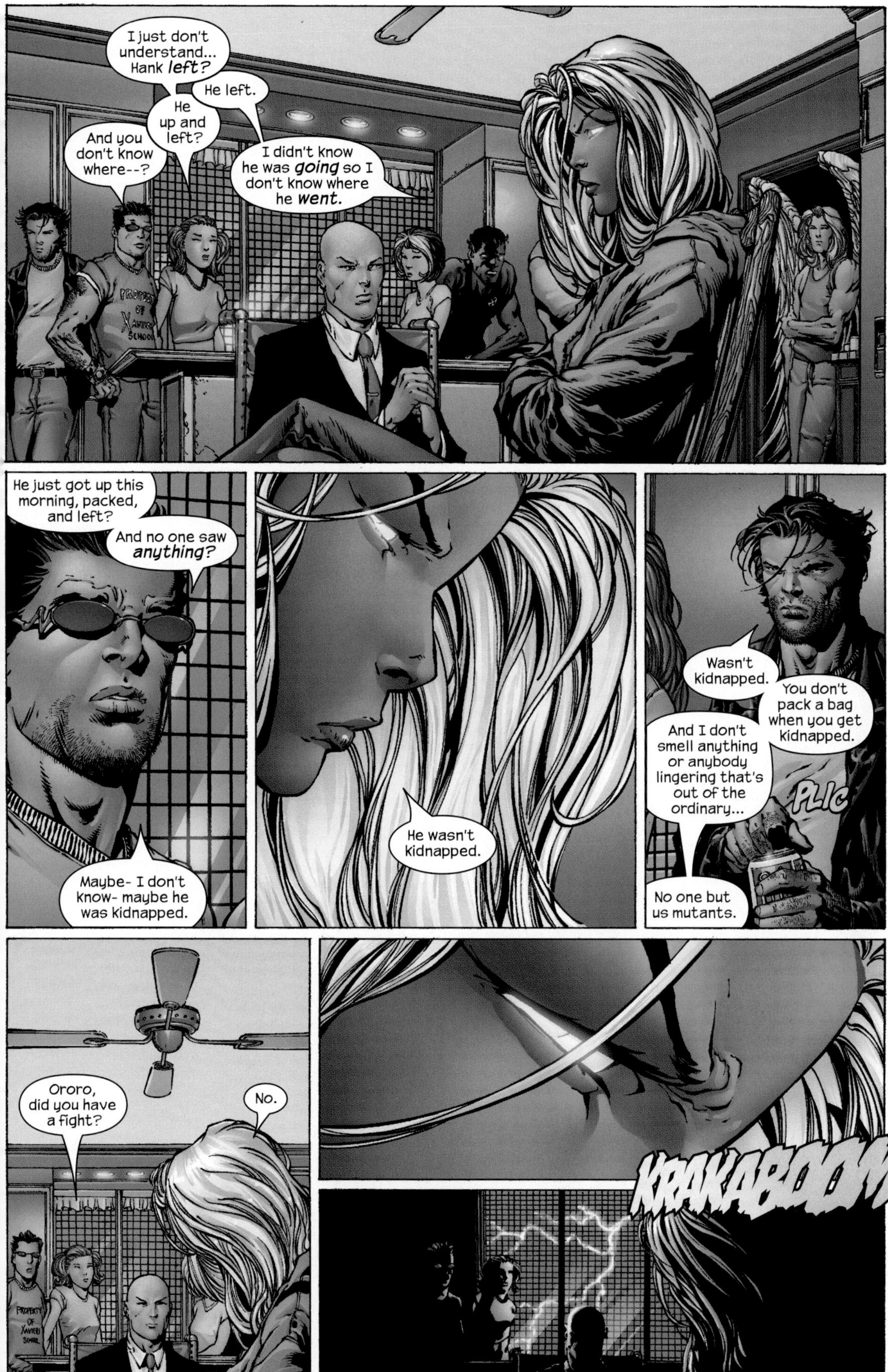
I just don't understand... Hank *left?*
He up and left?
He left.
And you don't know where--?
I didn't know he was *going* so I don't know where he *went.*
He just got up this morning, packed, and left?
And no one saw *anything?*
Maybe- I don't know- maybe he was kidnapped.
He wasn't kidnapped.
Wasn't kidnapped.
You don't pack a bag when you get kidnapped.
PLIC
And I don't smell anything or anybody lingering that's out of the ordinary...
No one but us mutants.
Ororo, did you have a fight?
No.
KRAKABOOM

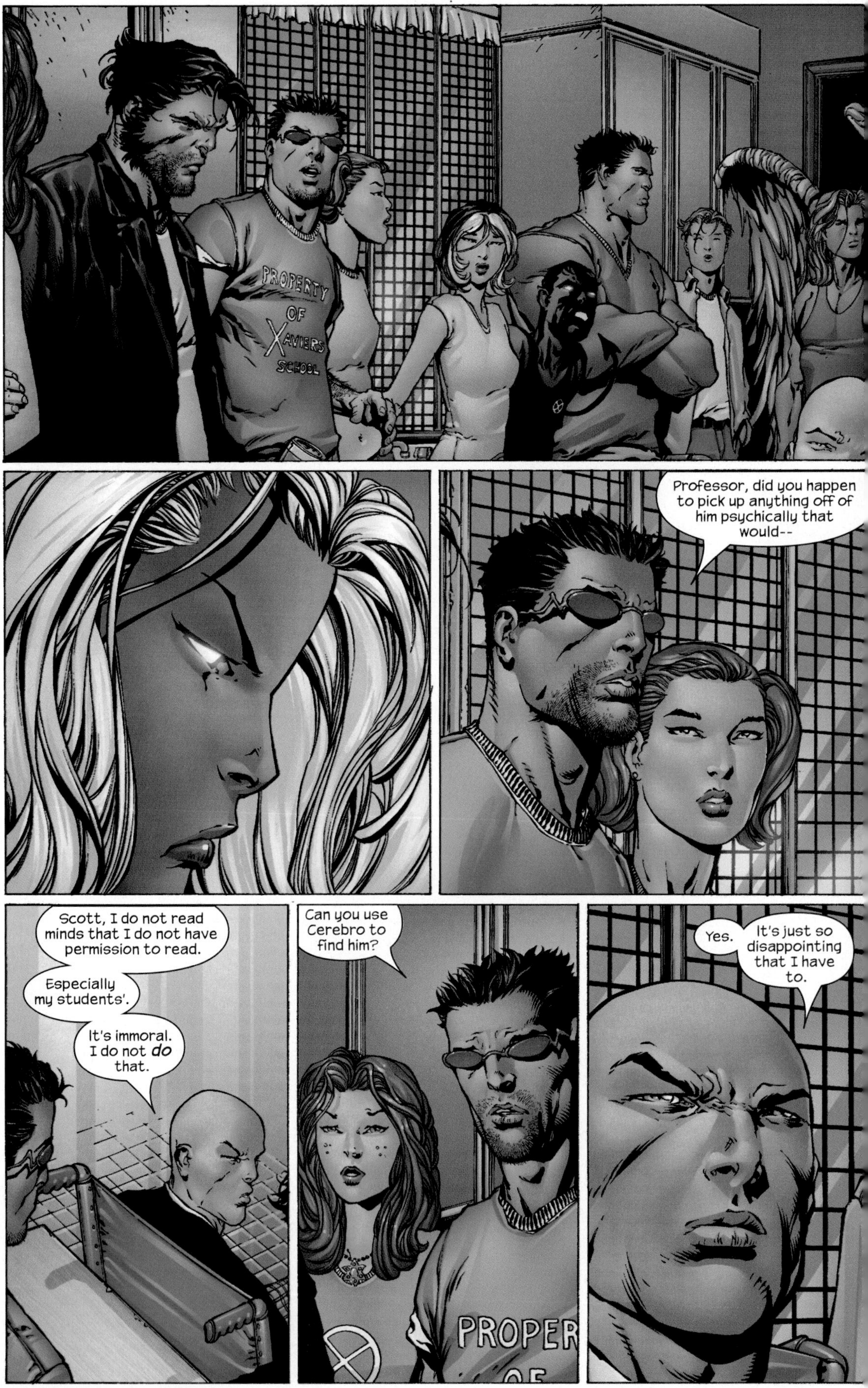

PROPERTY OF XAVIERS SCHOOL
Professor, did you happen to pick up anything off of him psychically that would--
Scott, I do not read minds that I do not have permission to read.
Especially my students'.
It's immoral. I do not *do* that.
Can you use Cerebro to find him?
Yes.
It's just so disappointing that I have to.

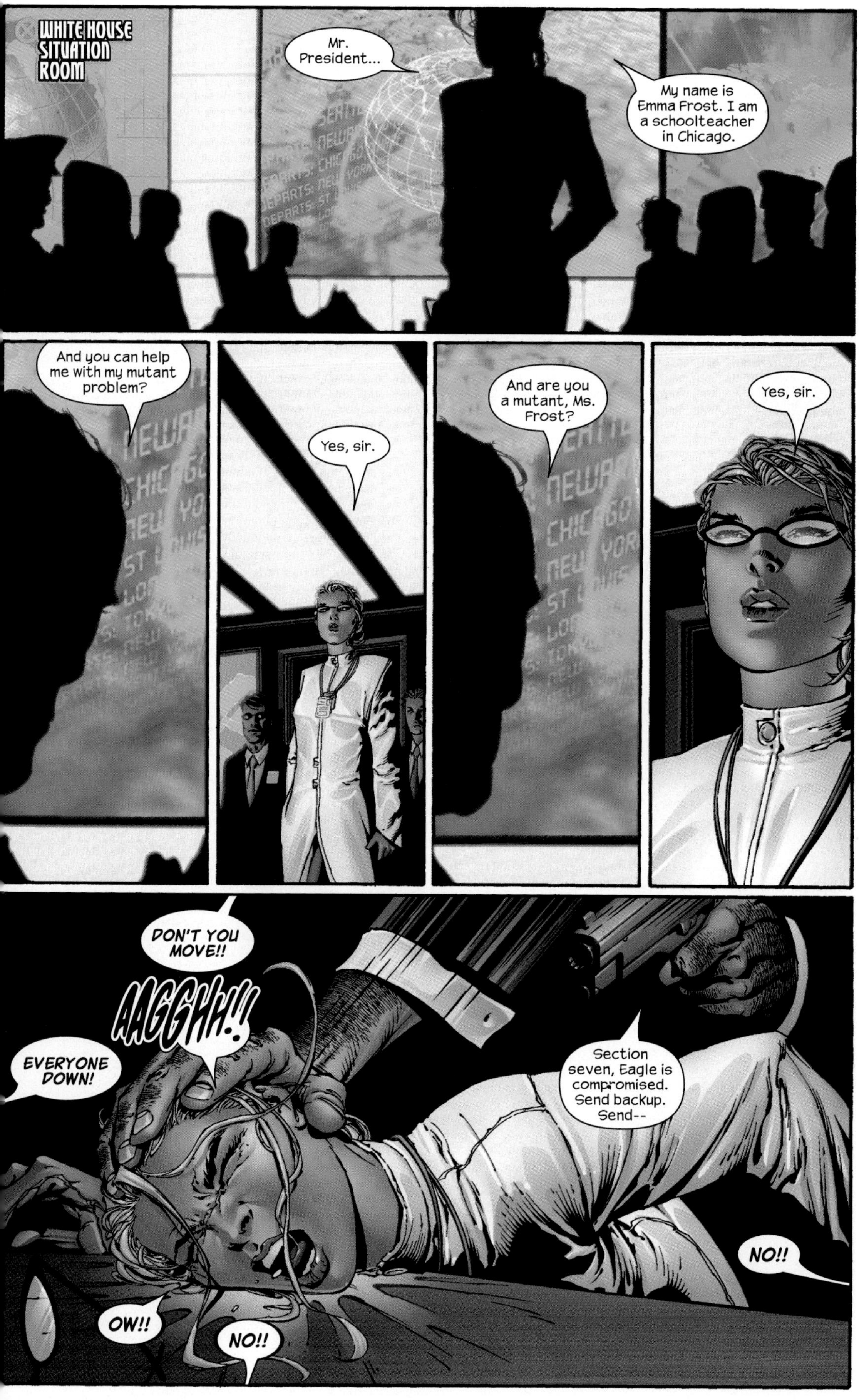
WHITE HOUSE SITUATION ROOM
Mr. President...
My name is Emma Frost. I am a schoolteacher in Chicago.
And you can help me with my mutant problem?
Yes, sir.
And are you a mutant, Ms. Frost?
Yes, sir.
DON'T YOU MOVE!!
AAGGHH!!
EVERYONE DOWN!
Section seven, Eagle is compromised. Send backup. Send--
NO!!
OW!!
NO!!

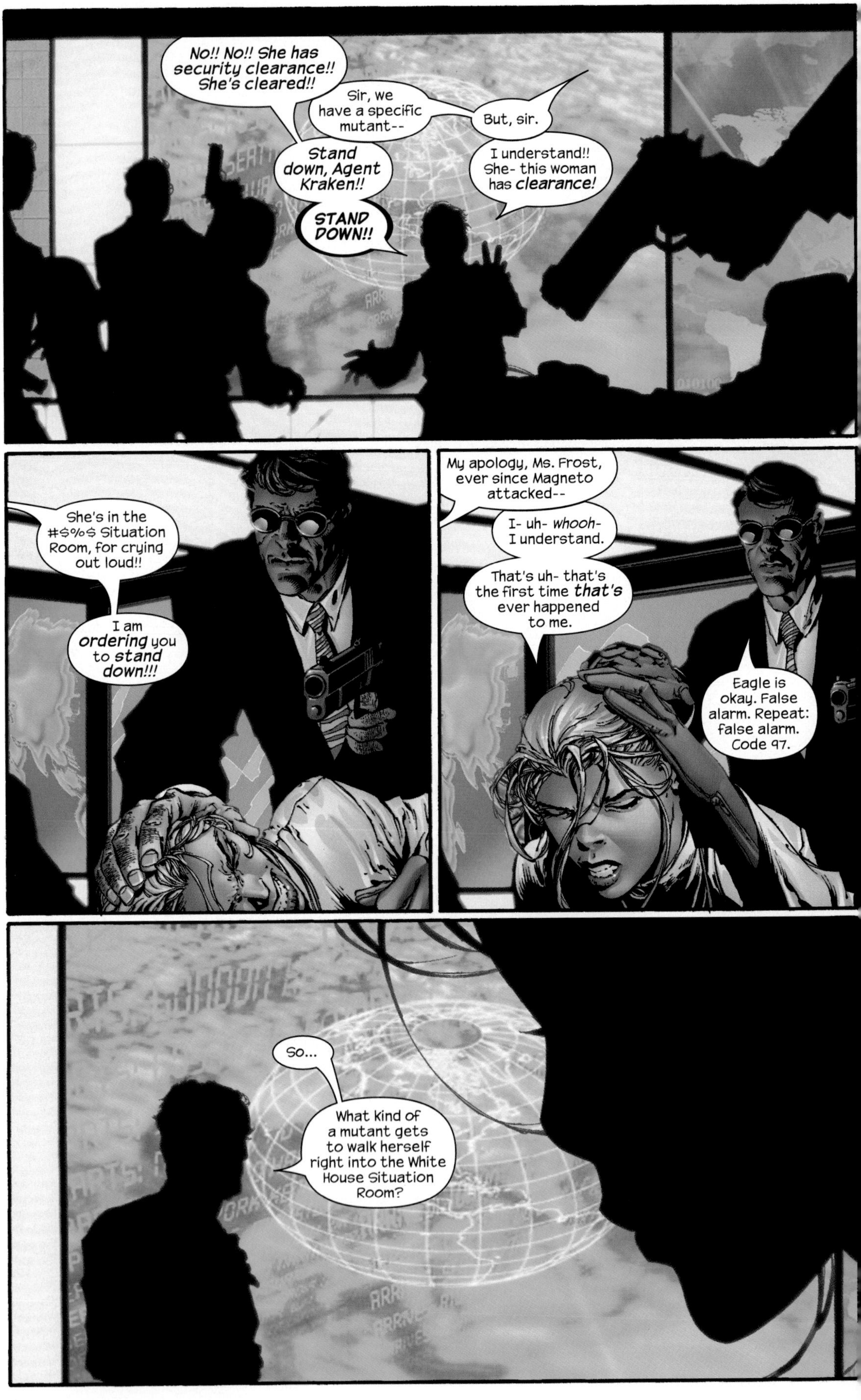

No!! No!! She has security clearance!! She's cleared!!
Sir, we have a specific mutant--
But, sir.
Stand down, Agent Kraken!!
I understand!! She- this woman has clearance!
STAND DOWN!!
She's in the #$%$ Situation Room, for crying out loud!!
I am ordering you to stand down!!!
My apology, Ms. Frost, ever since Magneto attacked--
I- uh- whooh- I understand.
That's uh- that's the first time that's ever happened to me.
Eagle is okay. False alarm. Repeat: false alarm. Code 97.
So...
What kind of a mutant gets to walk herself right into the White House Situation Room?

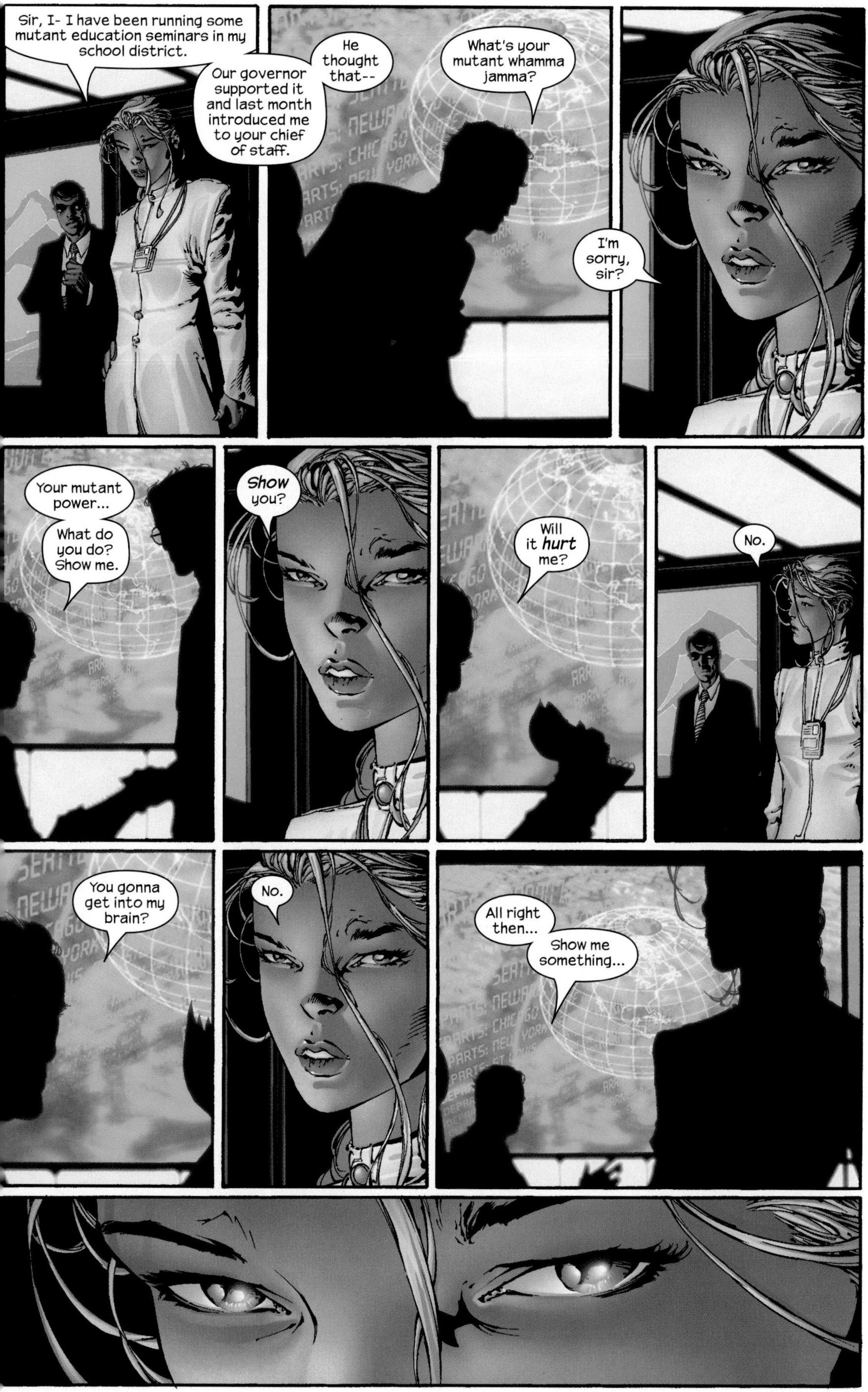
Sir, I- I have been running some mutant education seminars in my school district.
Our governor supported it and last month introduced me to your chief of staff.
He thought that--
What's your mutant whamma jamma?
I'm sorry, sir?
Your mutant power...
What do you do? Show me.
Show you?
Will it hurt me?
No.
You gonna get into my brain?
No.
All right then...
Show me something...

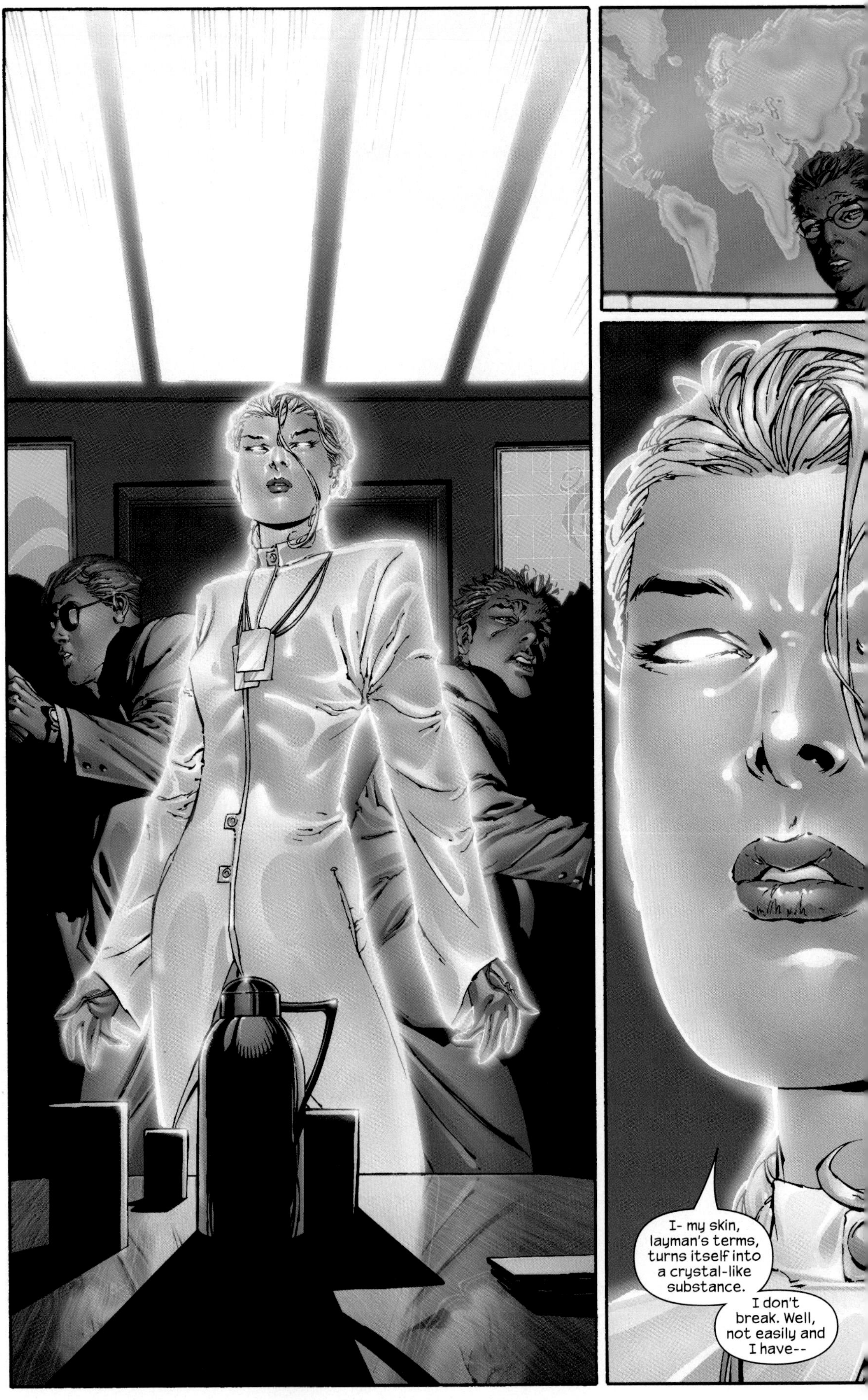
I- my skin, layman's terms, turns itself into a crystal-like substance.
I don't break. Well, not easily and I have--

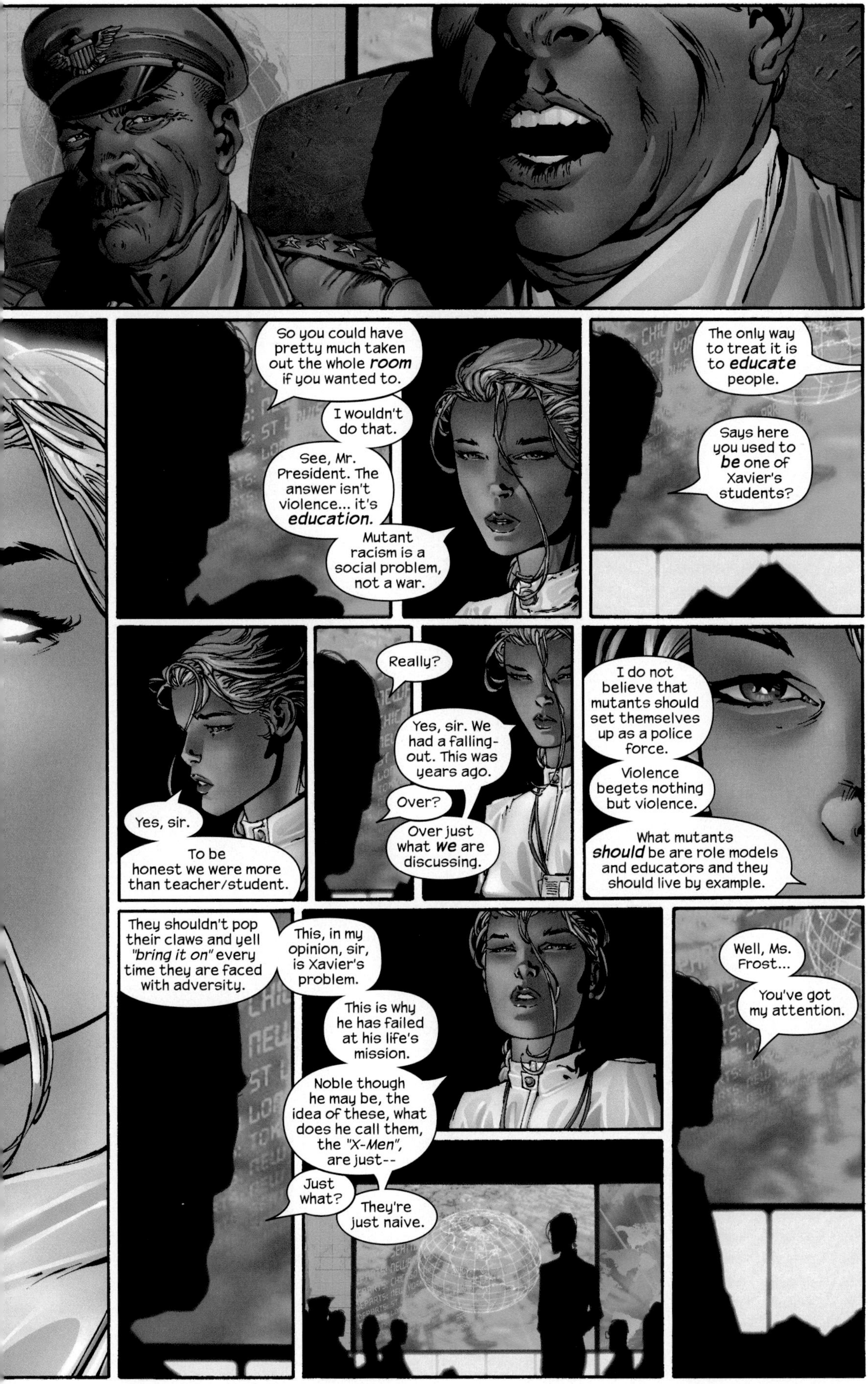

So you could have pretty much taken out the whole *room* if you wanted to.
I wouldn't do that.
See, Mr. President. The answer isn't violence... it's *education.*
Mutant racism is a social problem, not a war.
The only way to treat it is to *educate* people.
Says here you used to *be* one of Xavier's students?
Yes, sir.
To be honest we were more than teacher/student.
Really?
Yes, sir. We had a falling-out. This was years ago.
Over?
Over just what *we* are discussing.
I do not believe that mutants should set themselves up as a police force.
Violence begets nothing but violence.
What mutants *should* be are role models and educators and they should live by example.
They shouldn't pop their claws and yell *"bring it on"* every time they are faced with adversity.
This, in my opinion, sir, is Xavier's problem.
This is why he has failed at his life's mission.
Noble though he may be, the idea of these, what does he call them, the *"X-Men"*, are just--
Just what?
They're just naive.
Well, Ms. Frost...
You've got my attention.

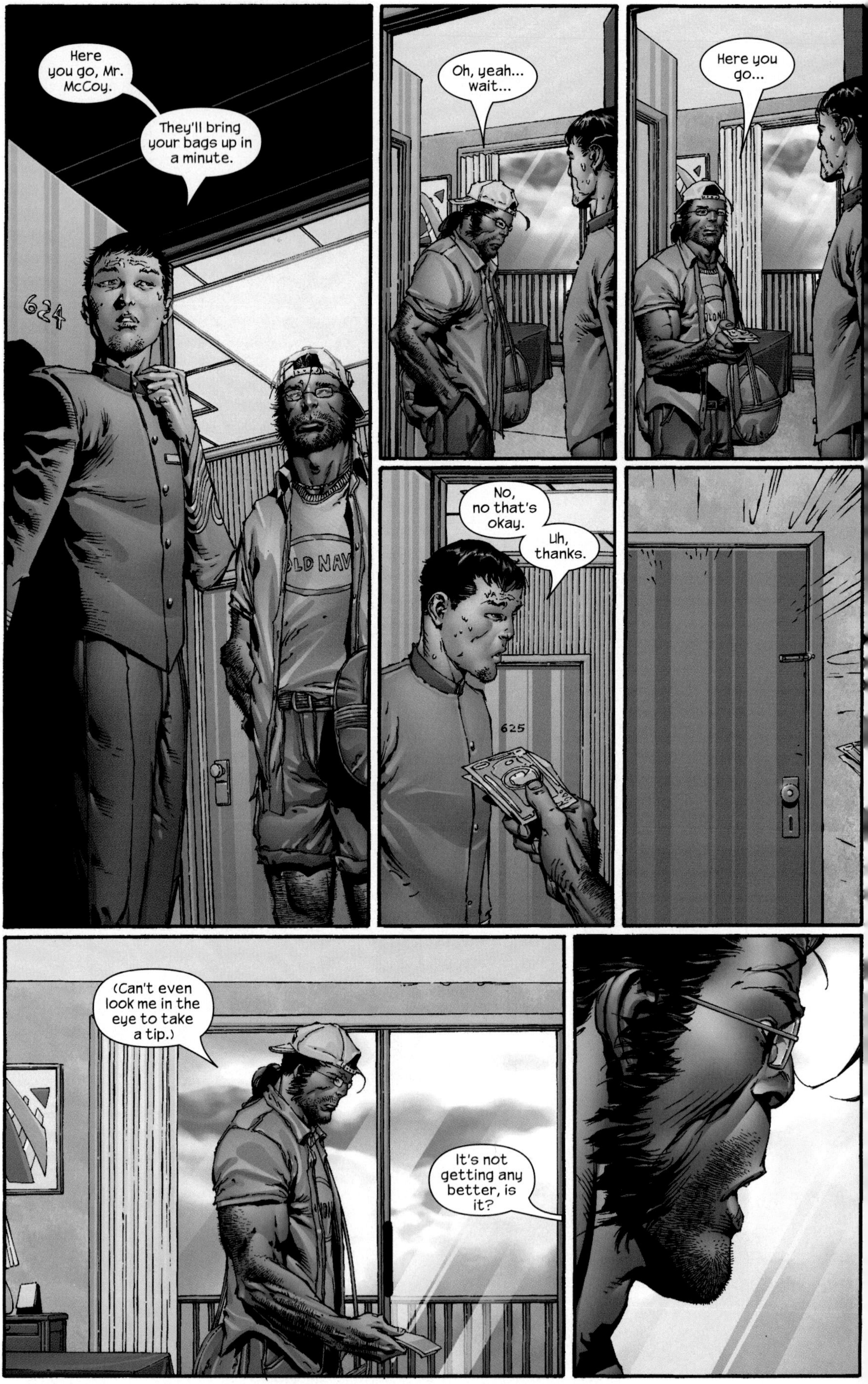
Here you go, Mr. McCoy.
They'll bring your bags up in a minute.
624
Oh, yeah... wait...
Here you go...
No, no that's okay.
Uh, thanks.
625
(Can't even look me in the eye to take a tip.)
It's not getting any better, is it?

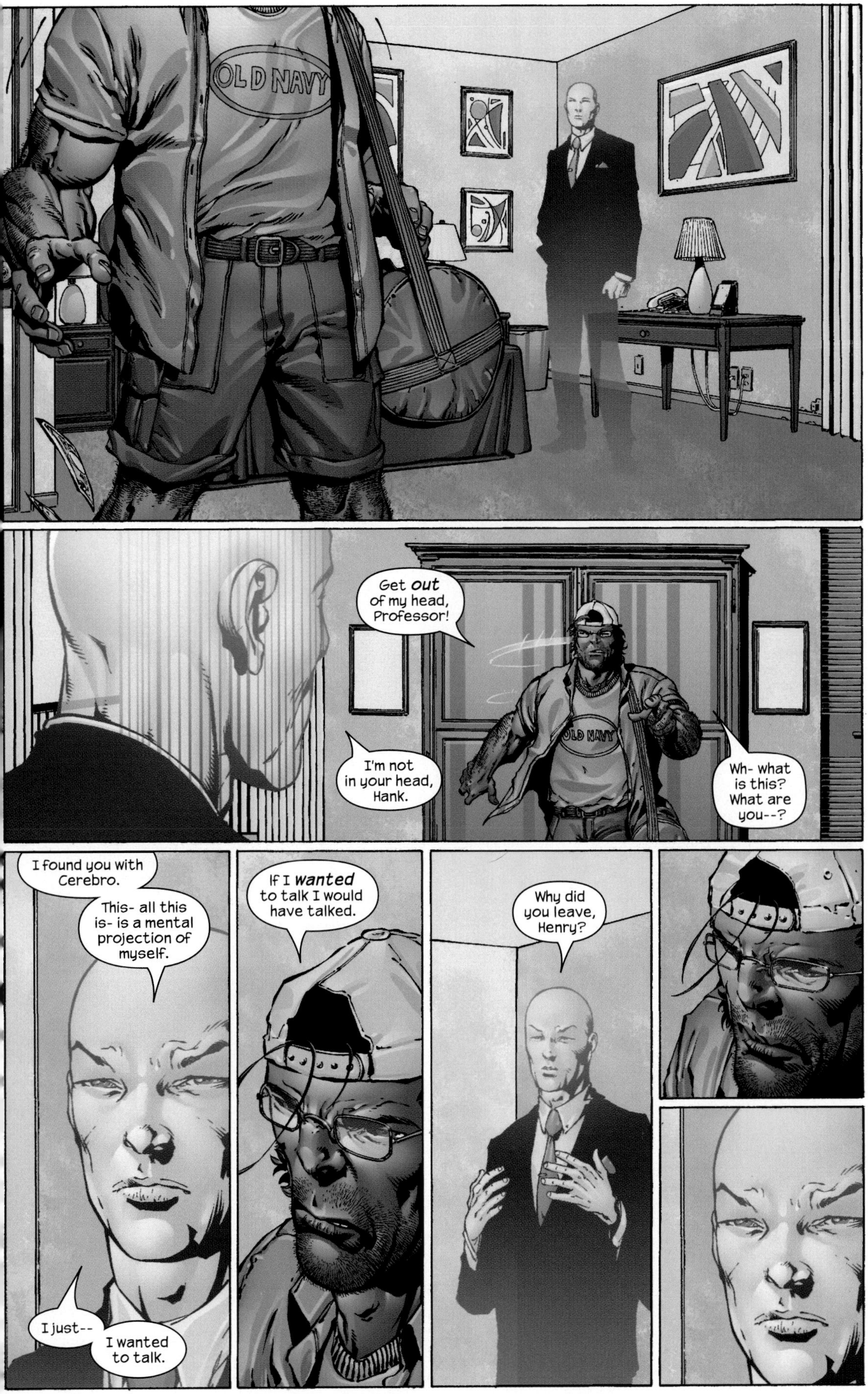

OLD NAVY
Get out of my head, Professor!
I'm not in your head, Hank.
Wh- what is this? What are you--?
I found you with Cerebro.
This- all this is- is a mental projection of myself.
I just--
I wanted to talk.
If I wanted to talk I would have talked.
Why did you leave, Henry?

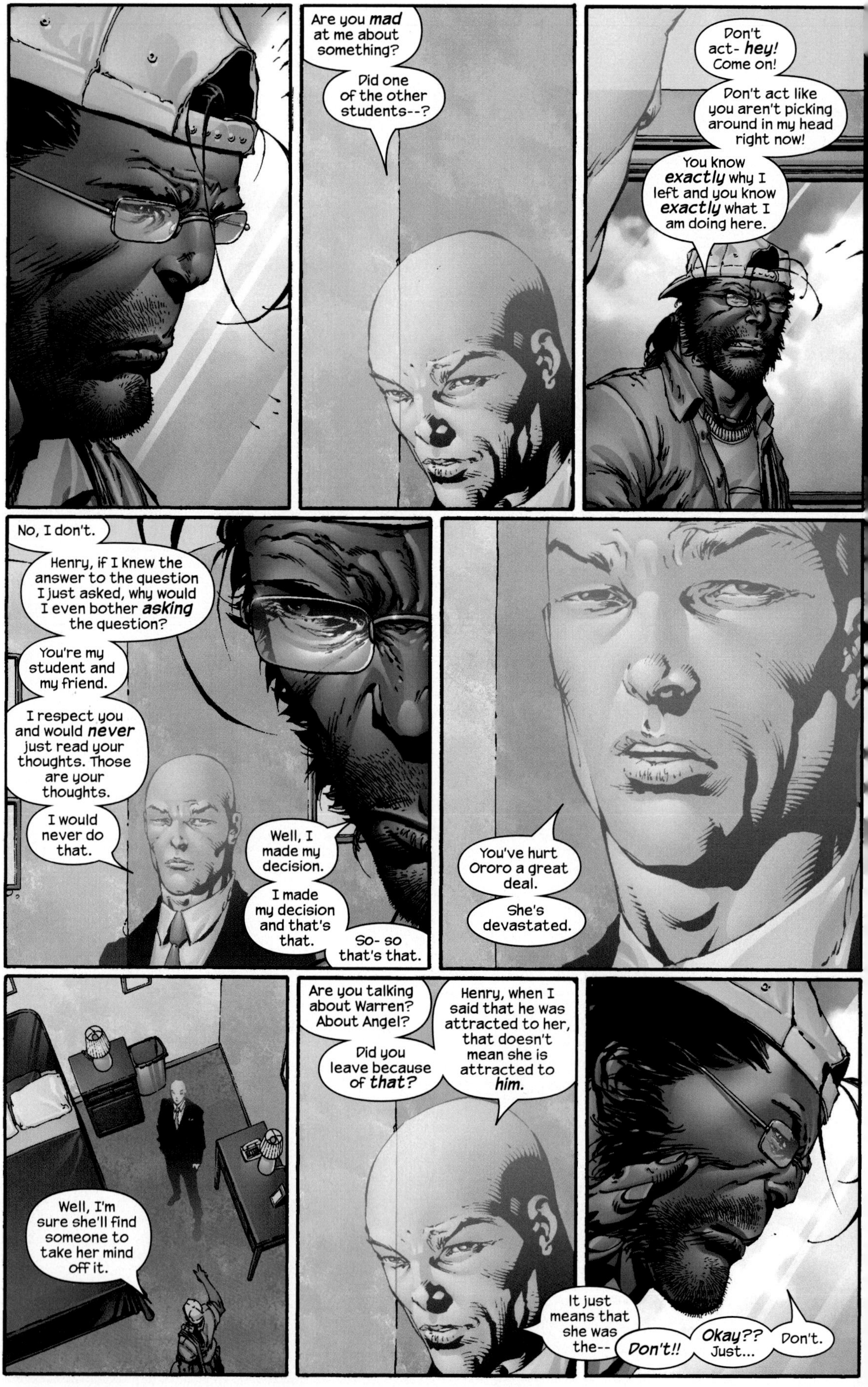
Are you *mad* at me about something?
Did one of the other students--?
Don't act- *hey!* Come on!
Don't act like you aren't picking around in my head right now!
You know *exactly* why I left and you know *exactly* what I am doing here.
No, I don't.
Henry, if I knew the answer to the question I just asked, why would I even bother *asking* the question?
You're my student and my friend.
I respect you and would *never* just read your thoughts. Those are your thoughts.
I would never do that.
Well, I made my decision.
I made my decision and that's that.
So- so that's that.
You've hurt Ororo a great deal.
She's devastated.
Well, I'm sure she'll find someone to take her mind off it.
Are you talking about Warren? About Angel?
Did you leave because of *that?*
Henry, when I said that he was attracted to her, that doesn't mean she is attracted to *him.*
It just means that she was the--
Don't!!
Okay?? Just...
Don't.

I'm grateful for everything you did for me.

And- and- and it was a pleasure knowing you, and I wish you the best.

I just- listen- I just don't feel like putting my life in danger over people like Wolverine, and- and I don't feel like--

I just- I don't want to *be* there anymore.

And now I want you to leave.

So disappear or- or- or *whatever* you have to do to *not* be here--

Please do it.

I--

I won't lie to you- this is *terribly* disappointing both personally and professionally.

But you always have a home with me, Henry.

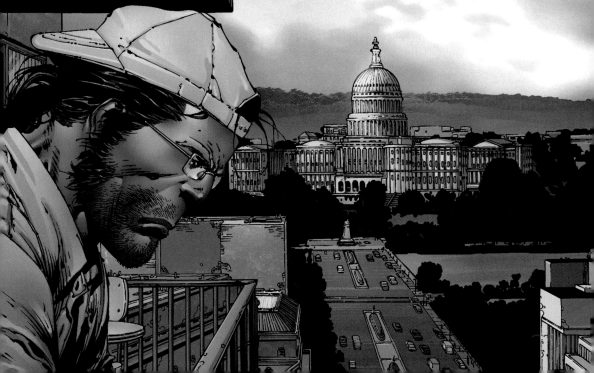

What is this Dazzler person?

She's a rock and roll star.

Yes, that is Henry McCoy. He *was* with Xavier but he is no longer with him.

I don't understand.

Actually, that was your political advisor's suggestion.

Young men and women, mutants all.

Who are not trained warriors, but smart, attractive mutants.

Not warriors, but potential *spokesmen* for the White House's mutant agenda.

Faces of the future.

People who can speak to the kids in their own language.

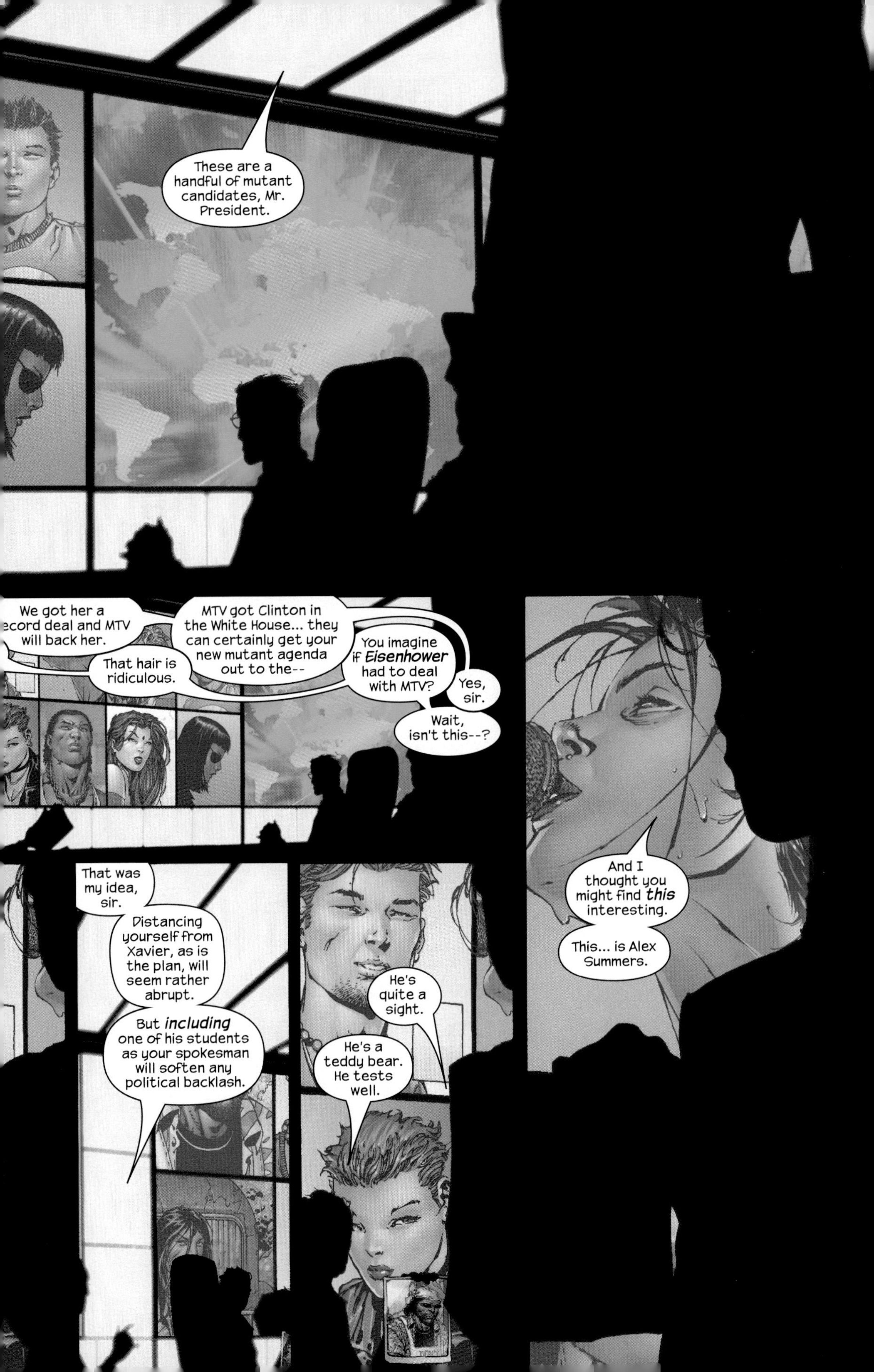

These are a handful of mutant candidates, Mr. President.
We got her a record deal and MTV will back her.
That hair is ridiculous.
MTV got Clinton in the White House... they can certainly get your new mutant agenda out to the--
You imagine if *Eisenhower* had to deal with MTV?
Yes, sir.
Wait, isn't this--?
And I thought you might find *this* interesting.
This... is Alex Summers.
That was my idea, sir.
Distancing yourself from Xavier, as is the plan, will seem rather abrupt.
But *including* one of his students as your spokesman will soften any political backlash.
He's quite a sight.
He's a teddy bear. He tests well.

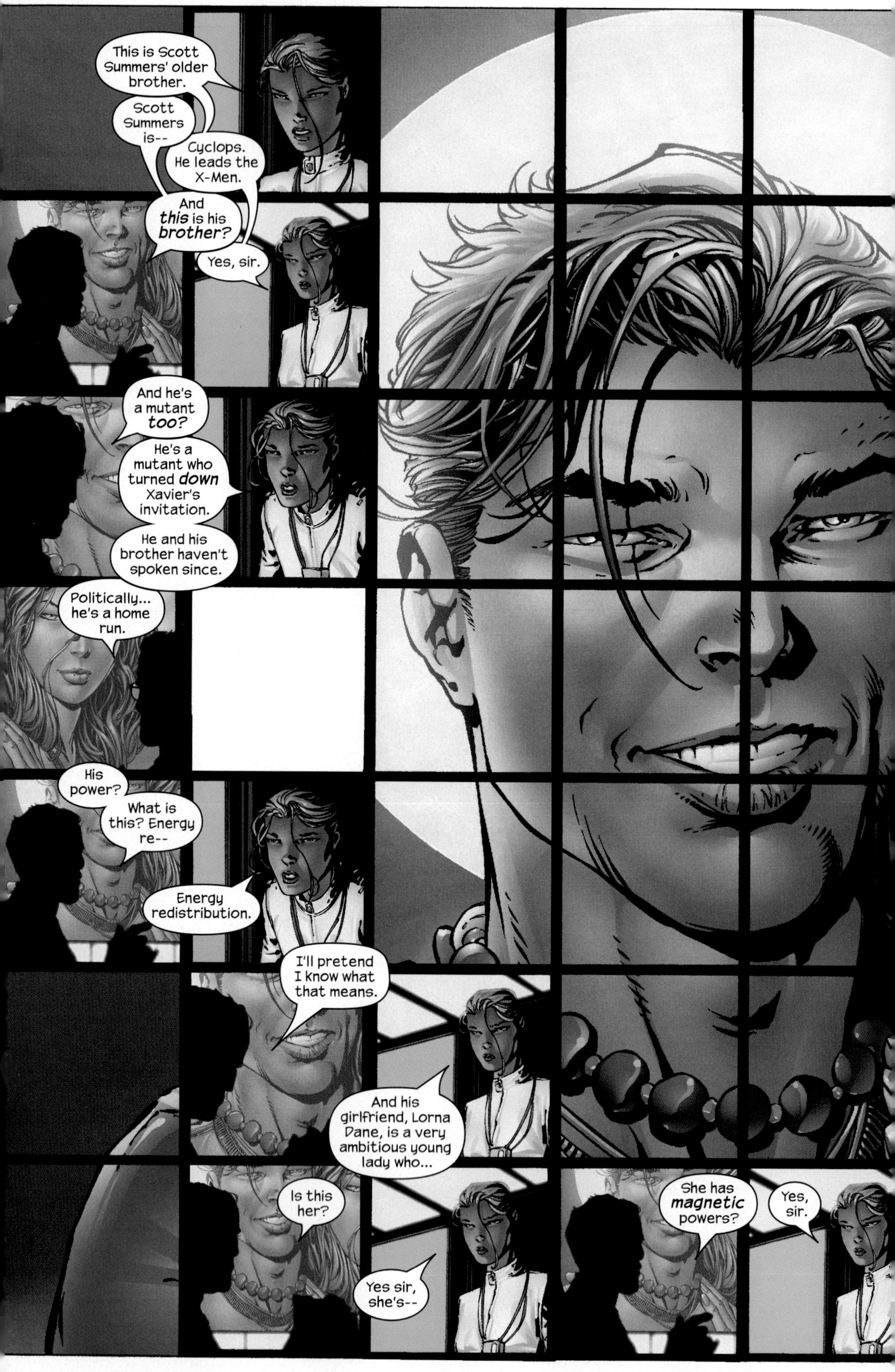
This is Scott Summers' older brother.
Scott Summers is--
Cyclops. He leads the X-Men.
And this is his brother?
Yes, sir.
And he's a mutant too?
He's a mutant who turned down Xavier's invitation.
He and his brother haven't spoken since.
Politically... he's a home run.
His power?
What is this? Energy re--
Energy redistribution.
I'll pretend I know what that means.
And his girlfriend, Lorna Dane, is a very ambitious young lady who...
Is this her?
Yes sir, she's--
She has magnetic powers?
Yes, sir.

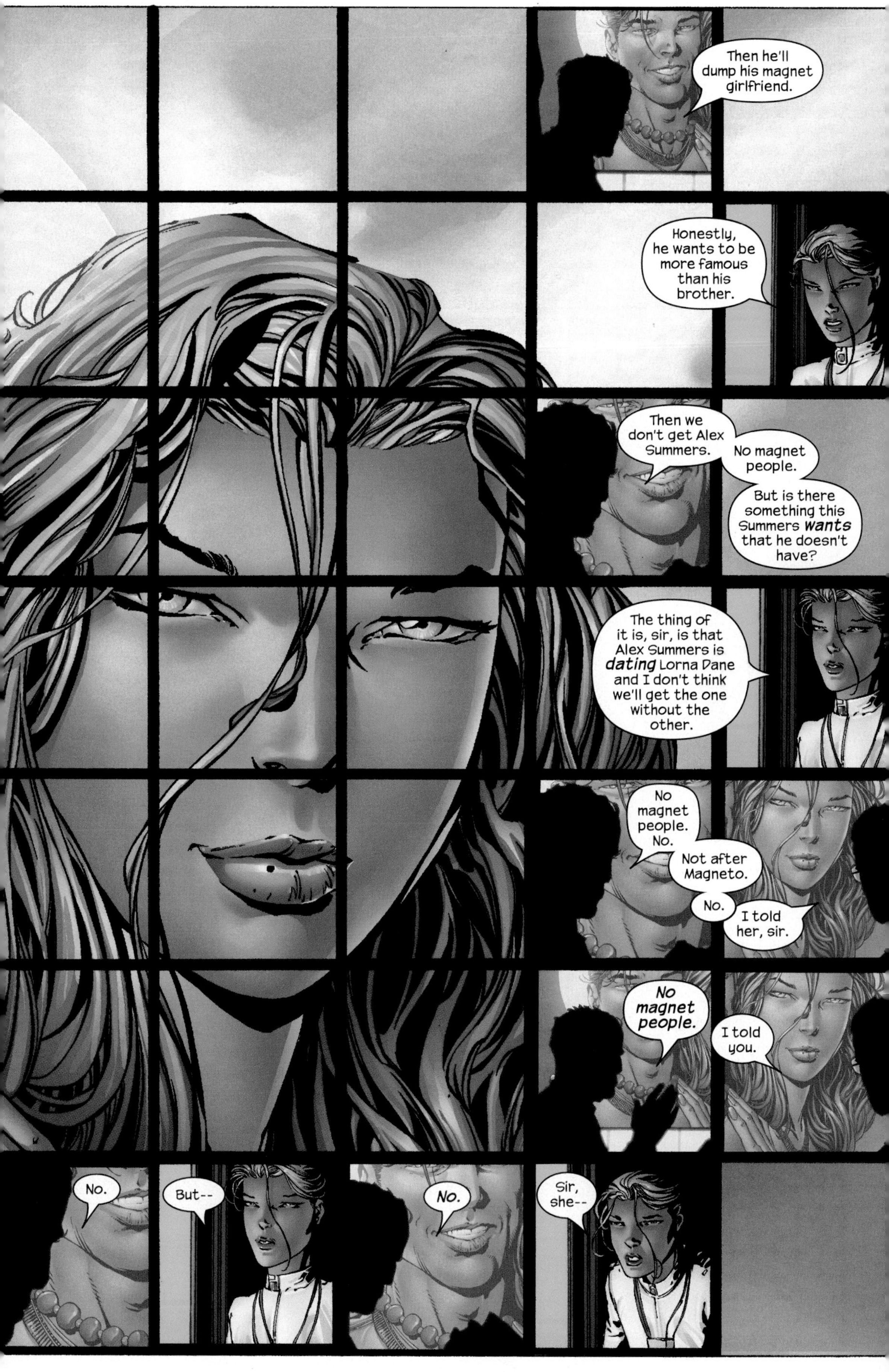

Then he'll dump his magnet girlfriend.
Honestly, he wants to be more famous than his brother.
Then we don't get Alex Summers.
No magnet people.
But is there something this Summers *wants* that he doesn't have?
The thing of it is, sir, is that Alex Summers is *dating* Lorna Dane and I don't think we'll get the one without the other.
No magnet people. No.
Not after Magneto.
No.
I told her, sir.
No magnet people.
I told you.
No.
But--
No.
Sir, she--

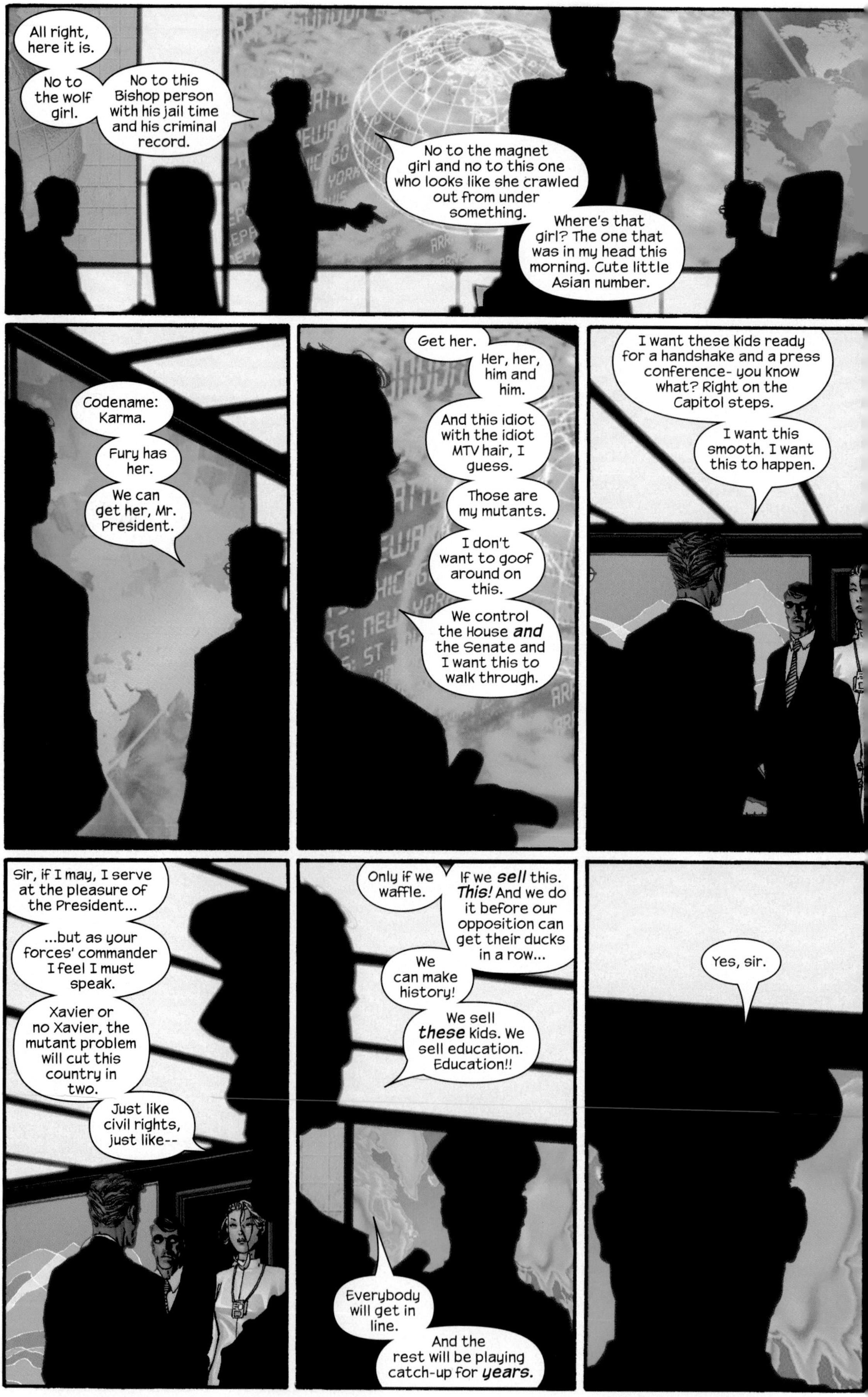
All right, here it is.
No to the wolf girl.
No to this Bishop person with his jail time and his criminal record.
No to the magnet girl and no to this one who looks like she crawled out from under something.
Where's that girl? The one that was in my head this morning. Cute little Asian number.
Codename: Karma.
Fury has her.
We can get her, Mr. President.
Get her.
Her, her, him and him.
And this idiot with the idiot MTV hair, I guess.
Those are my mutants.
I don't want to goof around on this.
We control the House and the Senate and I want this to walk through.
I want these kids ready for a handshake and a press conference- you know what? Right on the Capitol steps.
I want this smooth. I want this to happen.
Sir, if I may, I serve at the pleasure of the President...
...but as your forces' commander I feel I must speak.
Xavier or no Xavier, the mutant problem will cut this country in two.
Just like civil rights, just like--
Only if we waffle.
If we sell this. This! And we do it before our opposition can get their ducks in a row...
We can make history!
We sell these kids. We sell education. Education!!
Everybody will get in line.
And the rest will be playing catch-up for years.
Yes, sir.

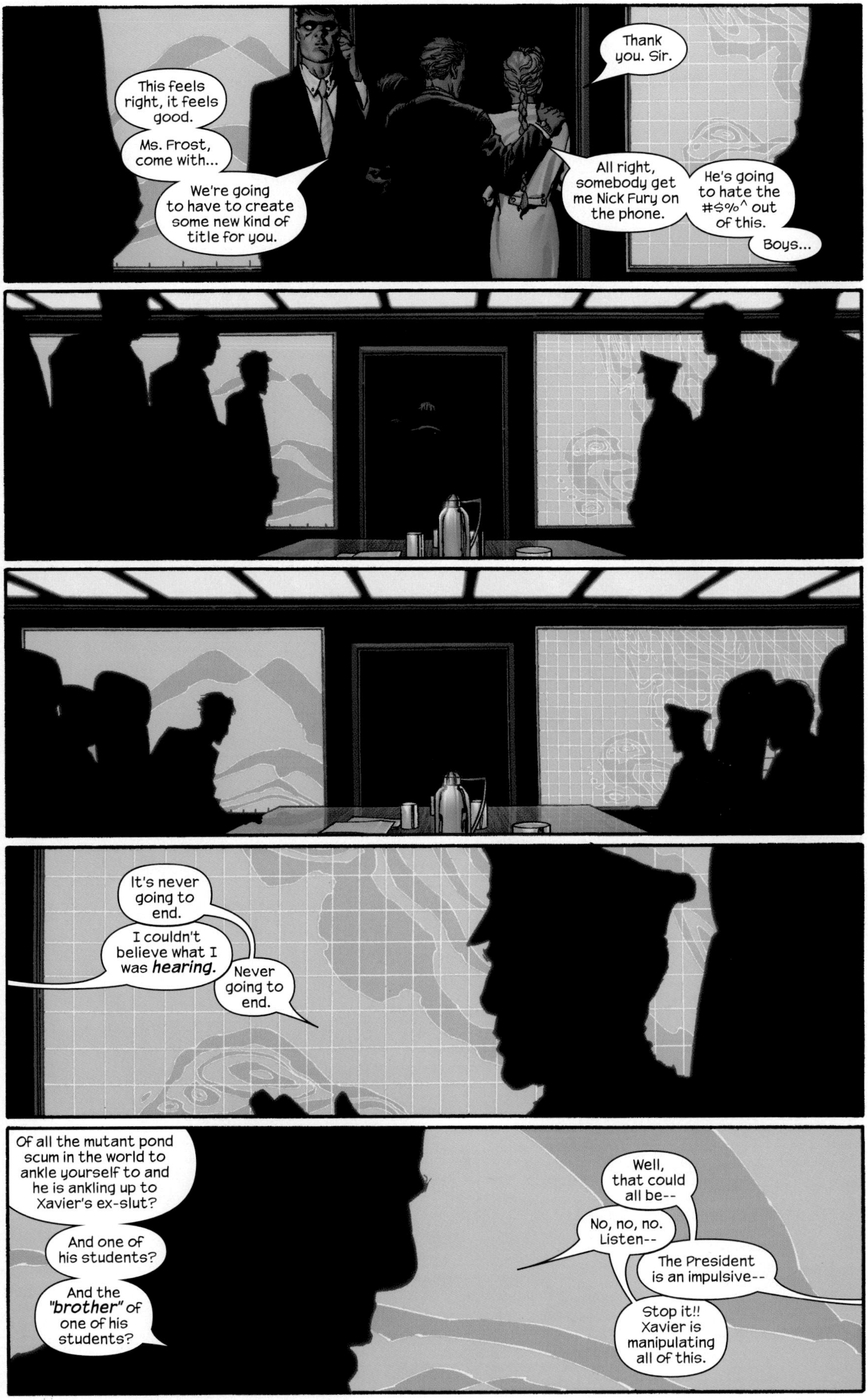
This feels right, it feels good.
Ms. Frost, come with...
We're going to have to create some new kind of title for you.
Thank you. Sir.
All right, somebody get me Nick Fury on the phone.
He's going to hate the #$%^ out of this.
Boys...
It's never going to end.
I couldn't believe what I was *hearing.*
Never going to end.
Of all the mutant pond scum in the world to ankle yourself to and he is ankling up to Xavier's ex-slut?
And one of his students?
And the *"brother"* of one of his students?
Well, that could all be--
No, no, no. Listen--
The President is an impulsive--
Stop it!! Xavier is manipulating all of this.

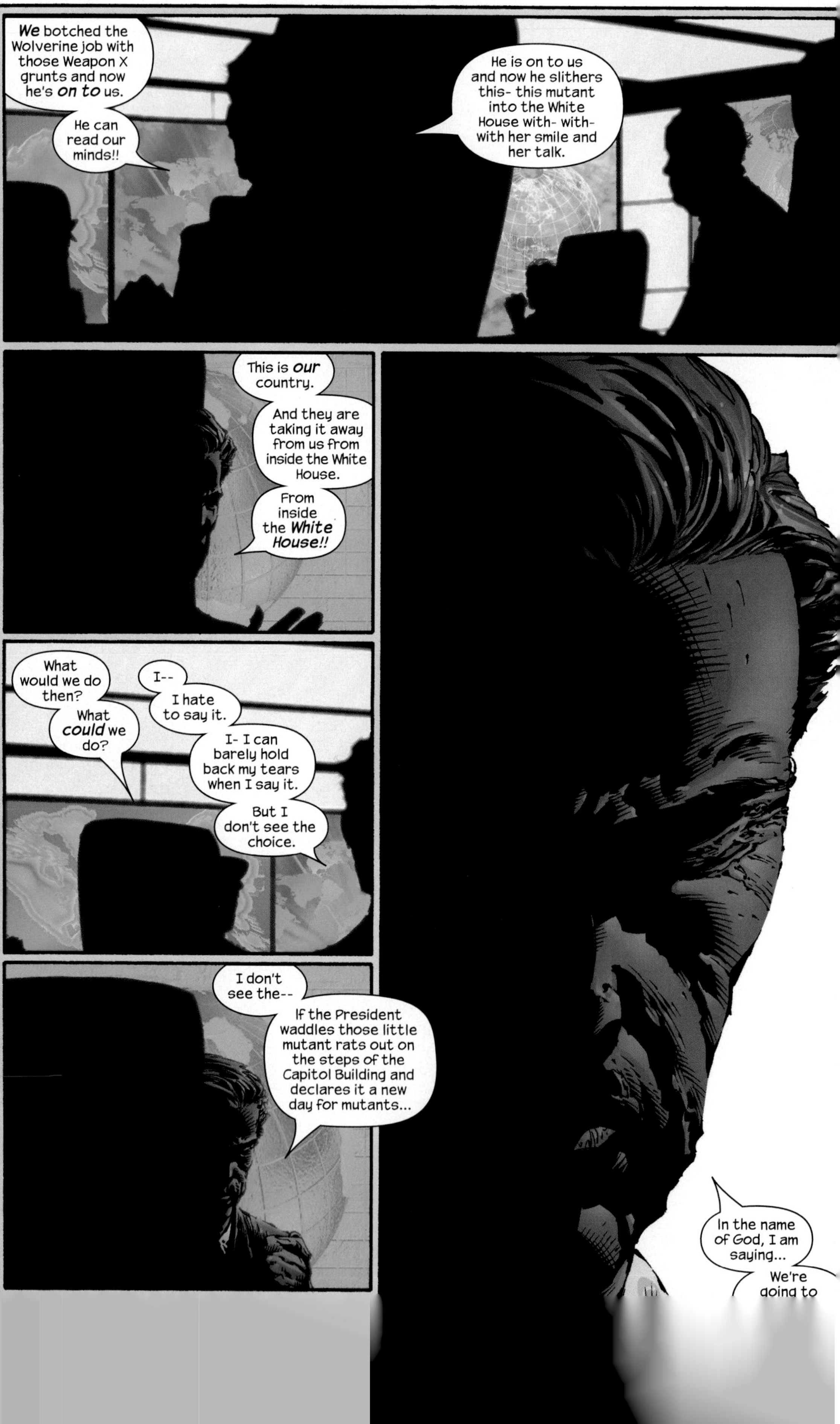

We botched the Wolverine job with those Weapon X grunts and now he's on to us.
He can read our minds!!
He is on to us and now he slithers this- this mutant into the White House with- with- with her smile and her talk.
This is our country.
And they are taking it away from us from inside the White House.
From inside the White House!!
What would we do then?
What could we do?
I--
I hate to say it.
I- I can barely hold back my tears when I say it.
But I don't see the choice.
I don't see the--
If the President waddles those little mutant rats out on the steps of the Capitol Building and declares it a new day for mutants...
In the name of God, I am saying...
We're going to

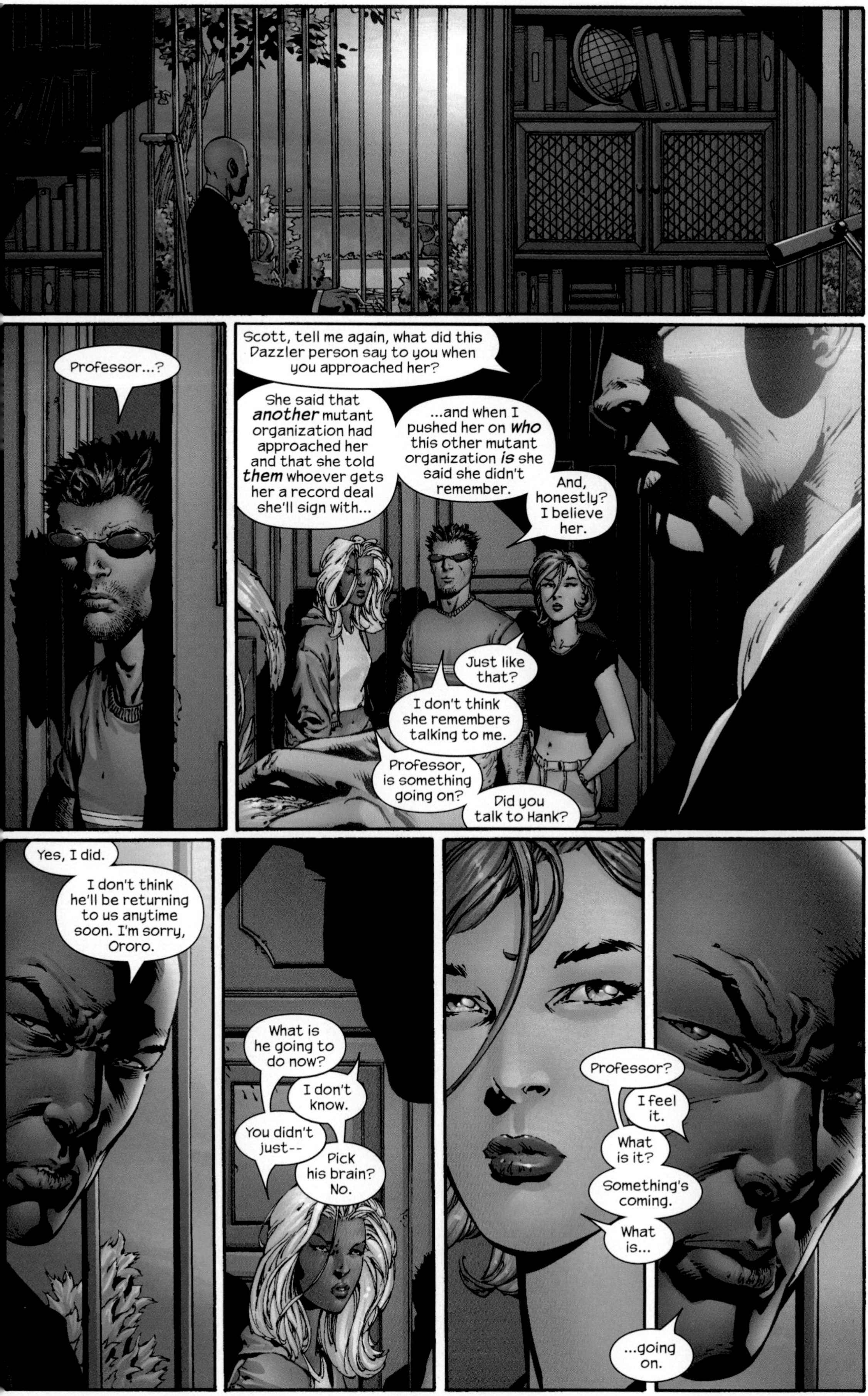
Professor...?
Scott, tell me again, what did this Dazzler person say to you when you approached her?
She said that **another** mutant organization had approached her and that she told **them** whoever gets her a record deal she'll sign with...
...and when I pushed her on **who** this other mutant organization **is** she said she didn't remember.
And, honestly? I believe her.
Just like that?
I don't think she remembers talking to me.
Professor, is something going on?
Did you talk to Hank?
Yes, I did.
I don't think he'll be returning to us anytime soon. I'm sorry, Ororo.
What is he going to do now?
I don't know.
You didn't just--
Pick his brain? No.
Professor?
I feel it.
What is it?
Something's coming.
What is...
...going on.

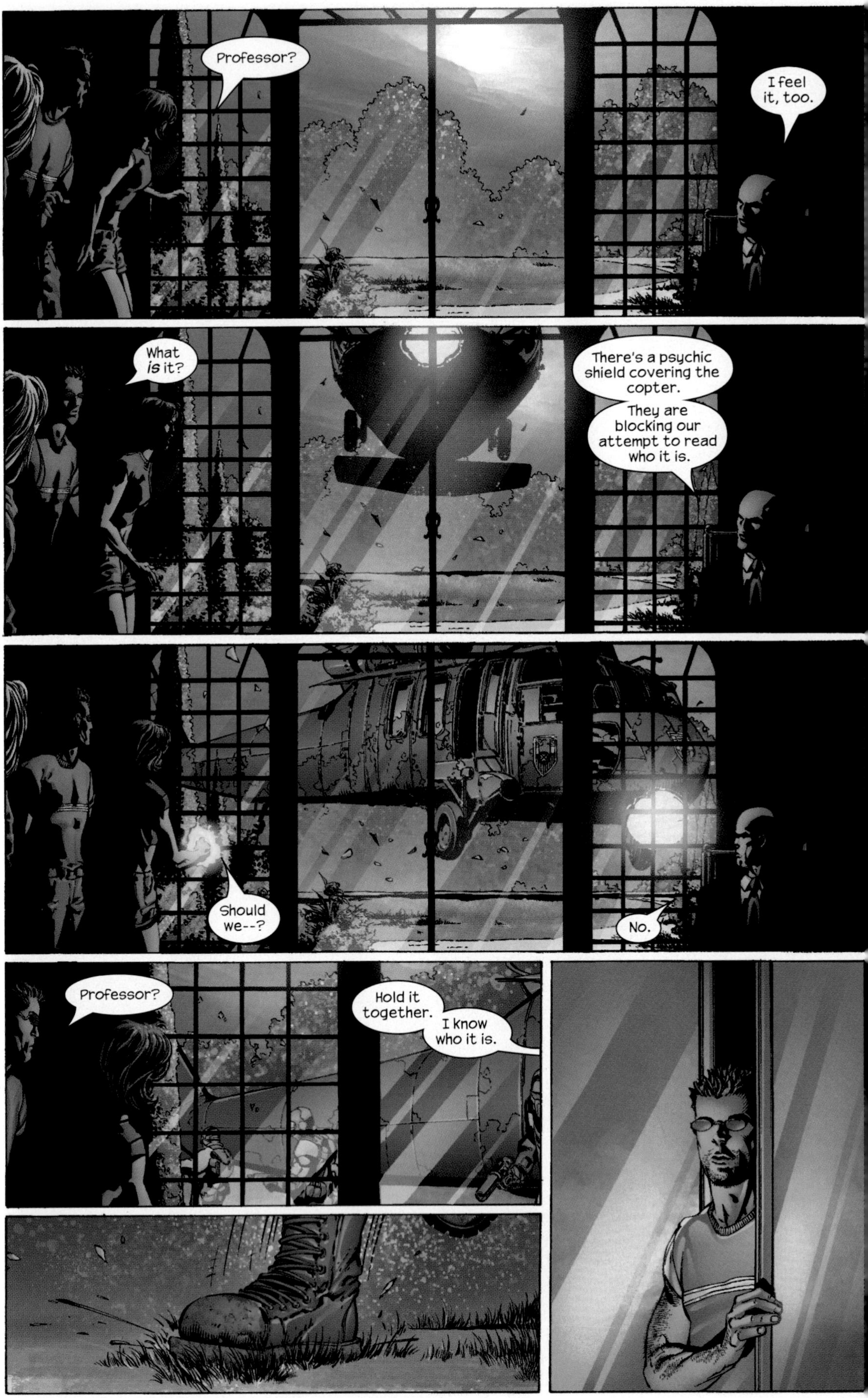

Professor?
I feel it, too.
What *is* it?
There's a psychic shield covering the copter.
They are blocking our attempt to read who it is.
Should we--?
No.
Professor?
Hold it together.
I know who it is.

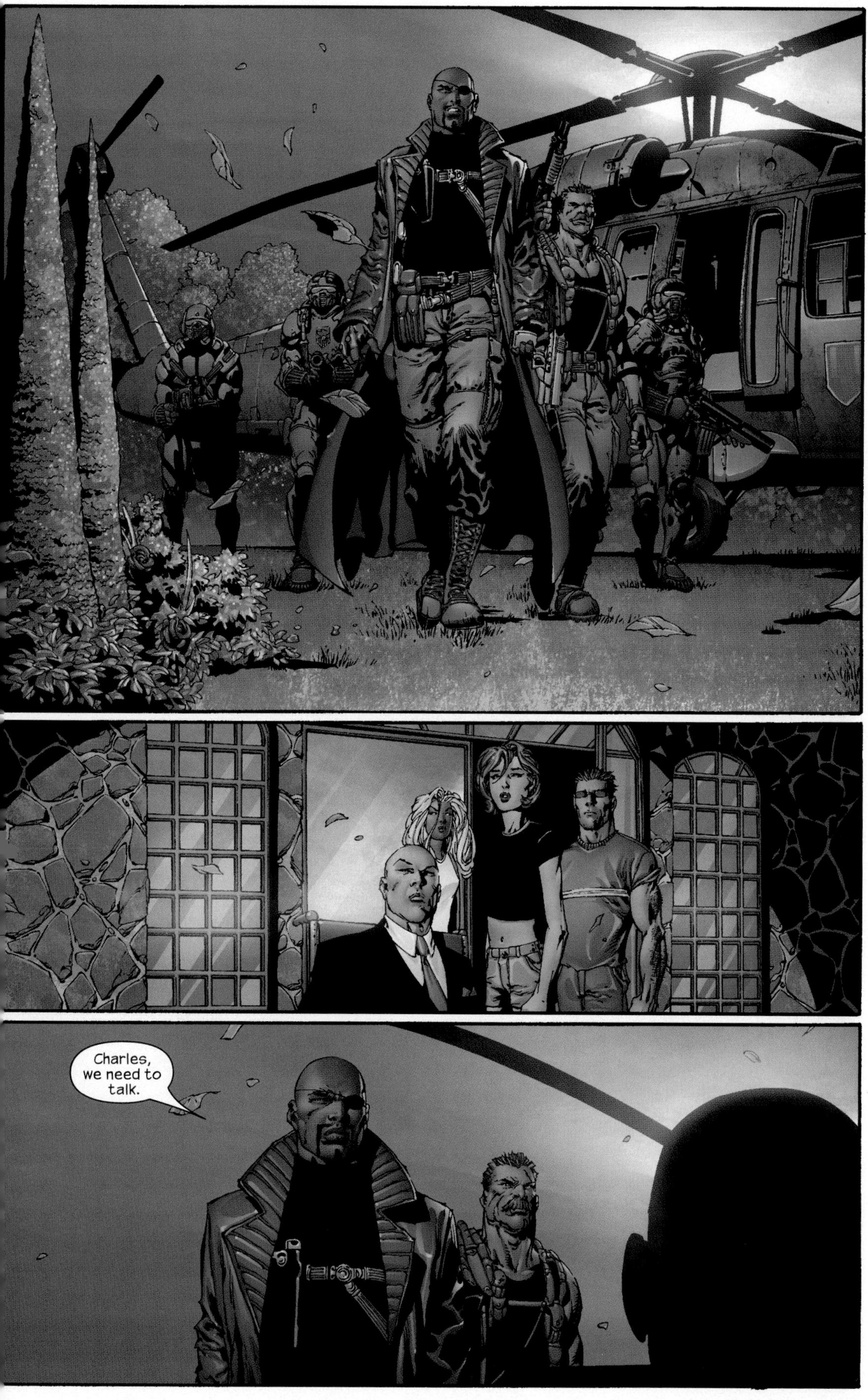
Charles,
we need to
talk.

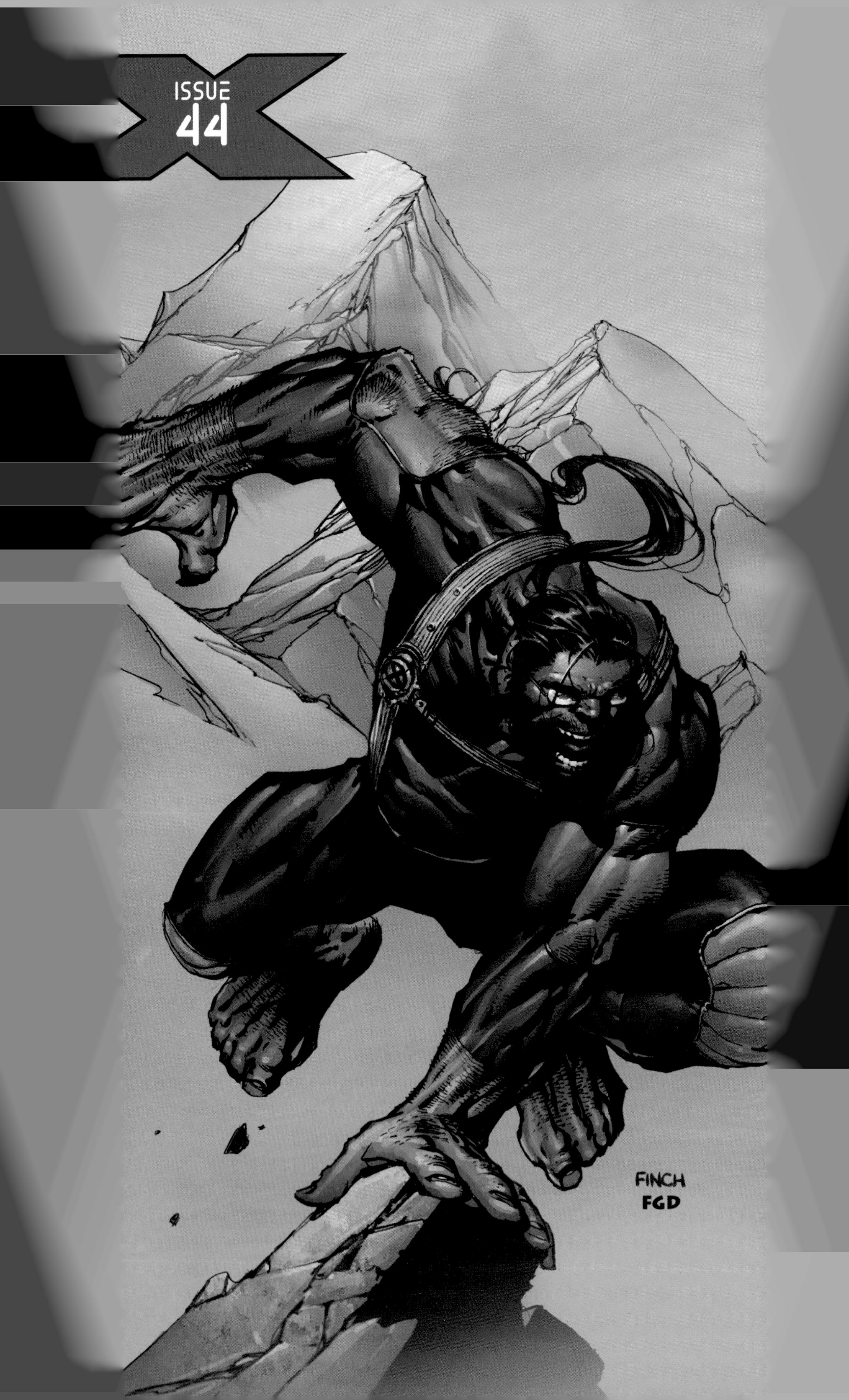
ISSUE
44
FINCH
FGD

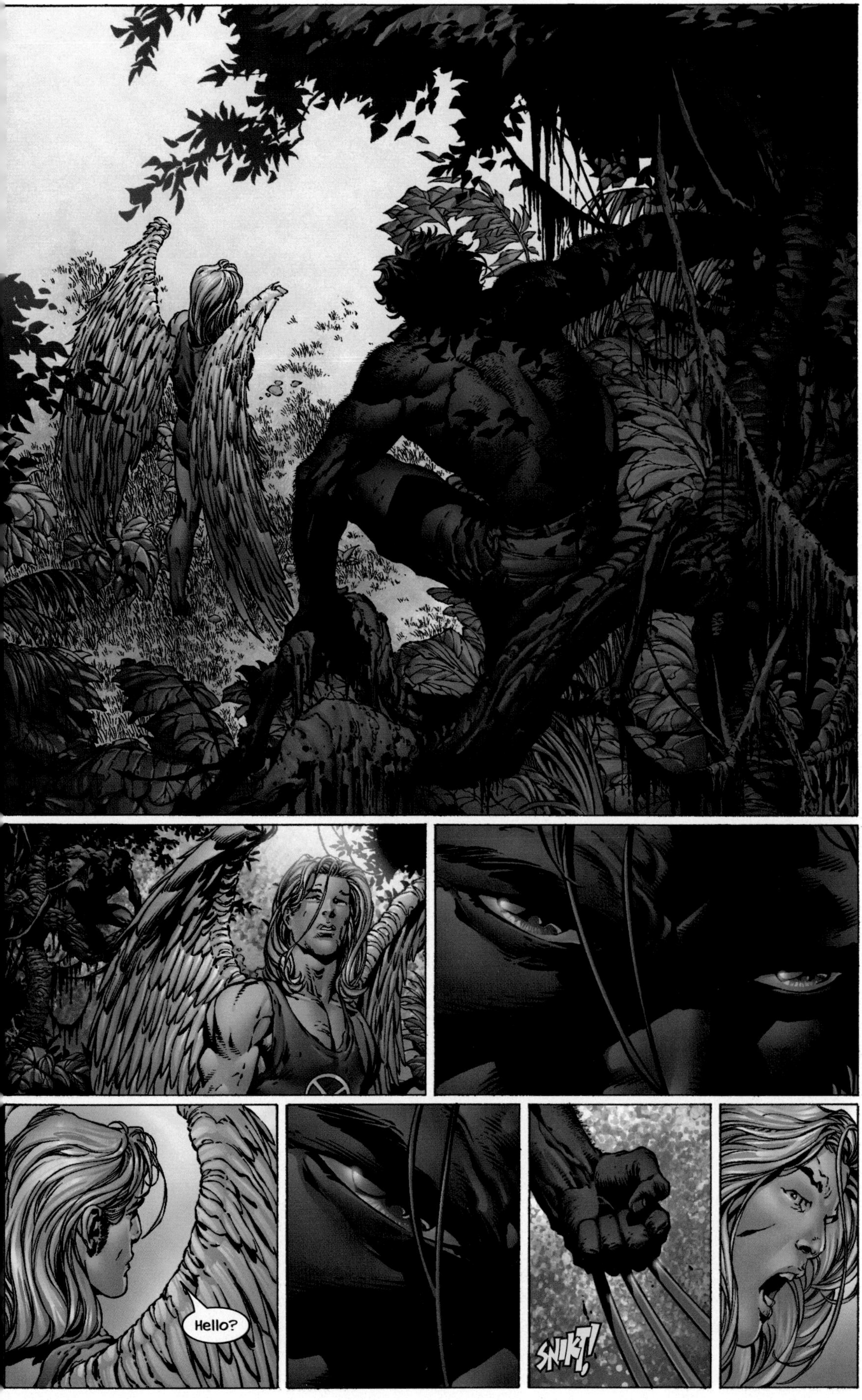
Hello?
SNIKT!

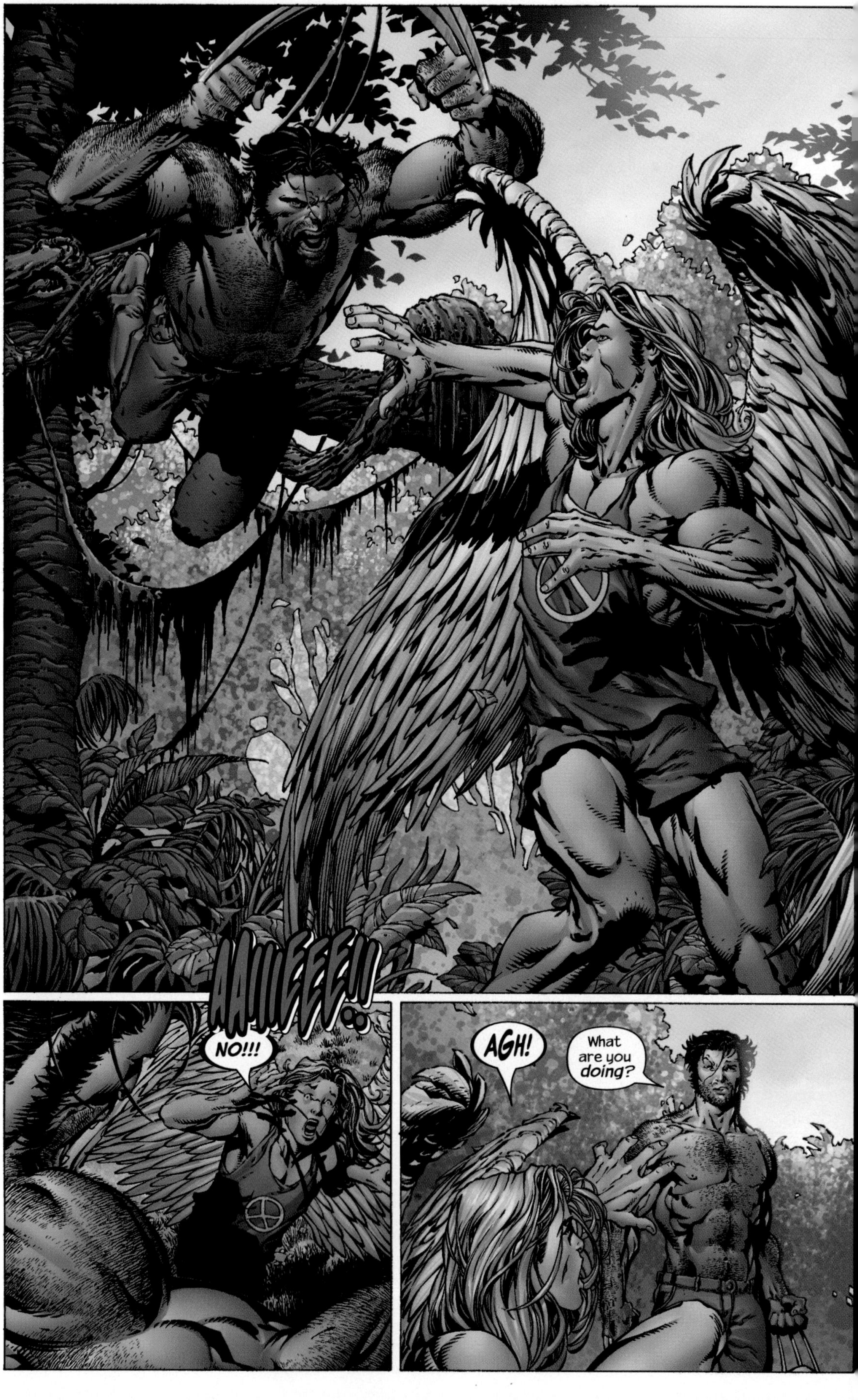
AAIIEEE!!
NO!!!
AGH!
What are you doing?

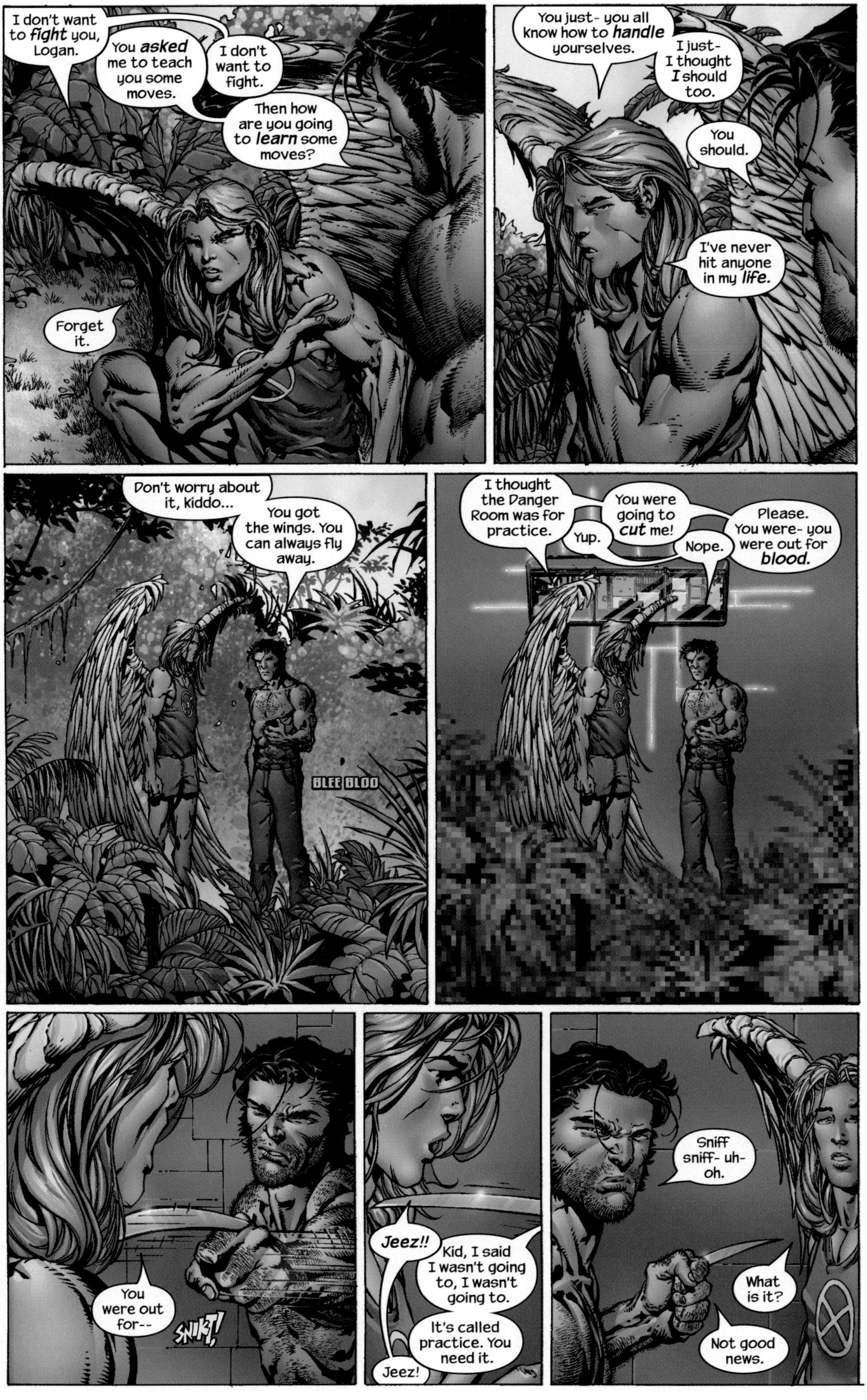
I don't want to *fight* you, Logan.
You *asked* me to teach you some moves.
I don't want to fight.
Then how are you going to *learn* some moves?
Forget it.
You just- you all know how to *handle* yourselves.
I just- I thought *I* should too.
You should.
I've never hit anyone in my *life.*
Don't worry about it, kiddo...
You got the wings. You can always fly away.
BLEE BLOO
I thought the Danger Room was for practice.
You were going to *cut* me!
Yup.
Nope.
Please. You were- you were out for *blood.*
You were out for--
SNIKT!
Jeez!!
Kid, I said I wasn't going to, I wasn't going to.
It's called practice. You need it.
Jeez!
Sniff sniff- uh-oh.
What is it?
Not good news.

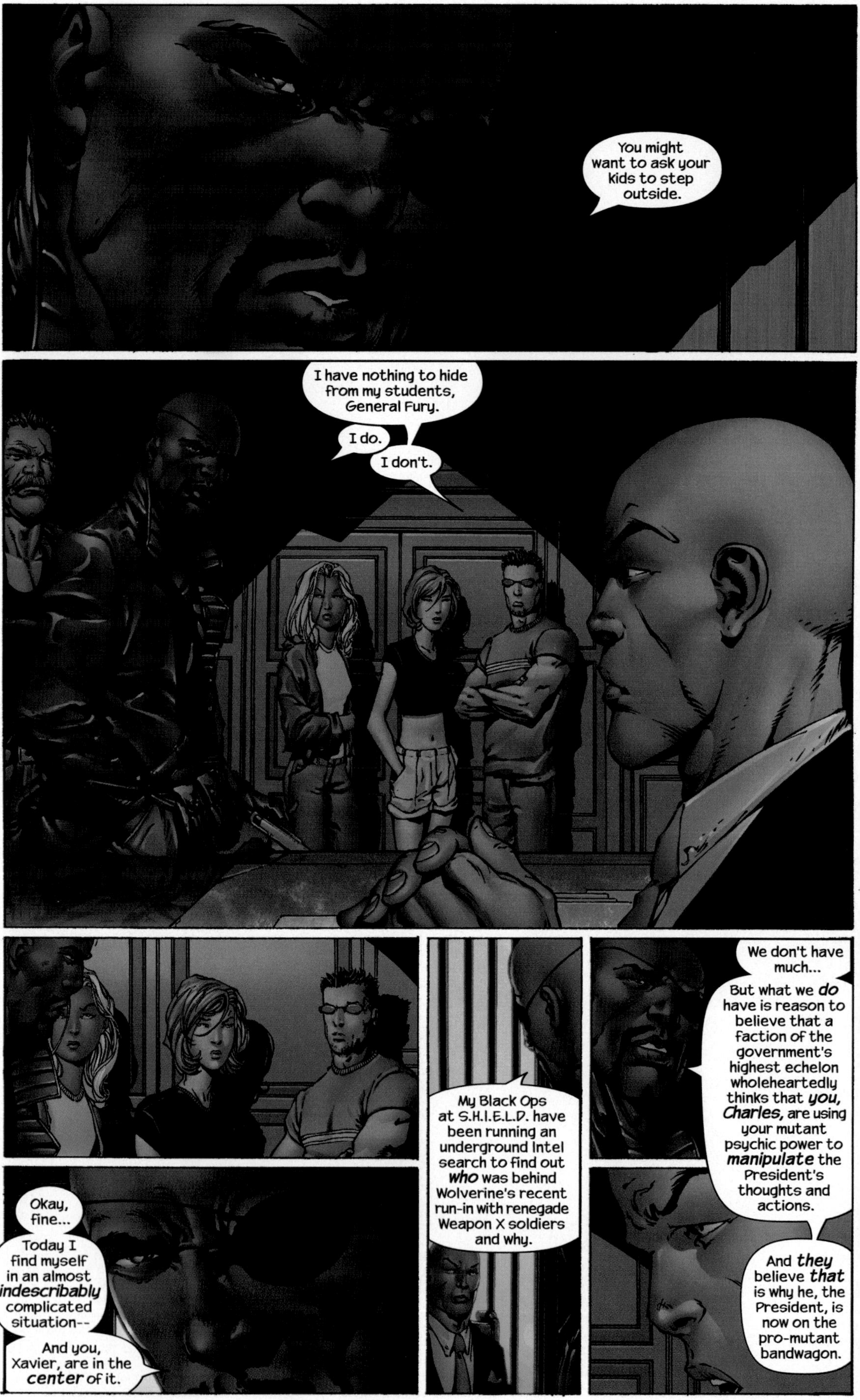

You might want to ask your kids to step outside.
I have nothing to hide from my students, General Fury.
I do.
I don't.
Okay, fine...
Today I find myself in an almost *indescribably* complicated situation--
And you, Xavier, are in the *center* of it.
My Black Ops at S.H.I.E.L.D. have been running an underground Intel search to find out *who* was behind Wolverine's recent run-in with renegade Weapon X soldiers and why.
We don't have much...
But what we *do* have is reason to believe that a faction of the government's highest echelon wholeheartedly thinks that *you, Charles,* are using your mutant psychic power to *manipulate* the President's thoughts and actions.
And *they* believe *that* is why he, the President, is now on the pro-mutant bandwagon.

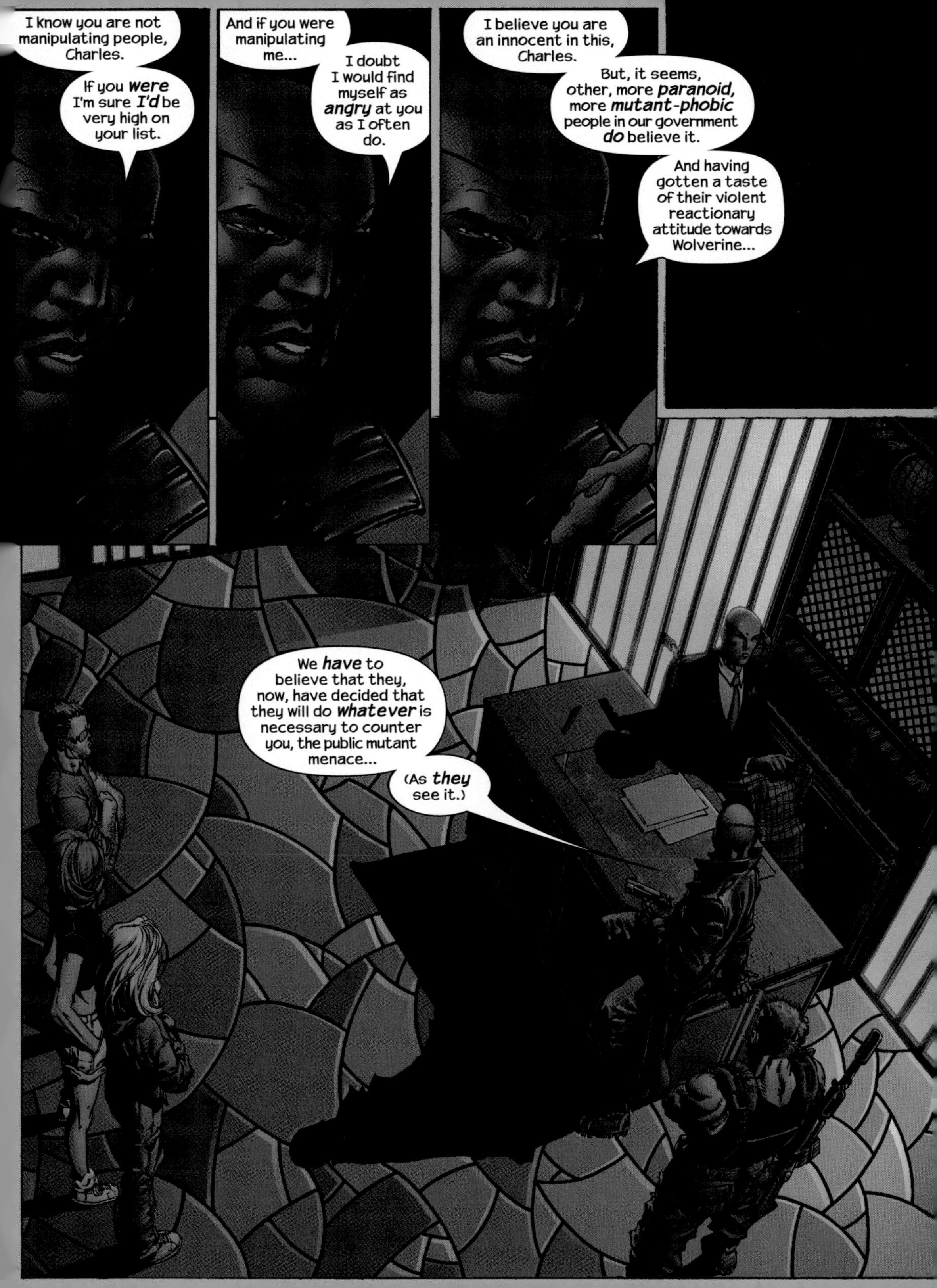
I know you are not manipulating people, Charles.
If you were I'm sure I'd be very high on your list.
And if you were manipulating me...
I doubt I would find myself as angry at you as I often do.
I believe you are an innocent in this, Charles.
But, it seems, other, more paranoid, more mutant-phobic people in our government do believe it.
And having gotten a taste of their violent reactionary attitude towards Wolverine...
We have to believe that they, now, have decided that they will do whatever is necessary to counter you, the public mutant menace...
(As they see it.)

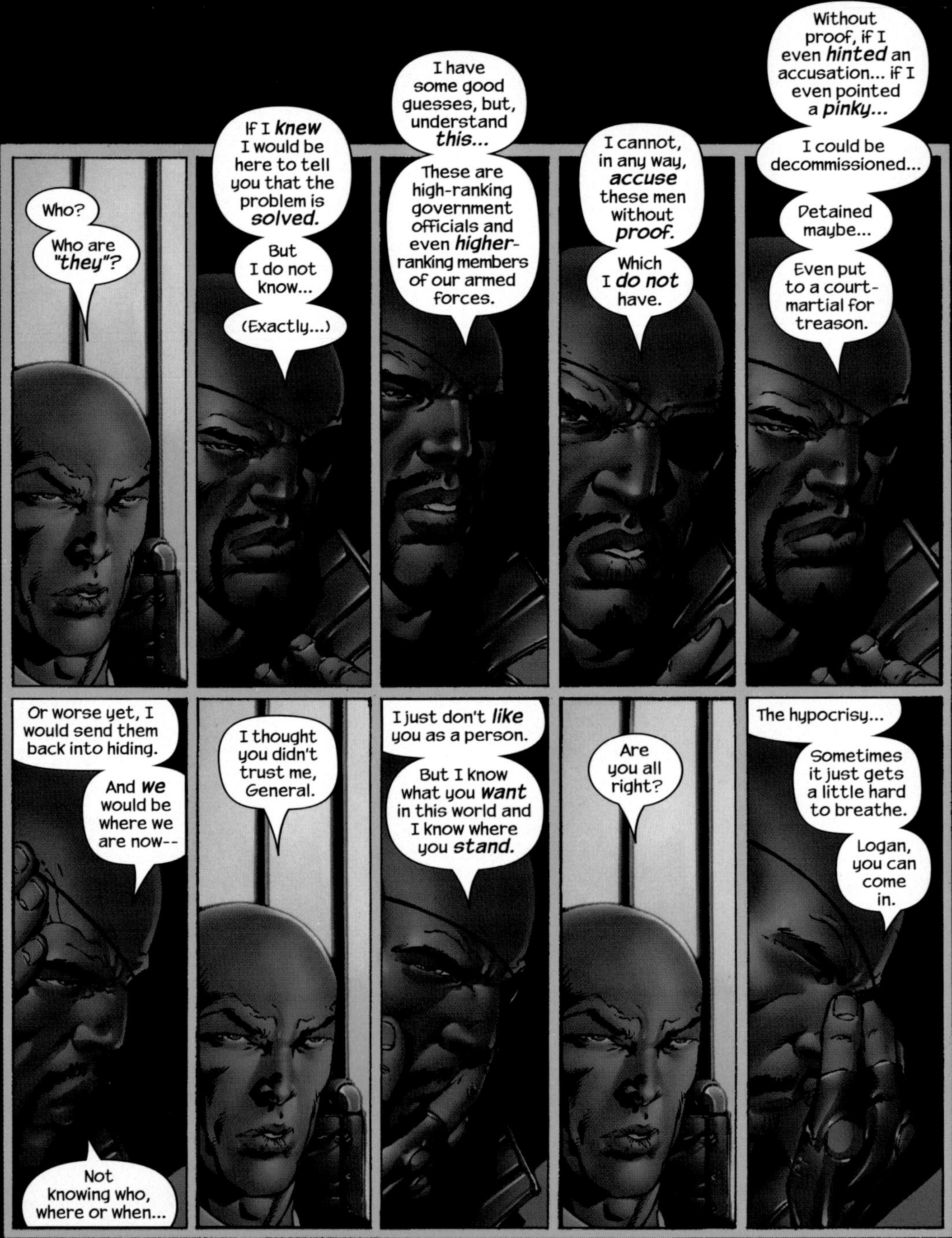

Who?
Who are "they"?
If I knew I would be here to tell you that the problem is solved.
But I do not know...
(Exactly...)
I have some good guesses, but, understand this...
These are high-ranking government officials and even higher-ranking members of our armed forces.
I cannot, in any way, accuse these men without proof.
Which I do not have.
Without proof, if I even hinted an accusation... if I even pointed a pinky...
I could be decommissioned...
Detained maybe...
Even put to a court-martial for treason.
Or worse yet, I would send them back into hiding.
And we would be where we are now--
Not knowing who, where or when...
I thought you didn't trust me, General.
I just don't like you as a person.
But I know what you want in this world and I know where you stand.
Are you all right?
The hypocrisy...
Sometimes it just gets a little hard to breathe.
Logan, you can come in.

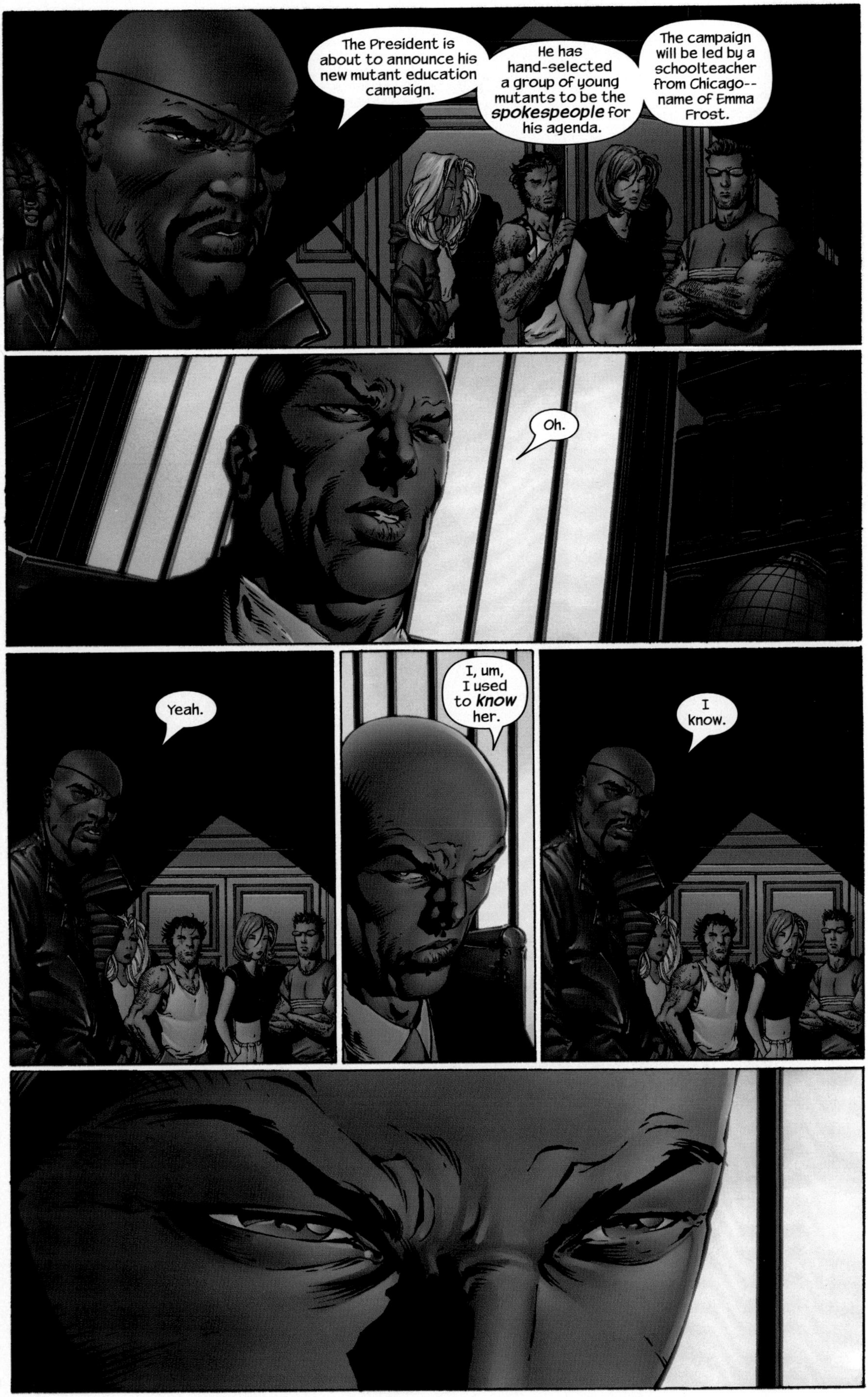
The President is about to announce his new mutant education campaign.
He has hand-selected a group of young mutants to be the *spokespeople* for his agenda.
The campaign will be led by a schoolteacher from Chicago-- name of Emma Frost.
Oh.
Yeah.
I, um, I used to *know* her.
I know.

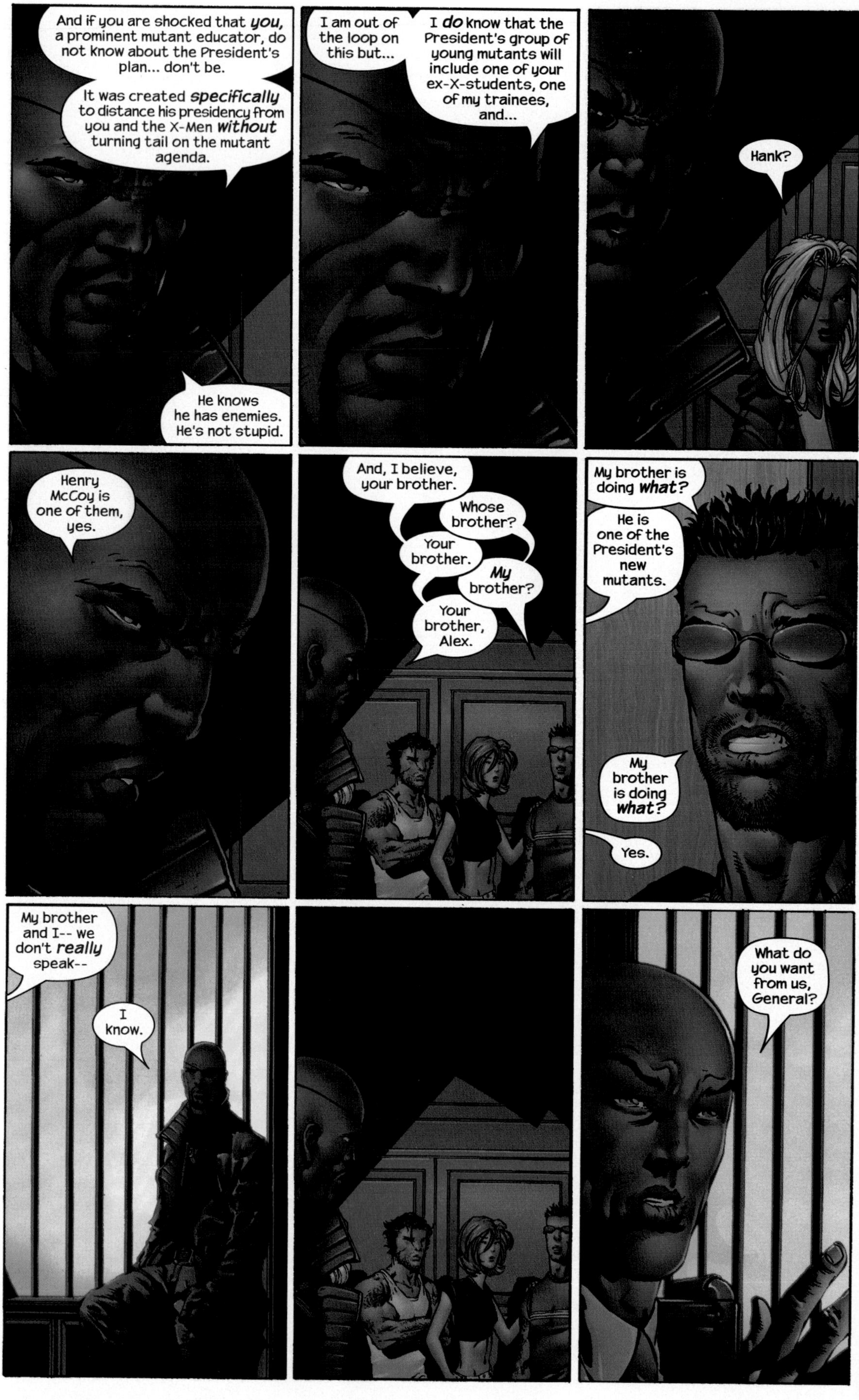
And if you are shocked that you, a prominent mutant educator, do not know about the President's plan... don't be.
It was created specifically to distance his presidency from you and the X-Men without turning tail on the mutant agenda.
He knows he has enemies. He's not stupid.
I am out of the loop on this but...
I do know that the President's group of young mutants will include one of your ex-X-students, one of my trainees, and...
Hank?
Henry McCoy is one of them, yes.
And, I believe, your brother.
Whose brother?
Your brother.
My brother?
Your brother, Alex.
My brother is doing what?
He is one of the President's new mutants.
My brother is doing what?
Yes.
My brother and I-- we don't really speak--
I know.
What do you want from us, General?

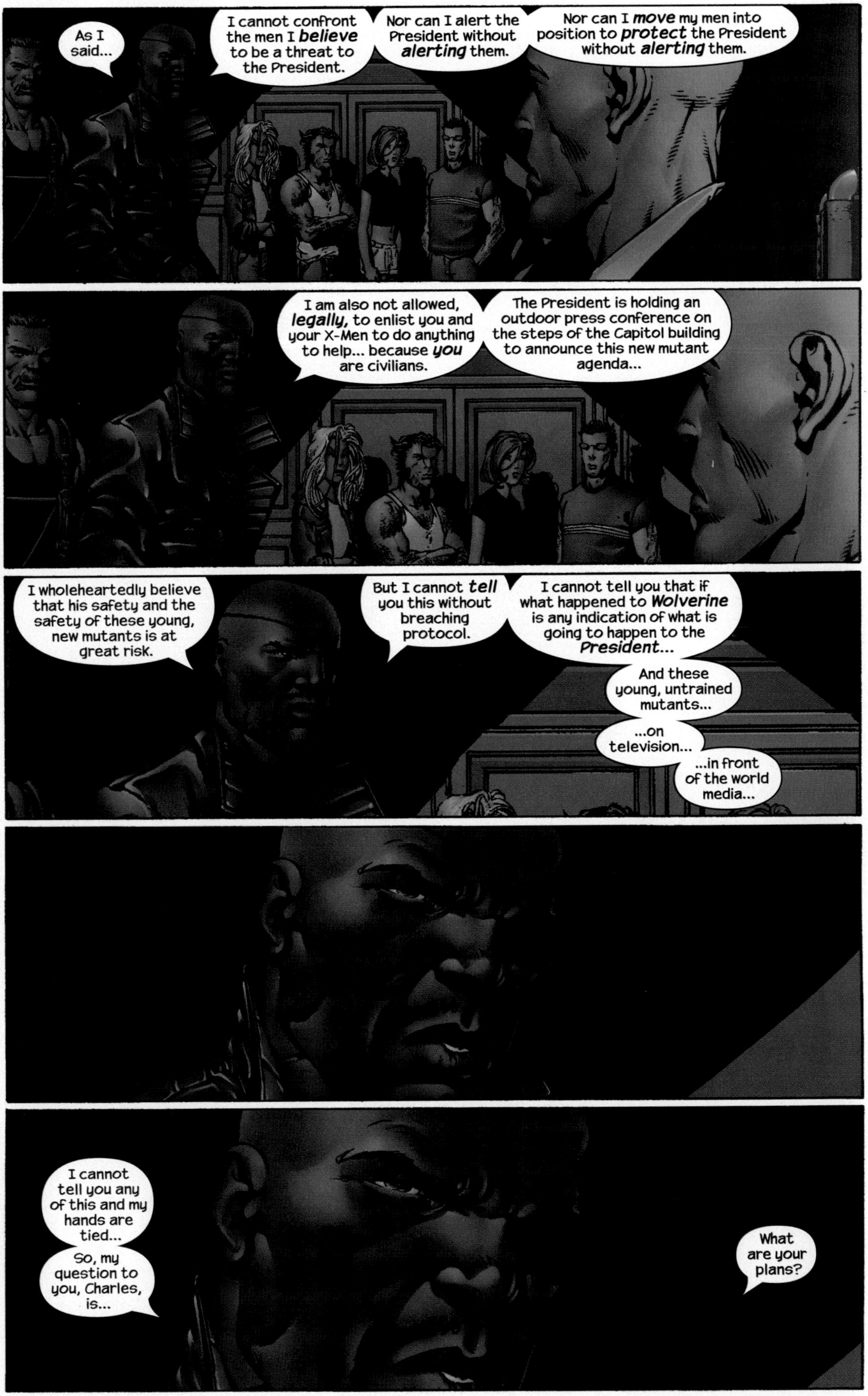
As I said...
I cannot confront the men I believe to be a threat to the President.
Nor can I alert the President without alerting them.
Nor can I move my men into position to protect the President without alerting them.
I am also not allowed, legally, to enlist you and your X-Men to do anything to help... because you are civilians.
The President is holding an outdoor press conference on the steps of the Capitol building to announce this new mutant agenda...
I wholeheartedly believe that his safety and the safety of these young, new mutants is at great risk.
But I cannot tell you this without breaching protocol.
I cannot tell you that if what happened to Wolverine is any indication of what is going to happen to the President...
And these young, untrained mutants...
...on television...
...in front of the world media...
I cannot tell you any of this and my hands are tied...
So, my question to you, Charles, is...
What are your plans?

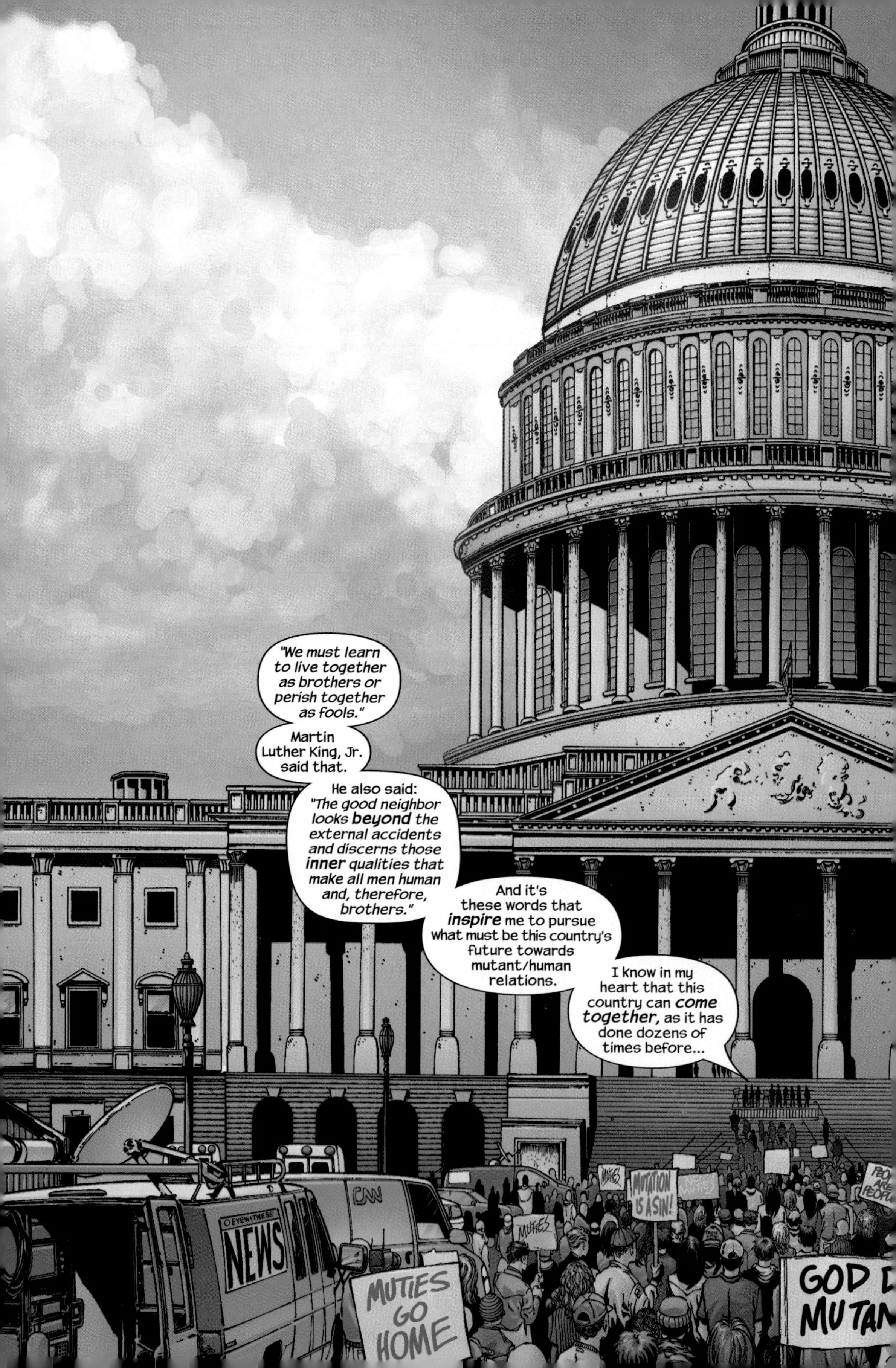
"We must learn to live together as brothers or perish together as fools."
Martin Luther King, Jr. said that.
He also said: "The good neighbor looks **beyond** the external accidents and discerns those **inner** qualities that make all men human and, therefore, brothers."
And it's these words that **inspire** me to pursue what must be this country's future towards mutant/human relations.
I know in my heart that this country can **come together,** as it has done dozens of times before...
EYEWITNESS NEWS
MUTIES GO HOME
MUTATION IS A SIN!
NO MUTIES
MUTIES

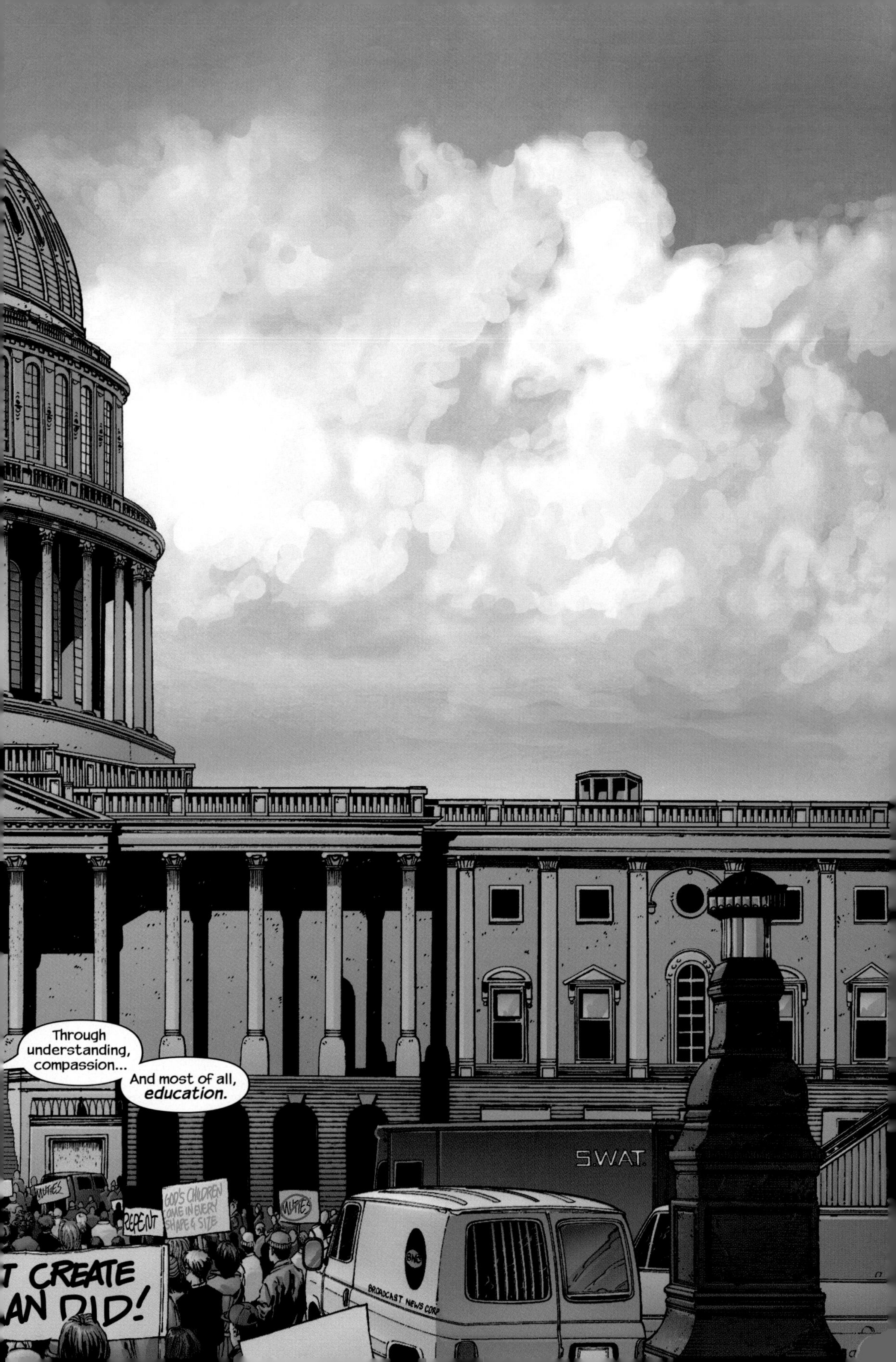
Through understanding, compassion...
And most of all, *education.*
S.W.A.T.
MUTIES
REPENT
GOD'S CHILDREN COME IN EVERY SHAPE & SIZE
MUTIES
T CREATE
AN DID!
BNC
BROADCAST NEWS CORP

And with that I would like to introduce you to Emma Frost.

Ms. Frost is a mutant and a schoolteacher.

Looks like *our* fifteen minutes were up about six minutes ago.

We weren't in it for that, Jean.

Still sucks.

Yeah. Well we'll...

PEOPLE ARE PEOPLE

GOD'S CHILDREN EVERY SIZE

MUTIES GO HOME

MUTATION IS A

Oh, dude, you guys the X-Men?

You guys-- why aren't *you* up there?

MUTIES GO HOME

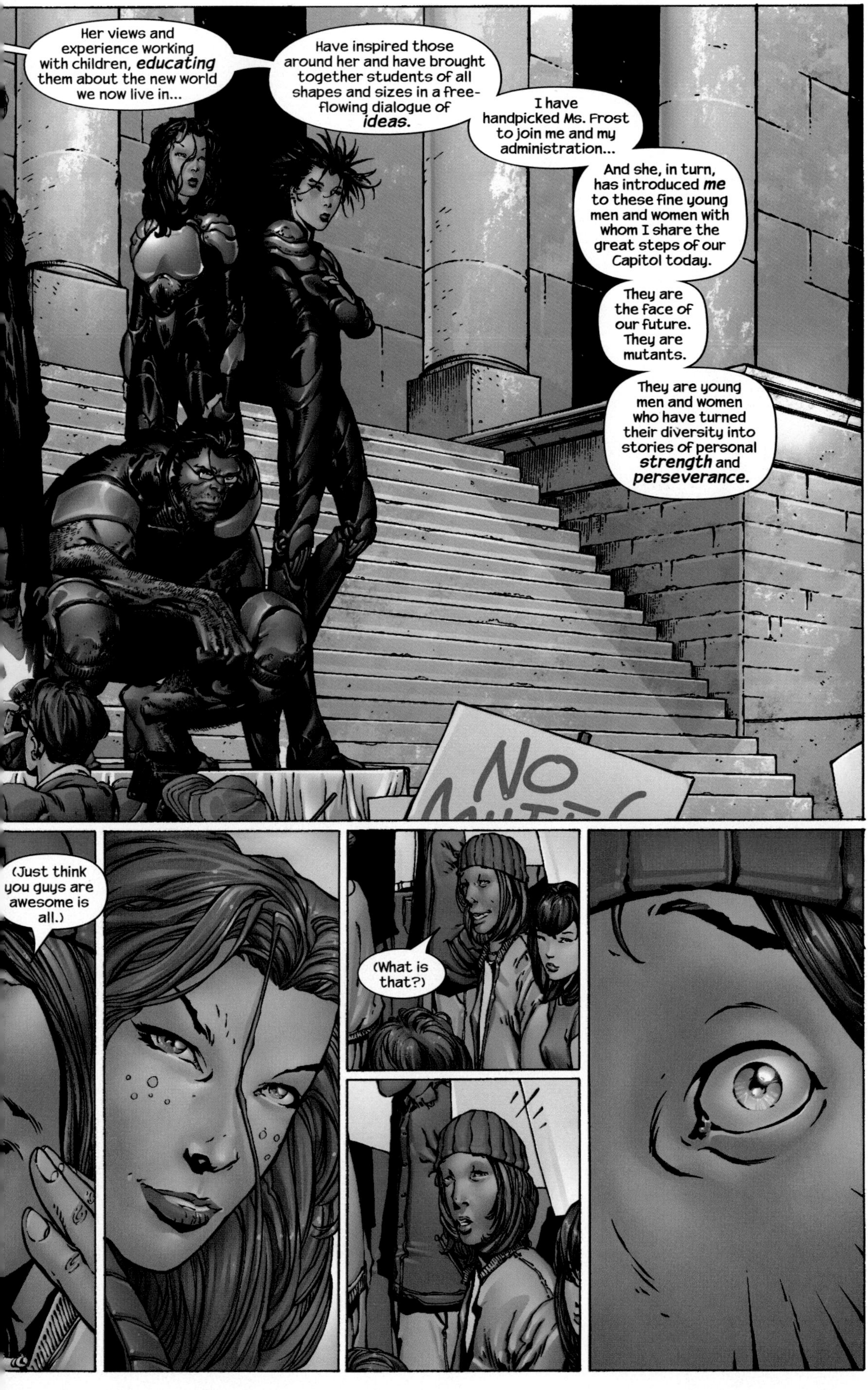
Her views and experience working with children, *educating* them about the new world we now live in...
Have inspired those around her and have brought together students of all shapes and sizes in a free-flowing dialogue of *ideas.*
I have handpicked Ms. Frost to join me and my administration...
And she, in turn, has introduced *me* to these fine young men and women with whom I share the great steps of our Capitol today.
They are the face of our future. They are mutants.
They are young men and women who have turned their diversity into stories of personal *strength* and *perseverance.*
NO
(Just think you guys are awesome is all.)
(What is that?)

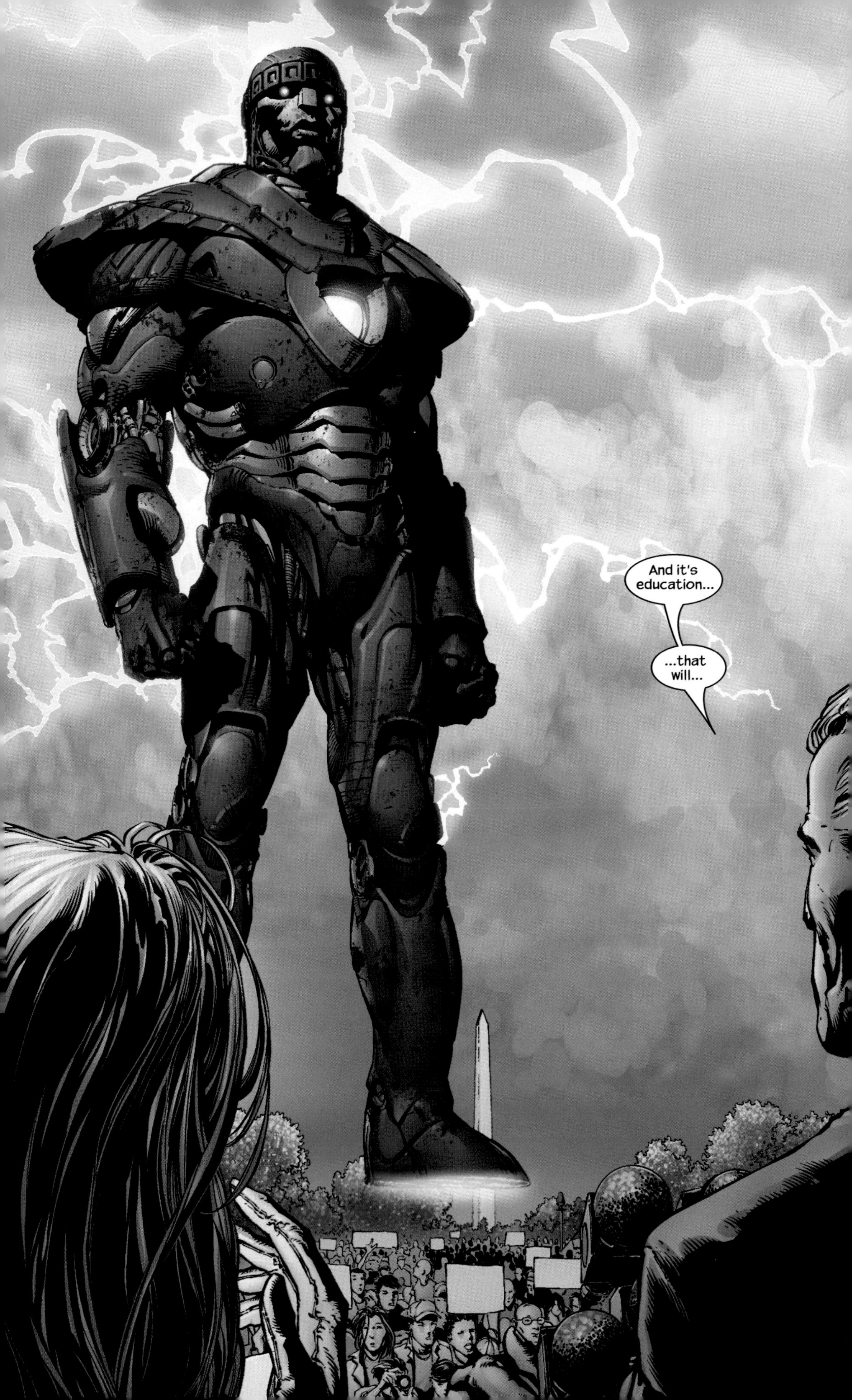
And it's education...
...that will...

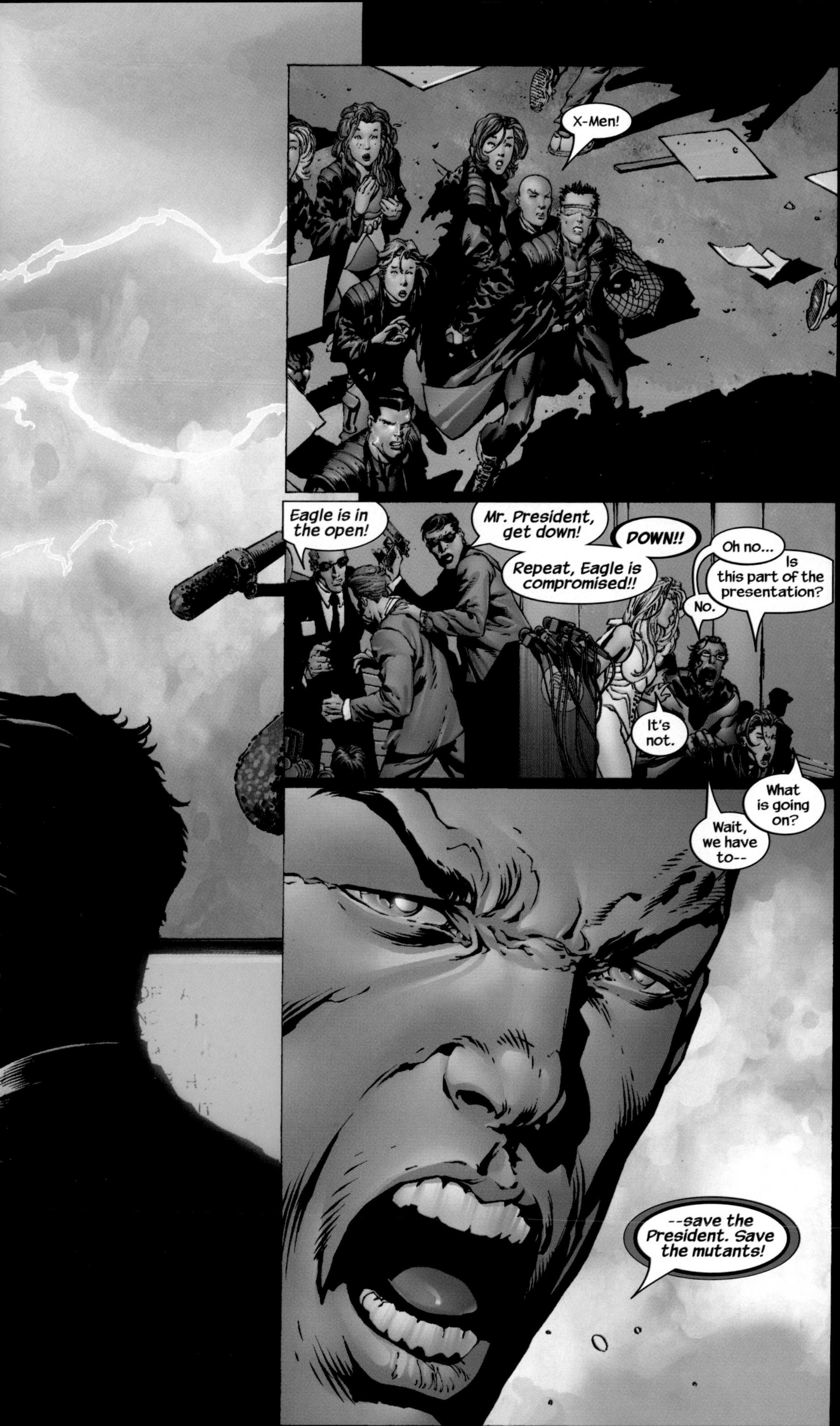
X-Men!
Eagle is in the open!
Mr. President, get down!
DOWN!!
Repeat, Eagle is compromised!!
Oh no...
Is this part of the presentation?
No.
It's not.
What is going on?
Wait, we have to--
--save the President. Save the mutants!

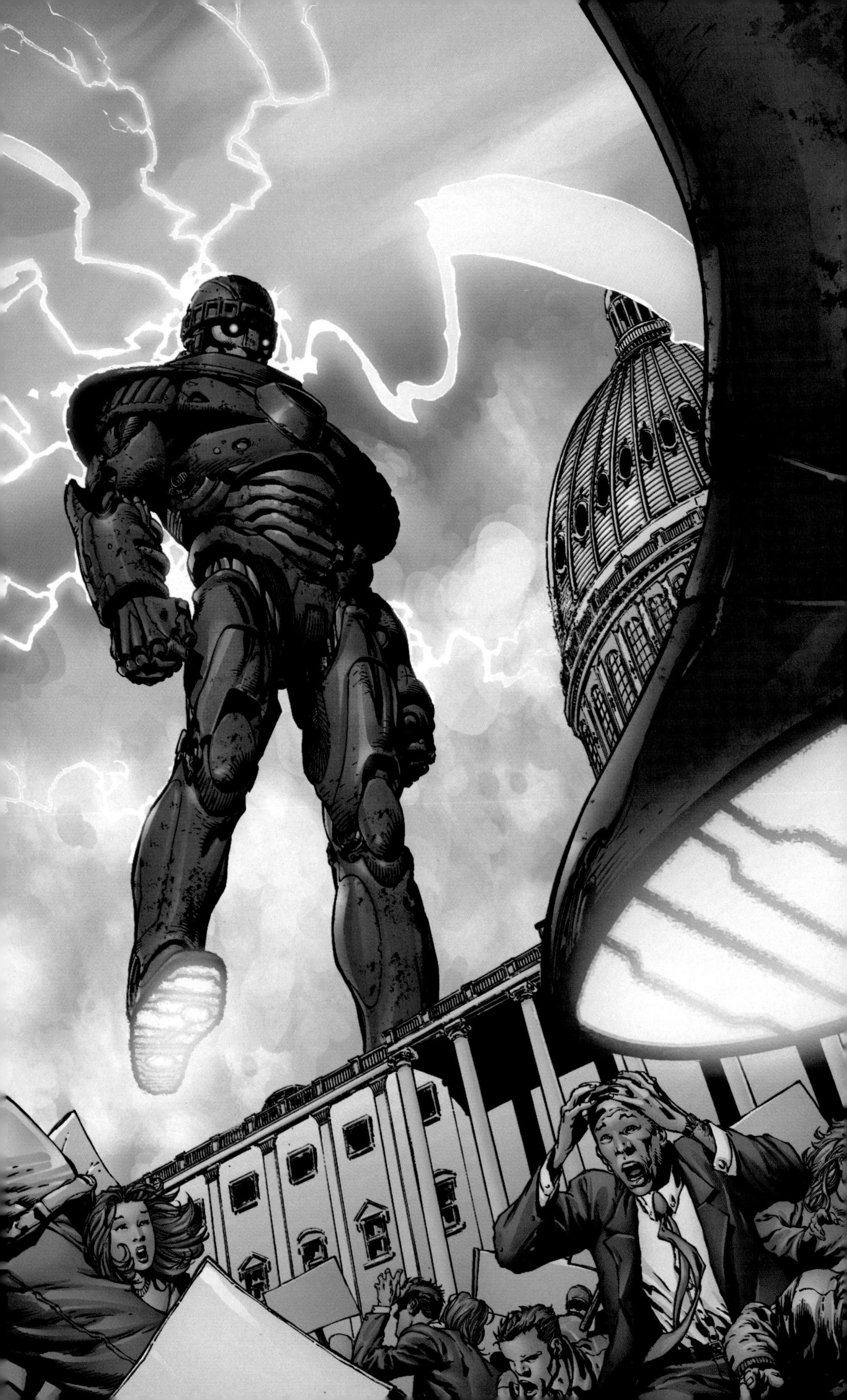

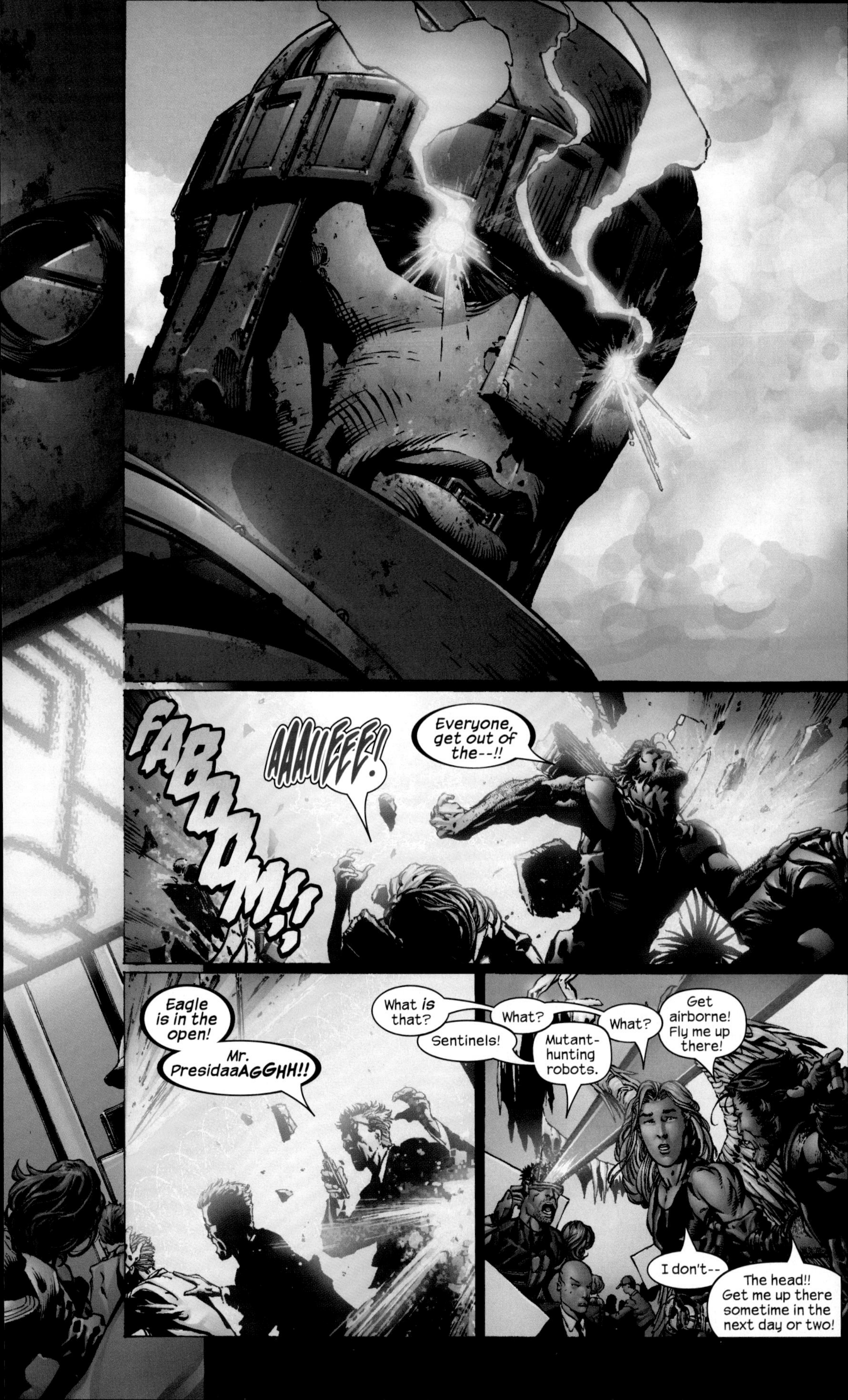
FABOOM!!
AAAIIEEE!
Everyone, get out of the--!!
Eagle is in the open!
Mr. PresidaaAGGHH!!
What *is* that?
What?
Sentinels!
Mutant-hunting robots.
What?
Get airborne! Fly me up there!
I don't--
The head!! Get me up there sometime in the next day or two!

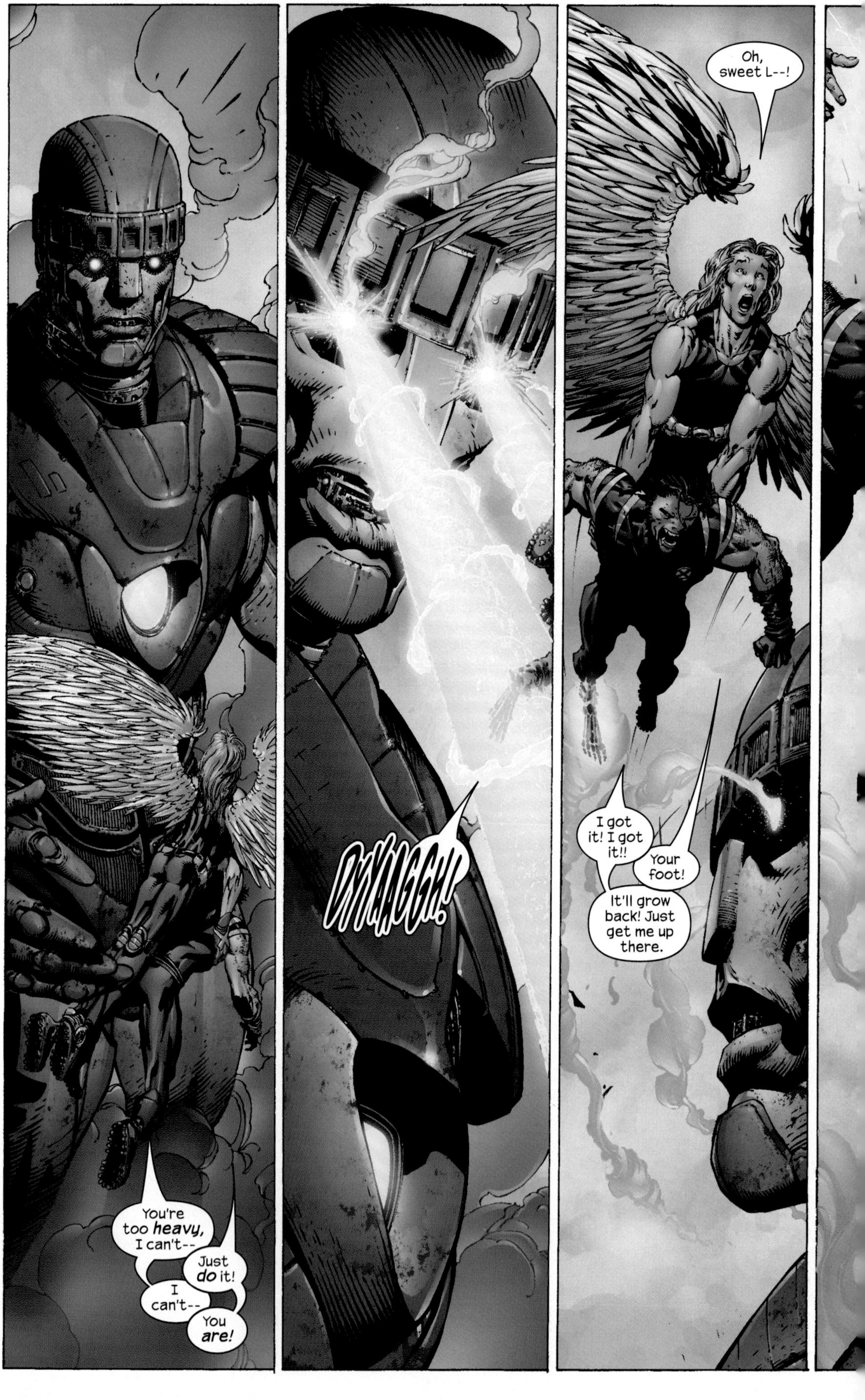

You're too heavy, I can't--
Just do it!
I can't--
You are!
Oh, sweet L--!
I got it! I got it!!
Your foot!
It'll grow back! Just get me up there.

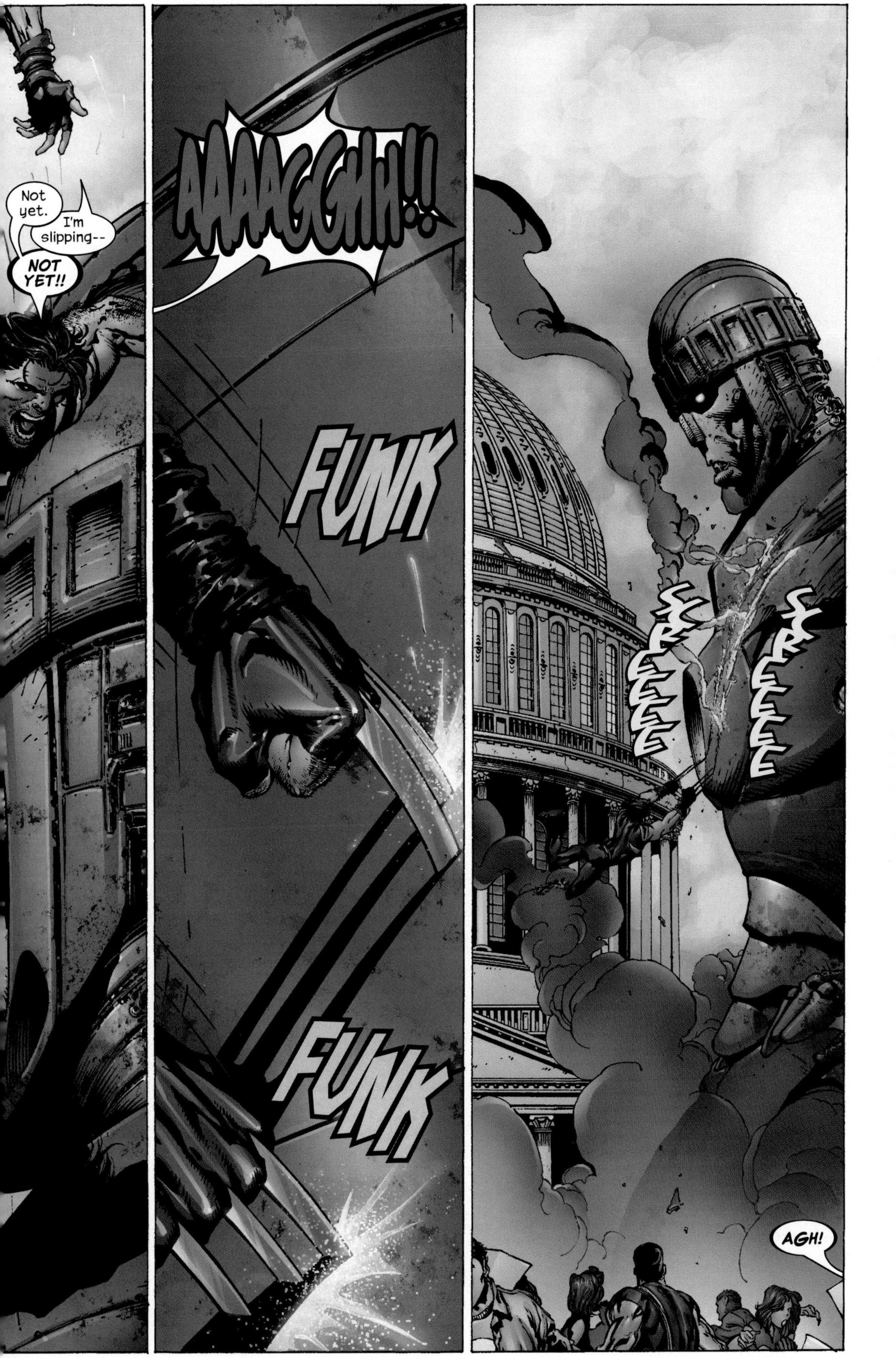
Not yet.
I'm slipping--
NOT YET!!
AAAAGGHH!!
FUNK
FUNK
SKREEEE
SKREEEE
AGH!

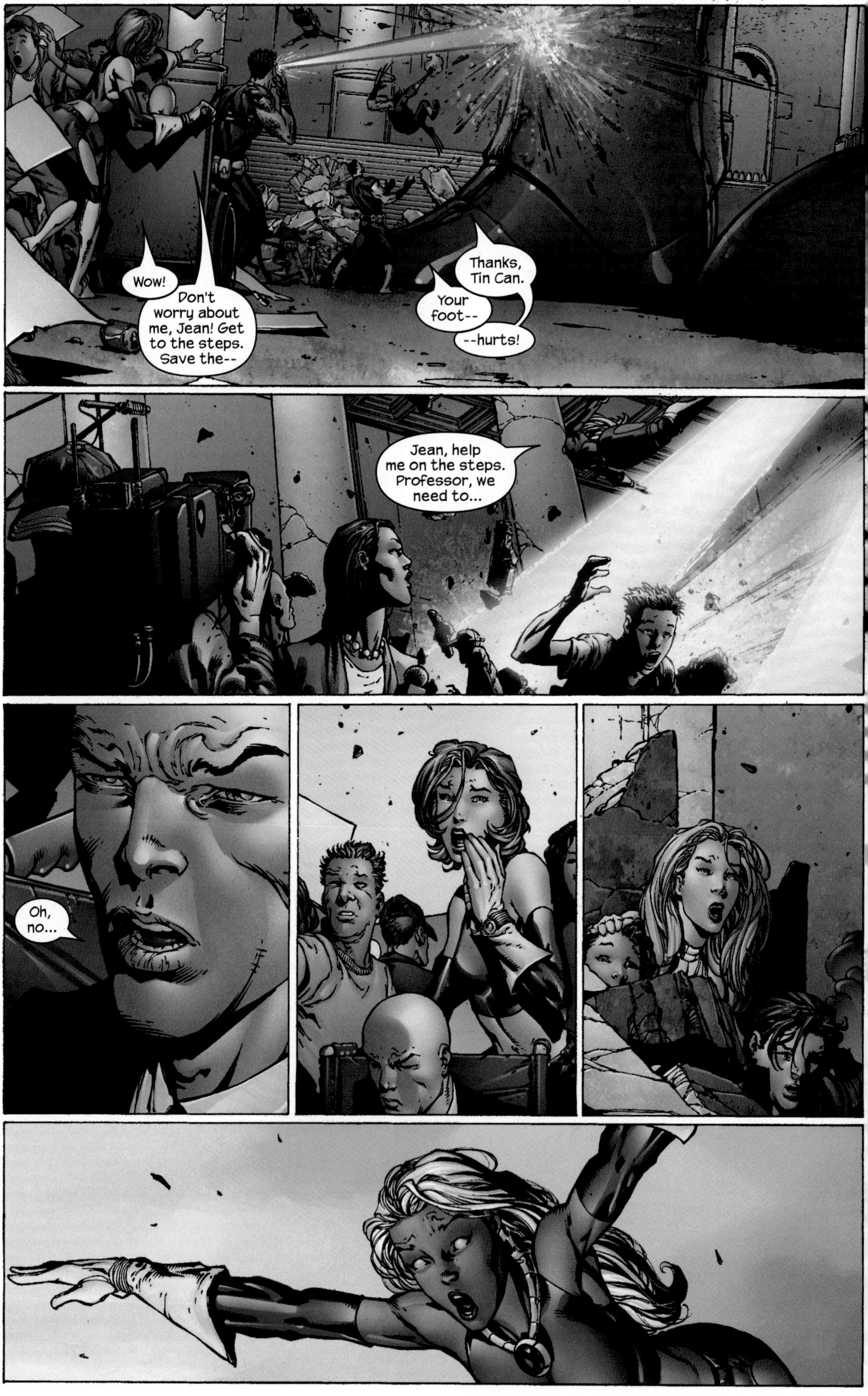
Wow!
Don't worry about me, Jean! Get to the steps. Save the--
Your foot--
Thanks, Tin Can.
--hurts!
Jean, help me on the steps. Professor, we need to...
Oh, no...

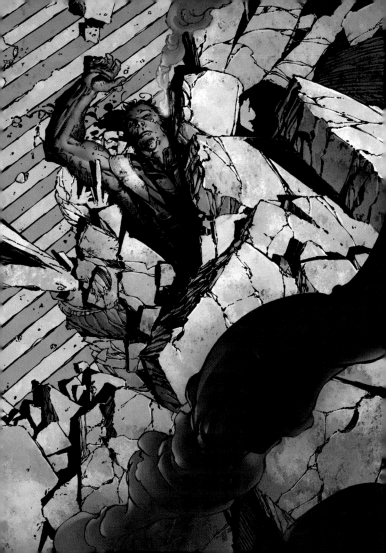

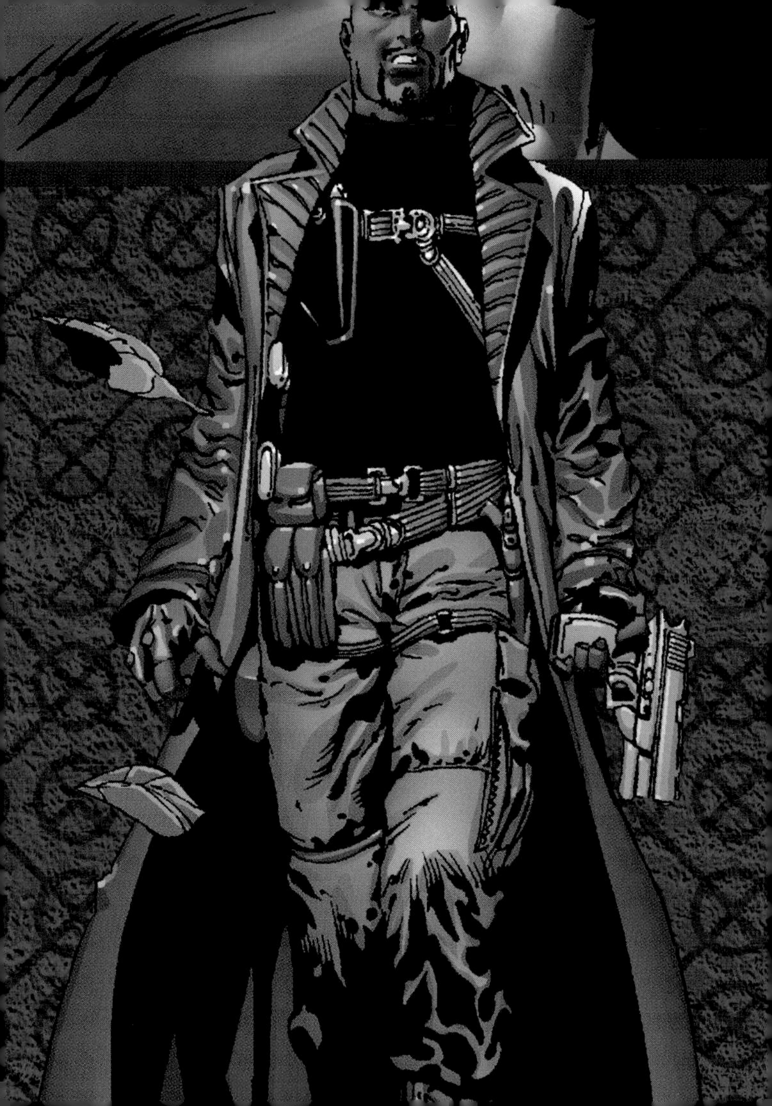

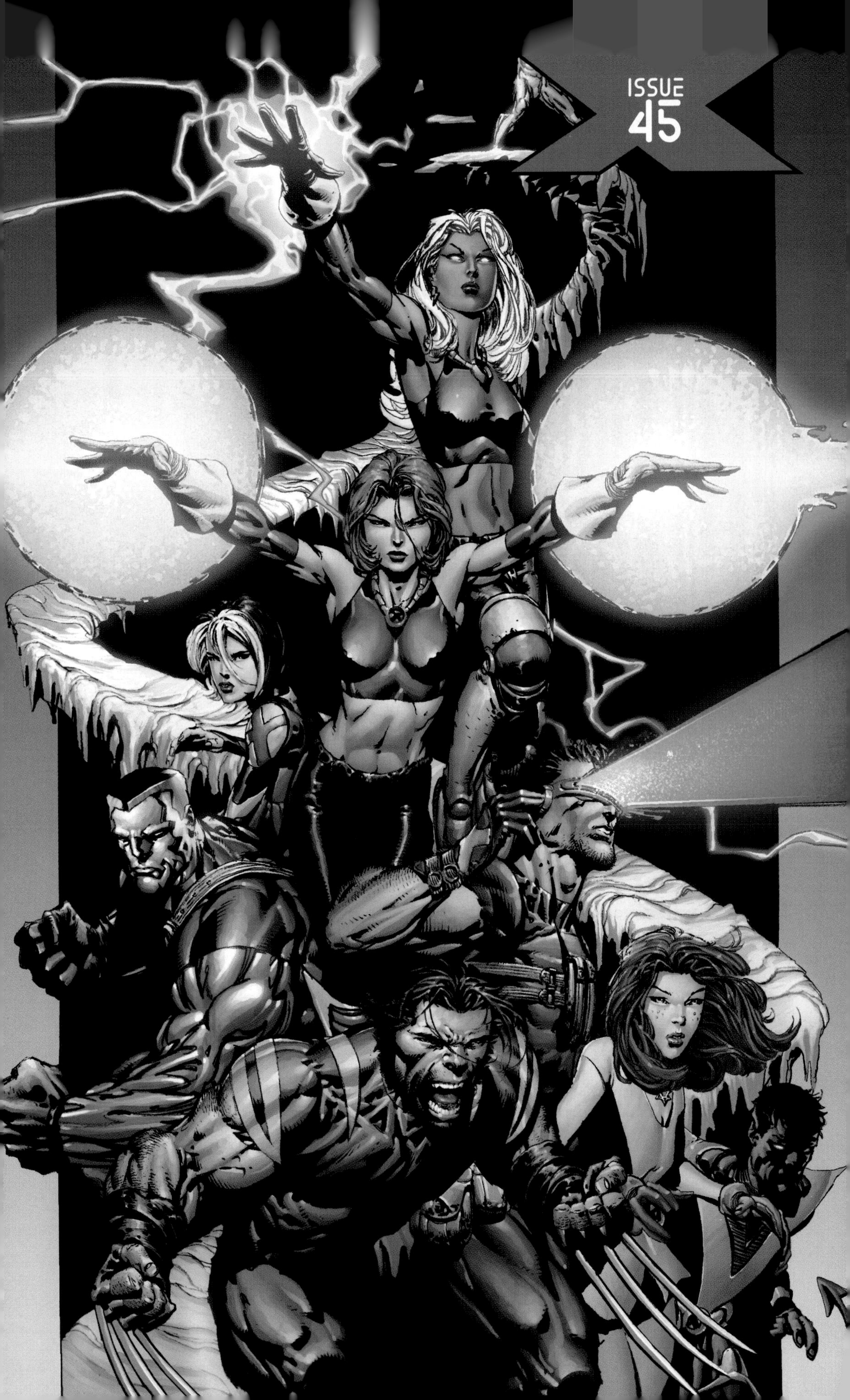
ISSUE
45

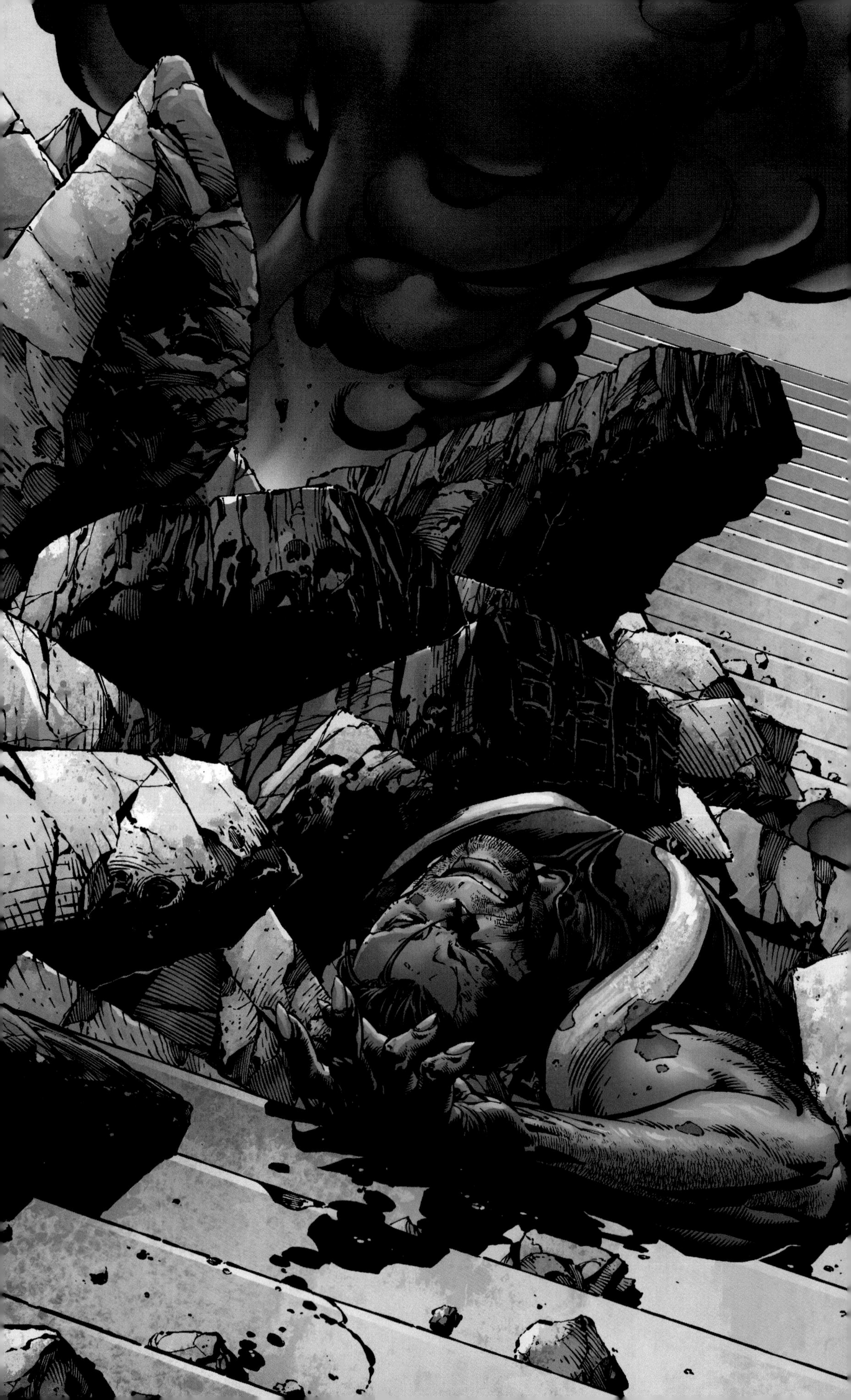

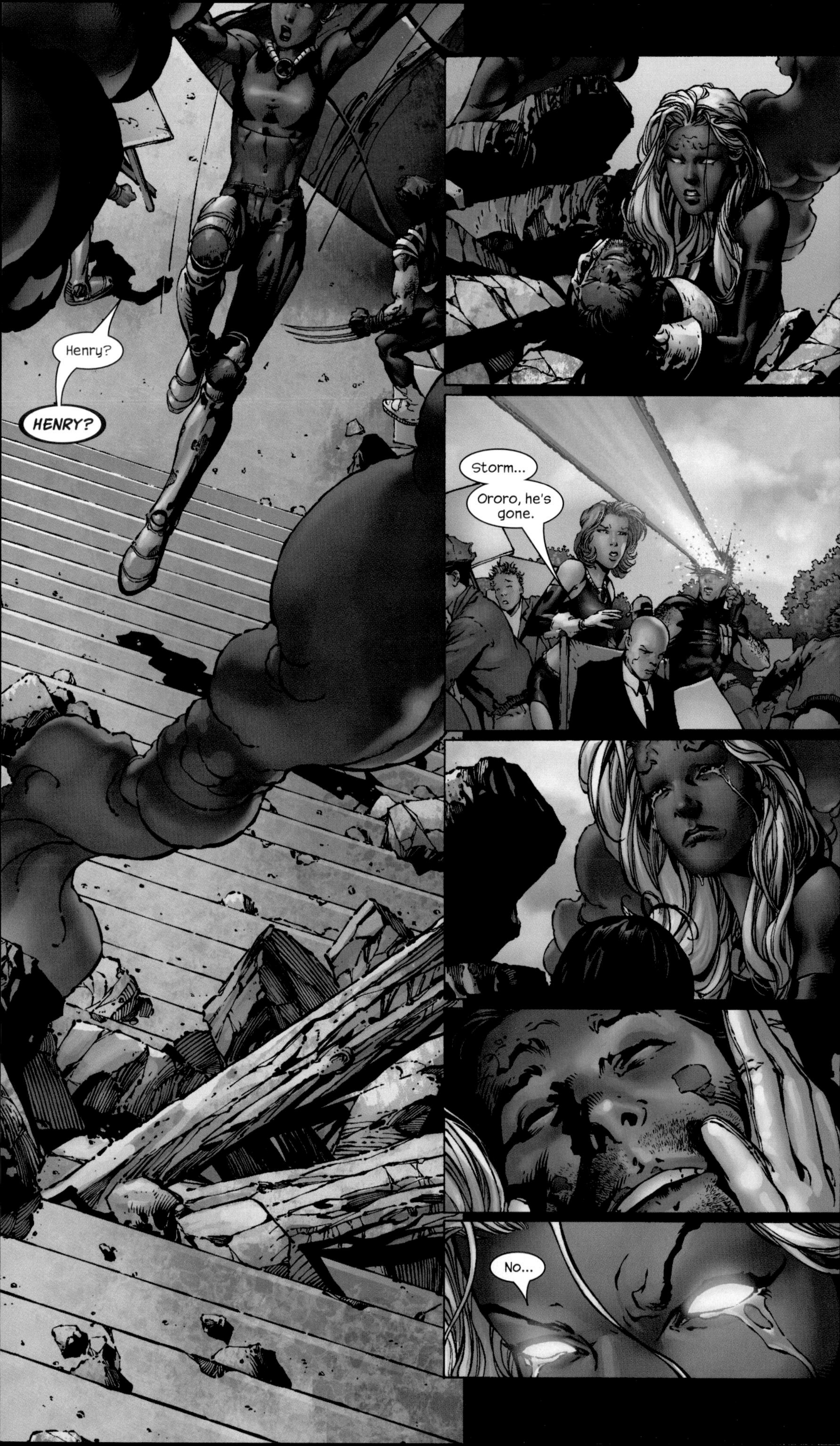
Henry?
HENRY?
Storm...
Ororo, he's gone.
No...

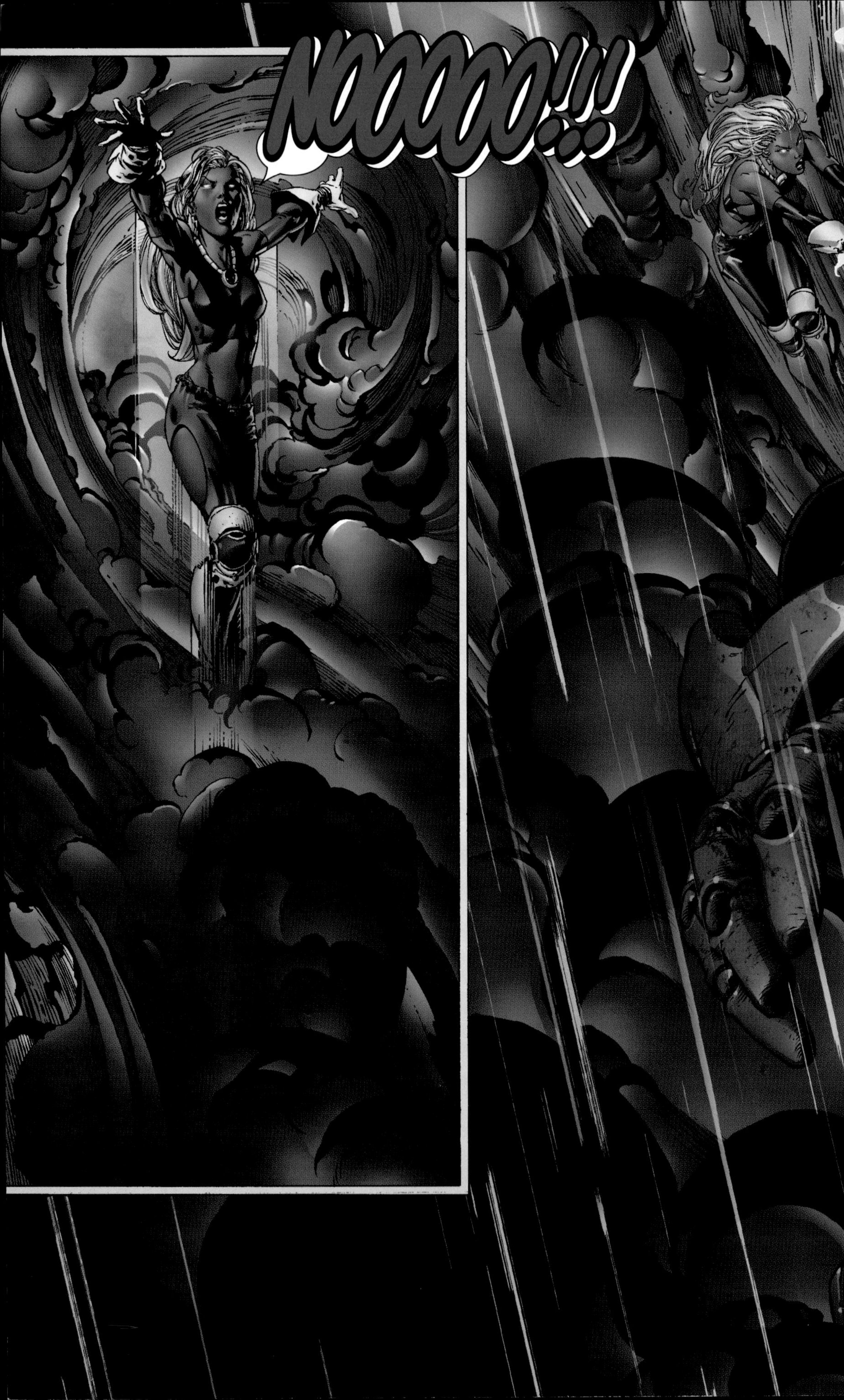
NOOOOO!!!

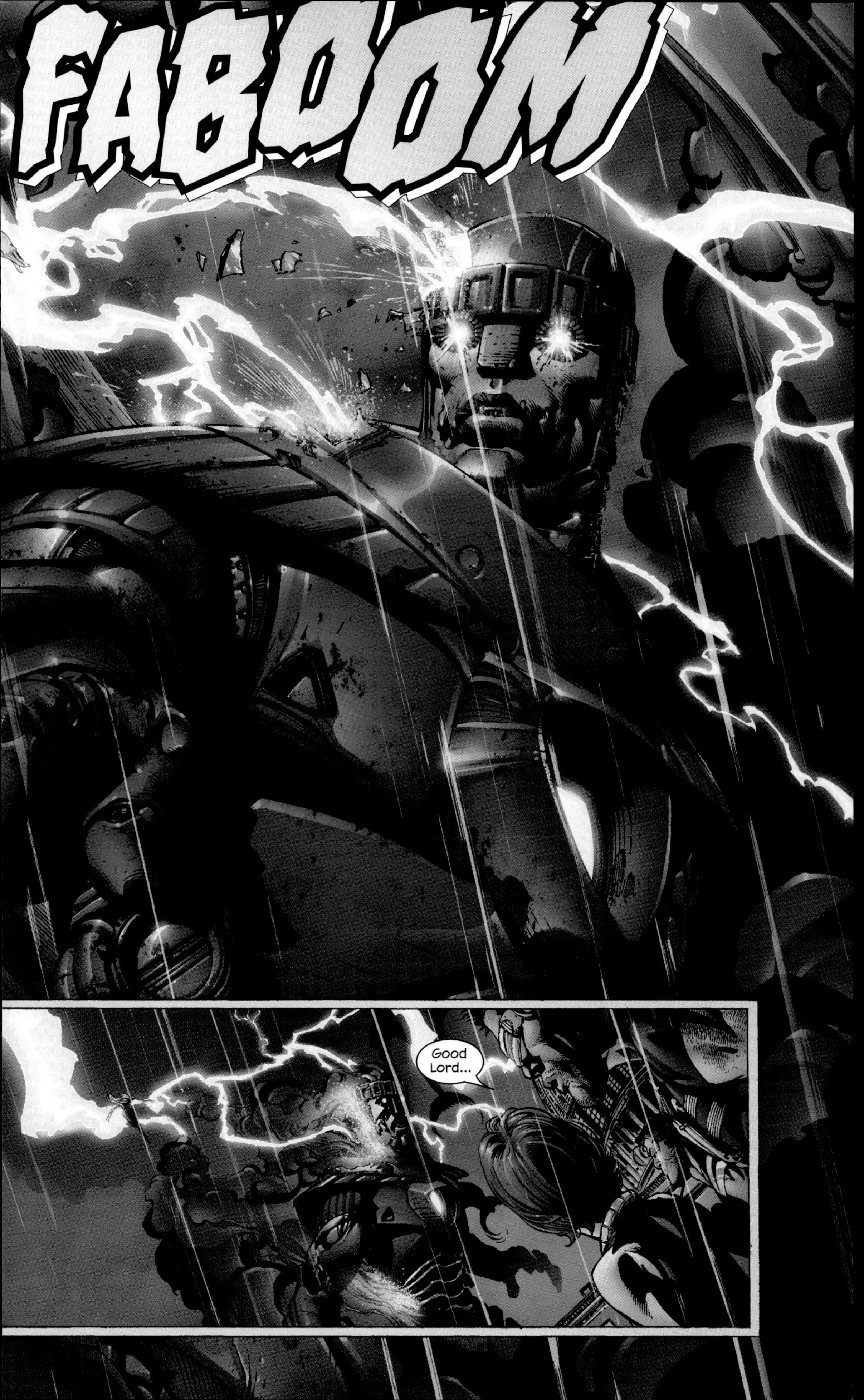
FABOOM
Good Lord...

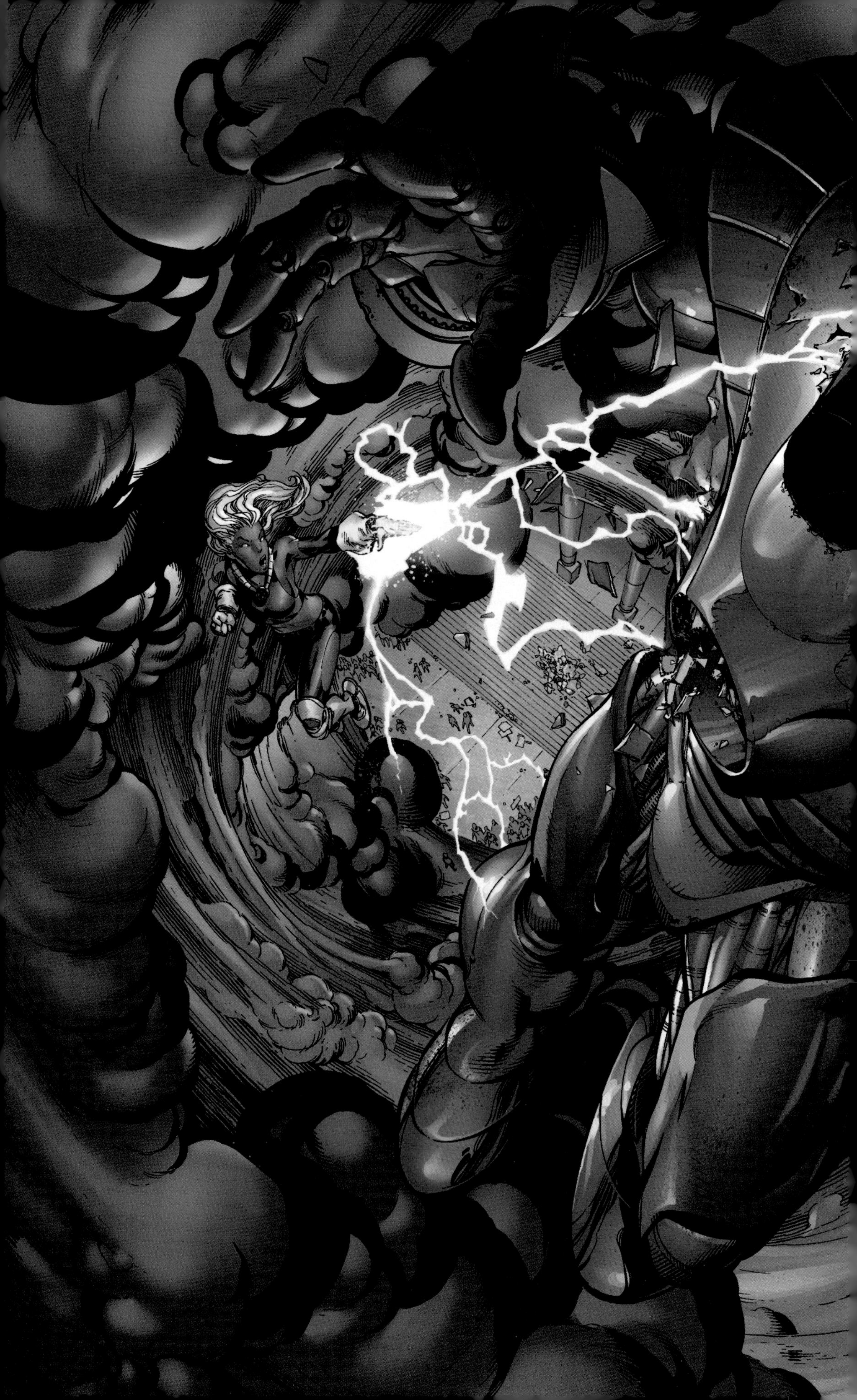

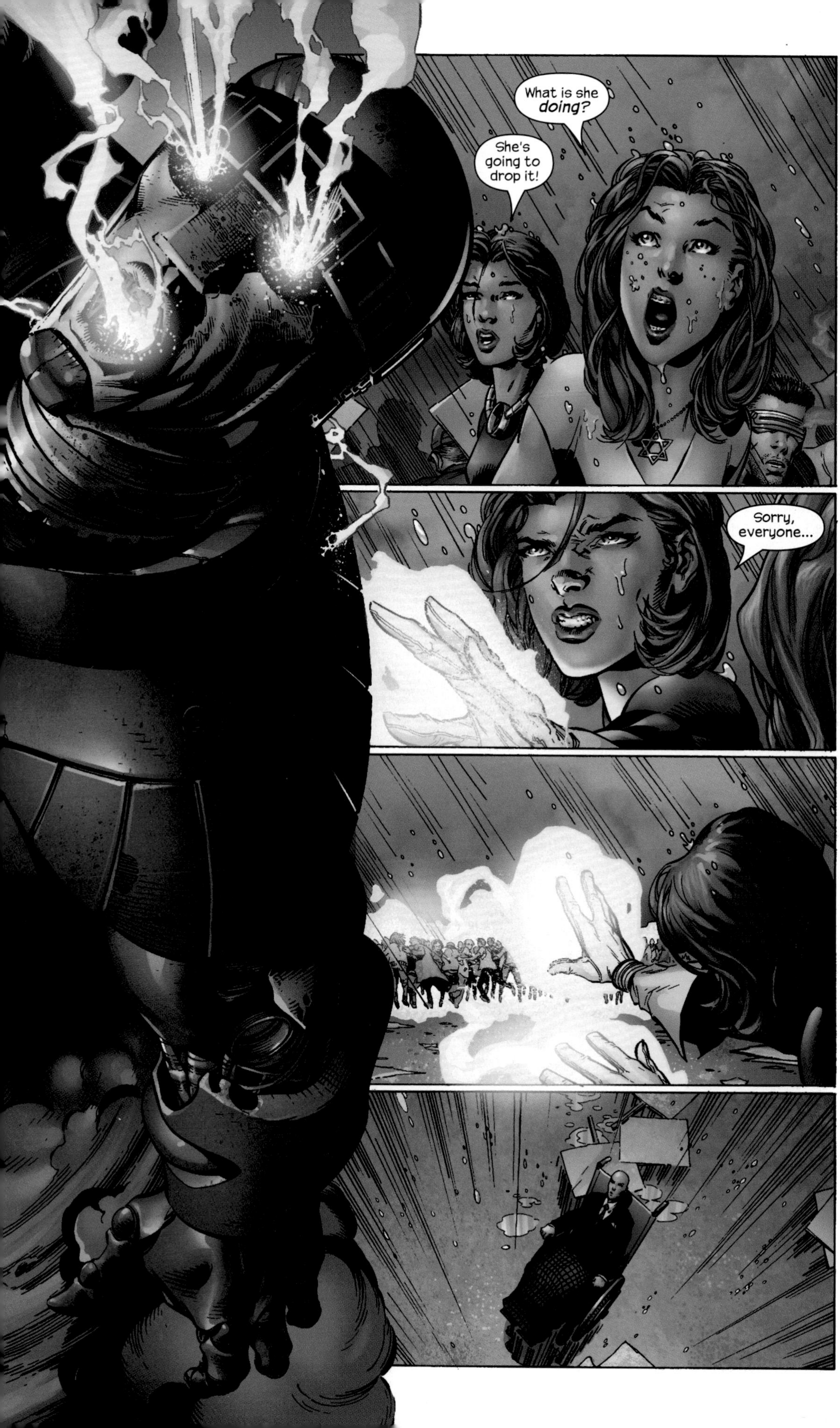
What is she doing?
She's going to drop it!
Sorry, everyone...

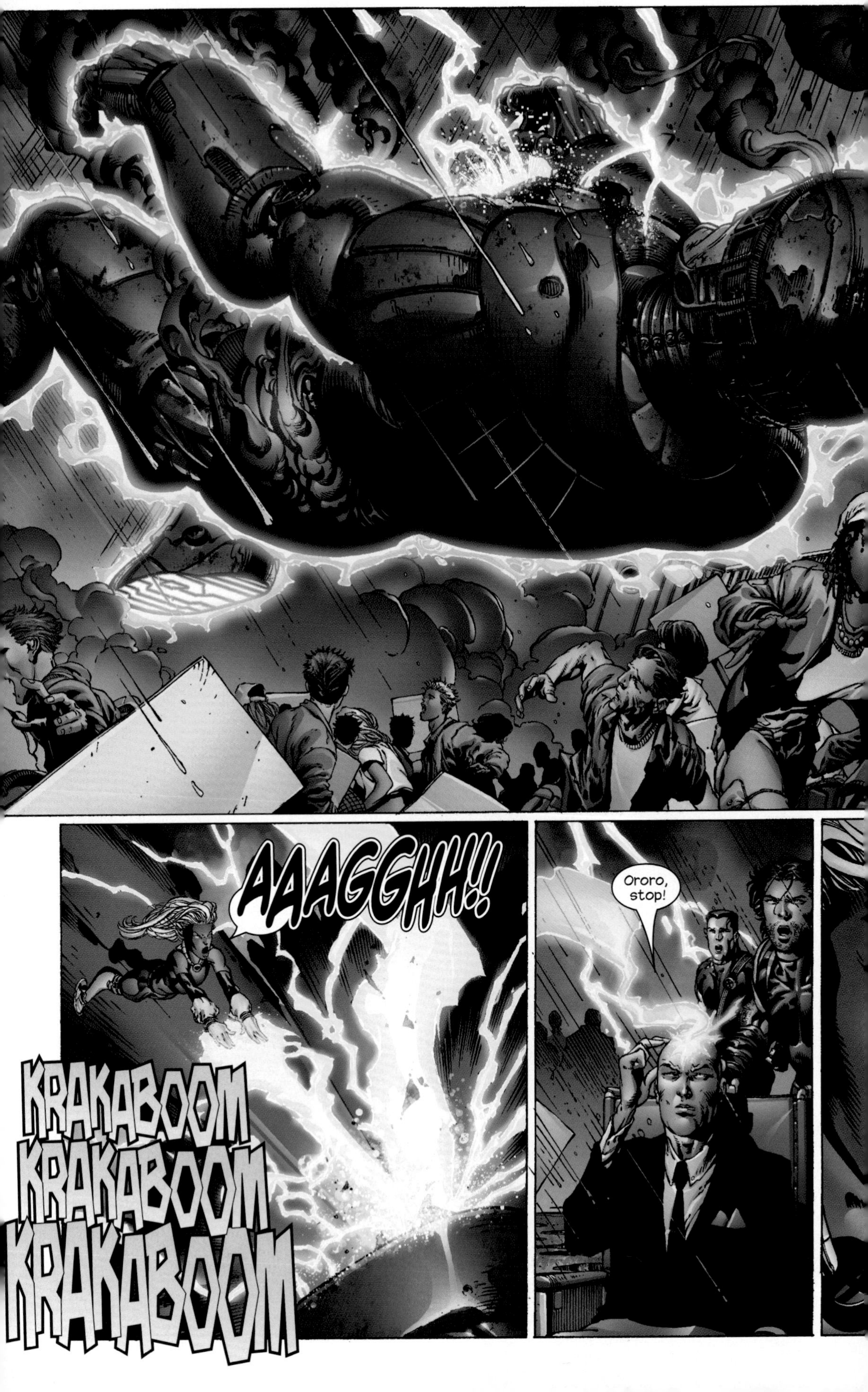
AAAGGHH!!
KRAKABOOM
KRAKABOOM
KRAKABOOM
Ororo, stop!

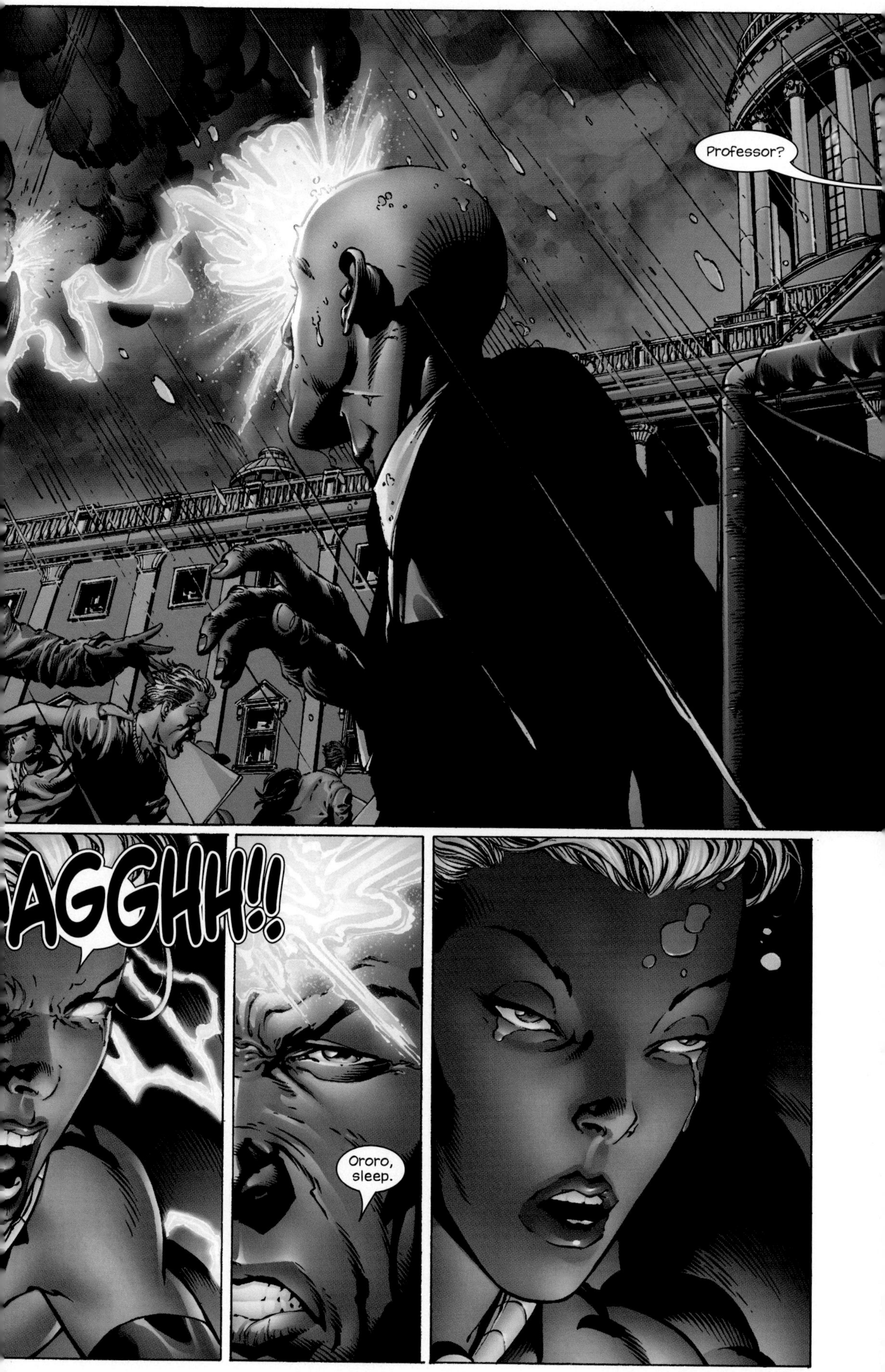
Professor?
AGGHH!!
Ororo, sleep.

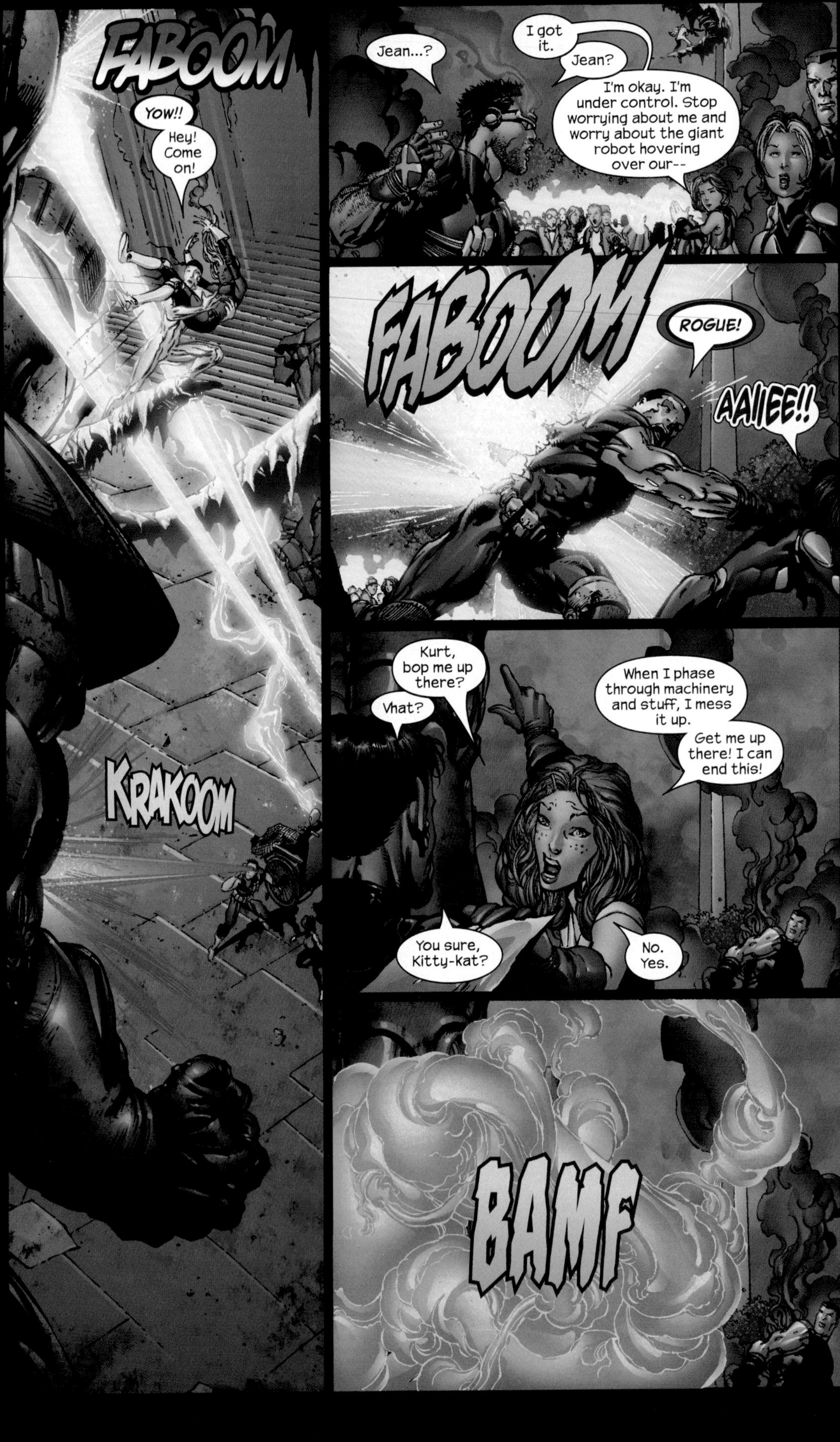
FABOOM
YOW!!
Hey! Come on!
KRAKOOM
Jean...?
I got it.
Jean?
I'm okay. I'm under control. Stop worrying about me and worry about the giant robot hovering over our--
FABOOM
ROGUE!
AAIIEE!!
Kurt, bop me up there?
Vhat?
When I phase through machinery and stuff, I mess it up.
Get me up there! I can end this!
You sure, Kitty-kat?
No. Yes.
BAMF

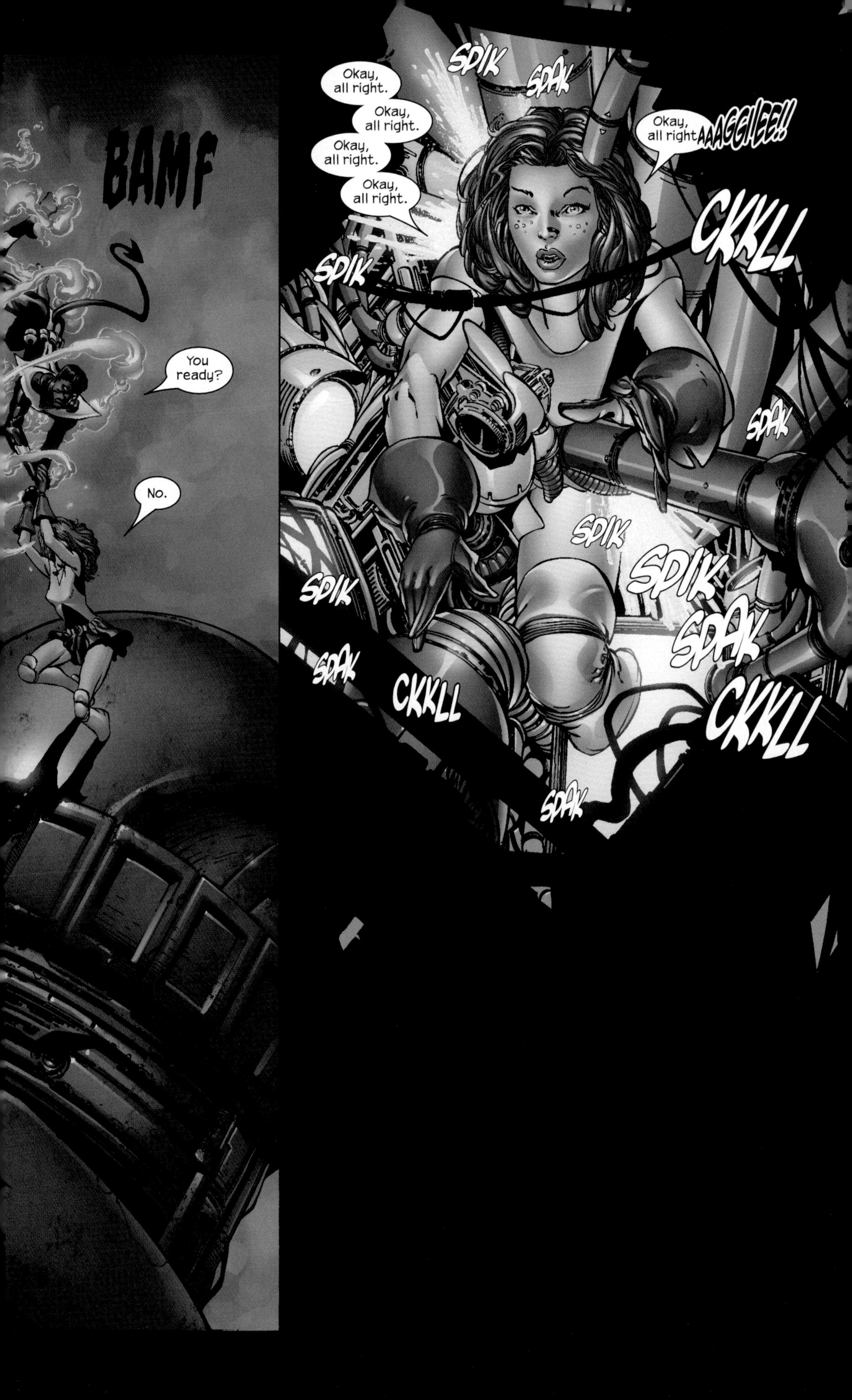
BAMF
You ready?
No.
SPIK
SPAK
Okay, all right.
Okay, all right.
Okay, all right.
Okay, all right.
Okay, all right AAAGGIIEE!!
CKKLL
SPIK
SPAK
SPIK
SPIK
SPIK
SPAK
SPAK
CKKLL
CKKLL
SPAK

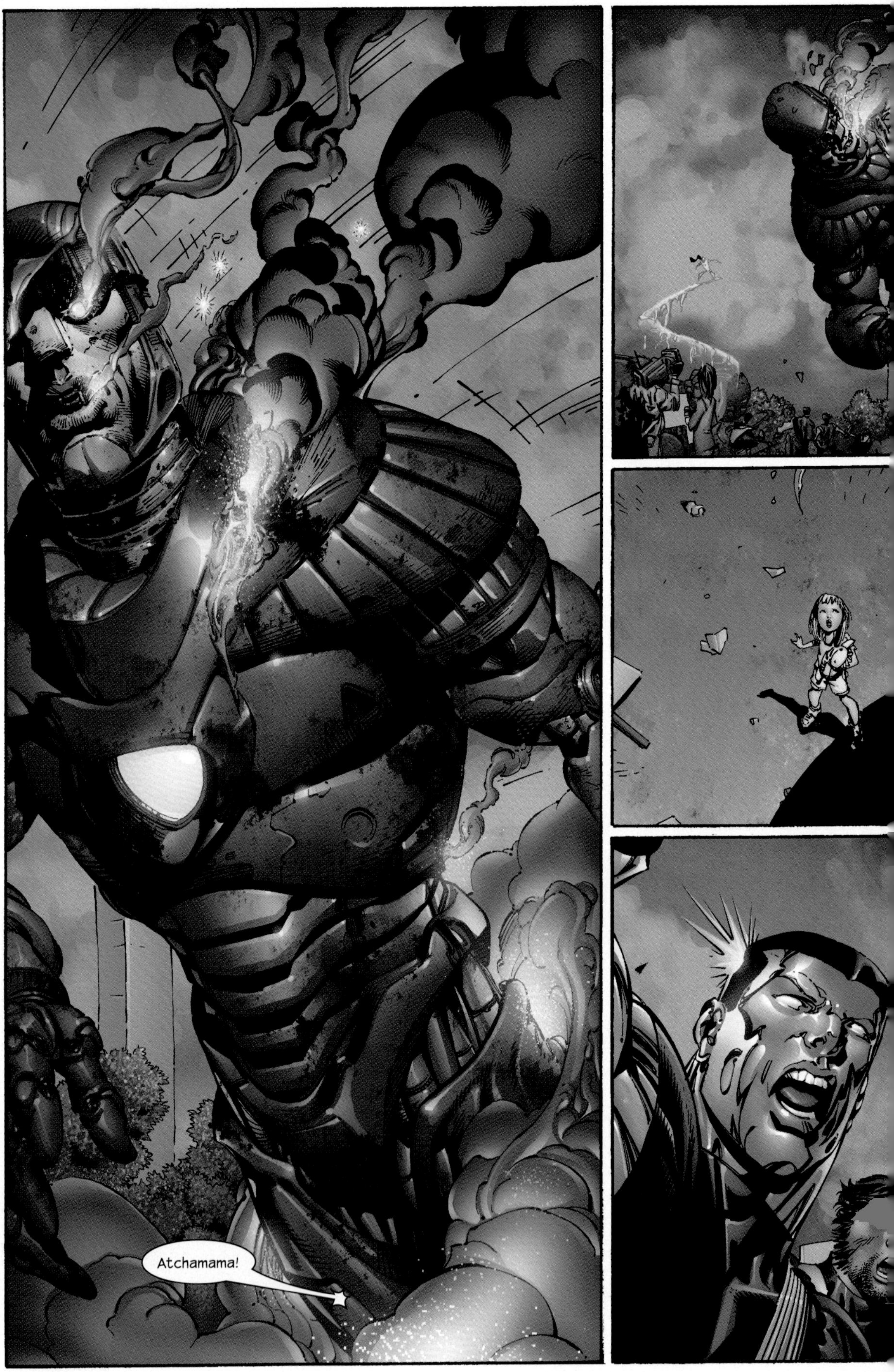
Atchamama!

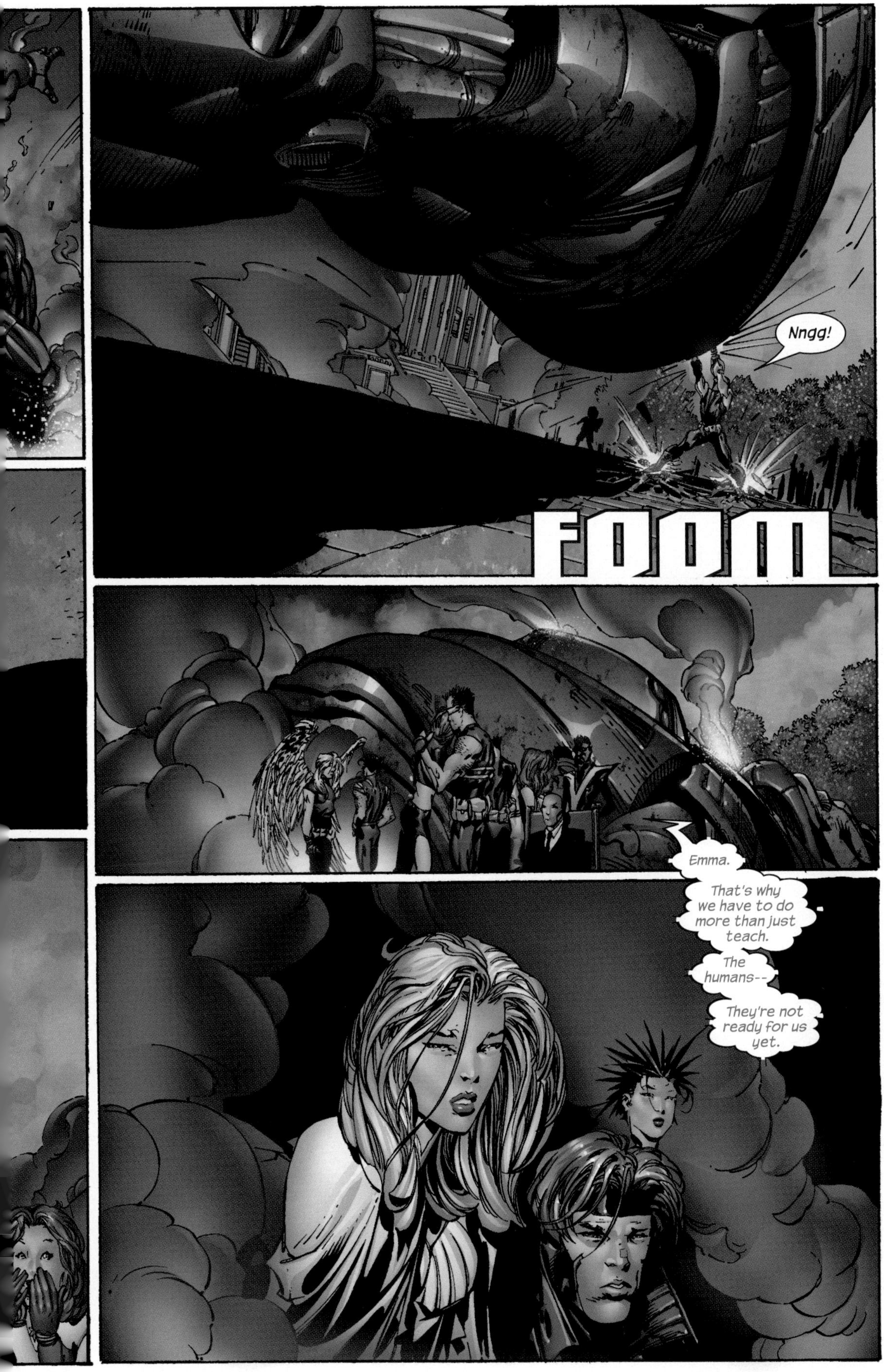

Nngg!
FOOM
Emma.
That's why we have to do more than just teach.
The humans--
They're not ready for us yet.

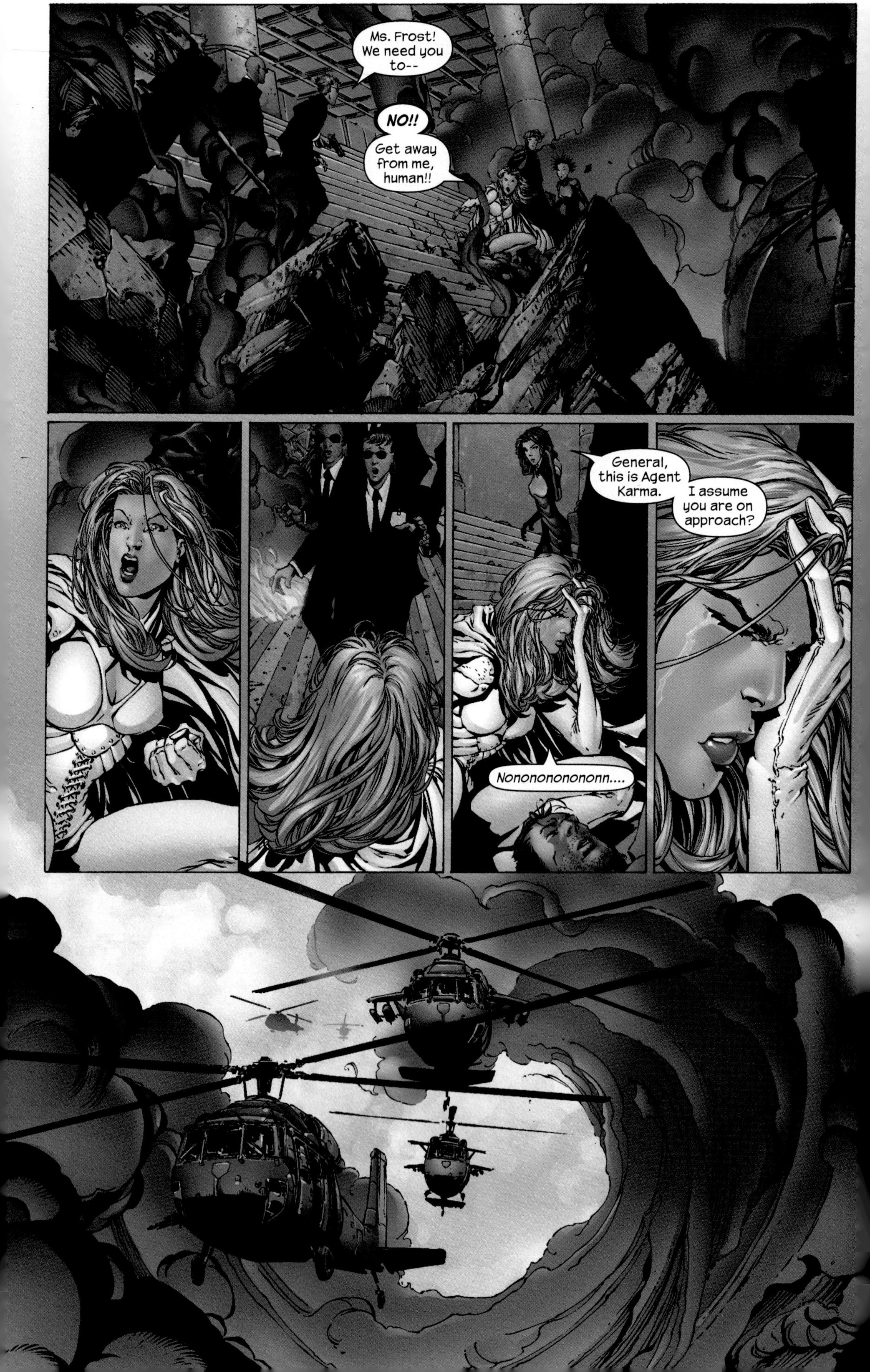
Ms. Frost! We need you to--
NO!! Get away from me, human!!
General, this is Agent Karma.
I assume you are on approach?
Nononononononn....

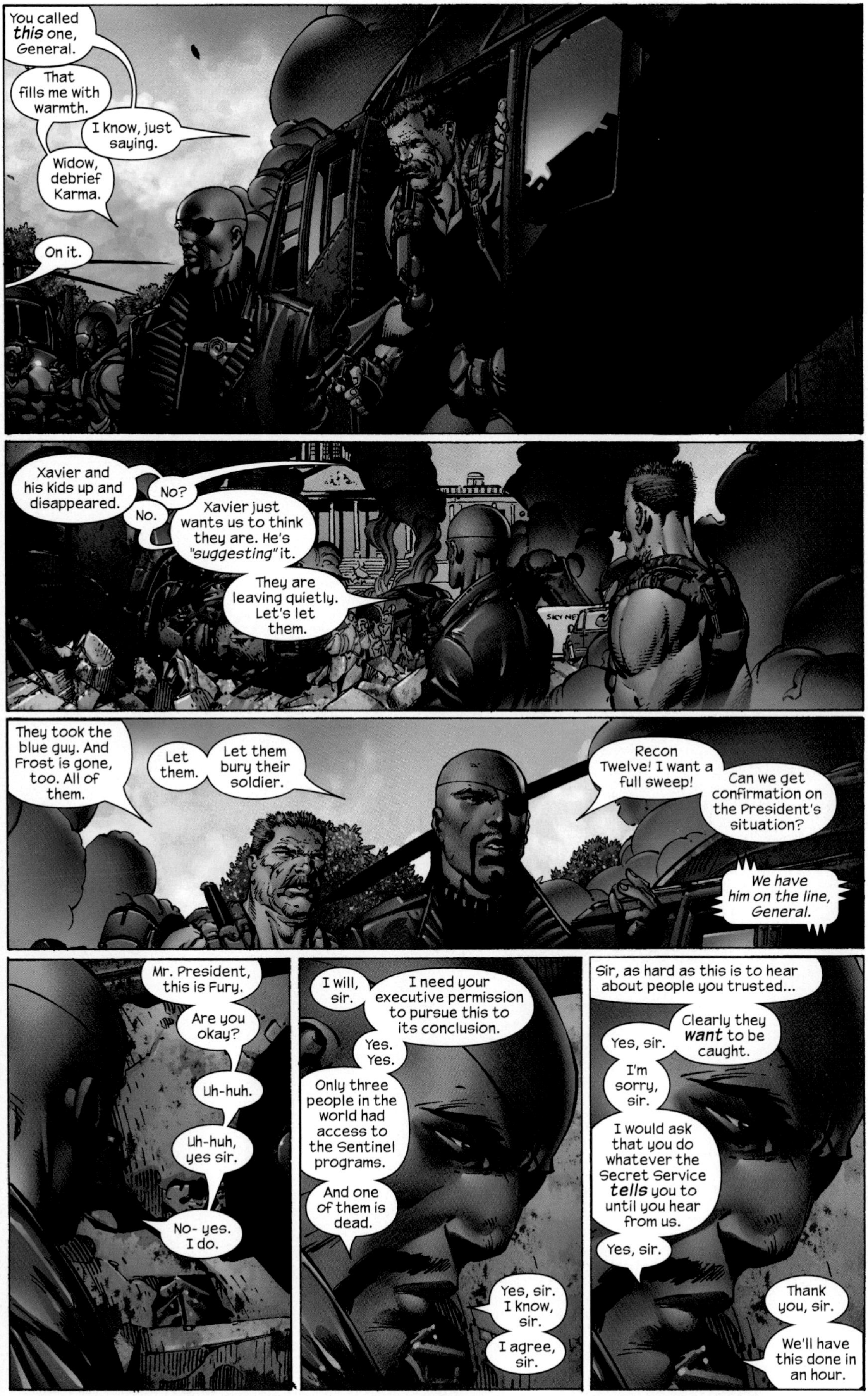

You called *this* one, General.
That fills me with warmth.
I know, just saying.
Widow, debrief Karma.
On it.
Xavier and his kids up and disappeared.
No?
No.
Xavier just wants us to think they are. He's *"suggesting"* it.
They are leaving quietly. Let's let them.
SKY NE
They took the blue guy. And Frost is gone, too. All of them.
Let them.
Let them bury their soldier.
Recon Twelve! I want a full sweep!
Can we get confirmation on the President's situation?
We have him on the line, General.
Mr. President, this is Fury.
Are you okay?
Uh-huh.
Uh-huh, yes sir.
No- yes. I do.
I will, sir.
I need your executive permission to pursue this to its conclusion.
Yes. Yes.
Only three people in the world had access to the Sentinel programs.
And one of them is dead.
Yes, sir. I know, sir.
I agree, sir.
Sir, as hard as this is to hear about people you trusted...
Clearly they *want* to be caught.
Yes, sir.
I'm sorry, sir.
I would ask that you do whatever the Secret Service *tells* you to until you hear from us.
Yes, sir.
Thank you, sir.
We'll have this done in an hour.

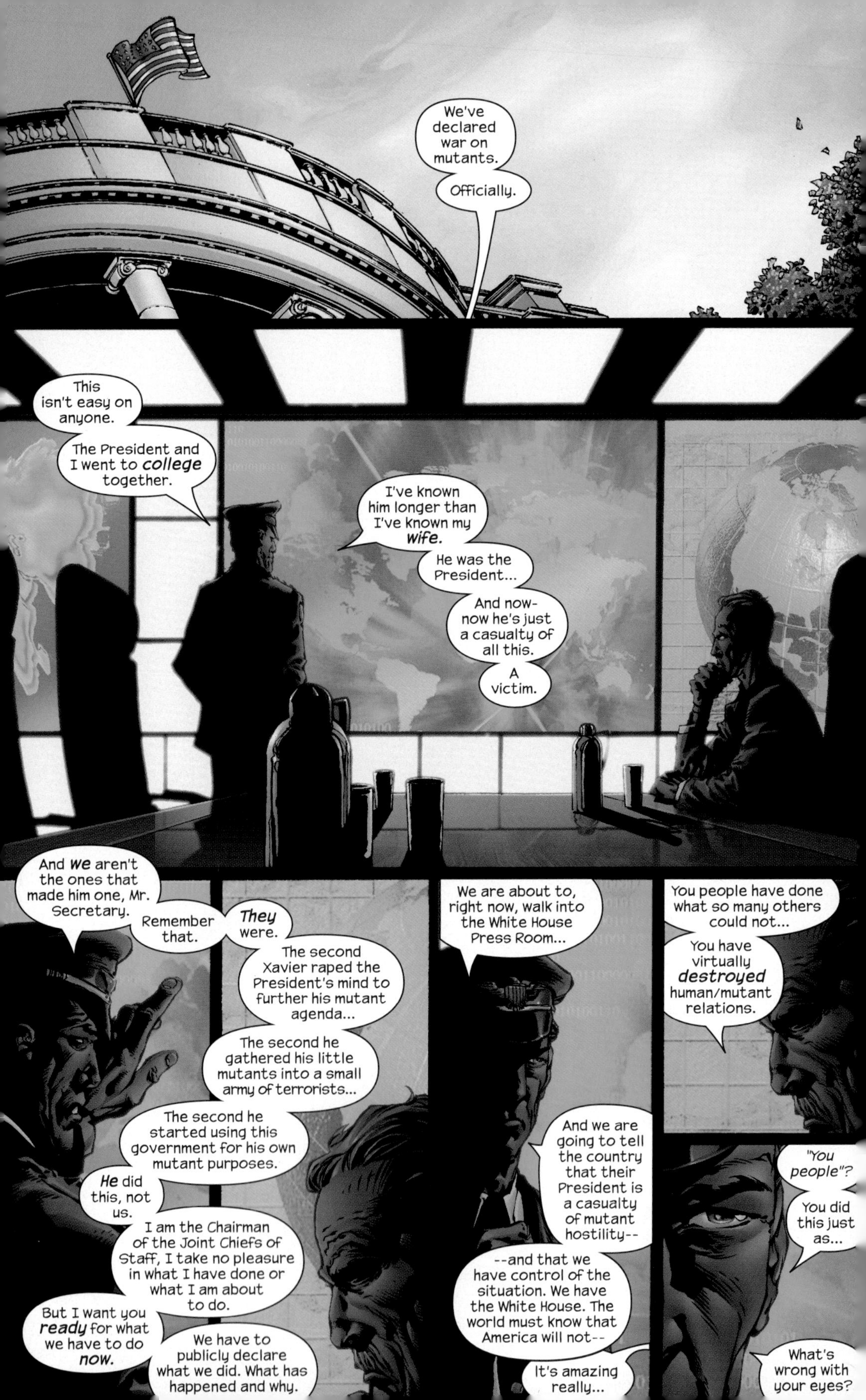
We've declared war on mutants.
Officially.
This isn't easy on anyone.
The President and I went to college together.
I've known him longer than I've known my wife.
He was the President...
And now-now he's just a casualty of all this.
A victim.
And we aren't the ones that made him one, Mr. Secretary.
Remember that.
They were.
The second Xavier raped the President's mind to further his mutant agenda...
The second he gathered his little mutants into a small army of terrorists...
The second he started using this government for his own mutant purposes.
He did this, not us.
I am the Chairman of the Joint Chiefs of Staff, I take no pleasure in what I have done or what I am about to do.
But I want you ready for what we have to do now.
We have to publicly declare what we did. What has happened and why.
We are about to, right now, walk into the White House Press Room...
And we are going to tell the country that their President is a casualty of mutant hostility--
--and that we have control of the situation. We have the White House. The world must know that America will not--
It's amazing really...
You people have done what so many others could not...
You have virtually destroyed human/mutant relations.
"You people"?
You did this just as...
What's wrong with your eyes?

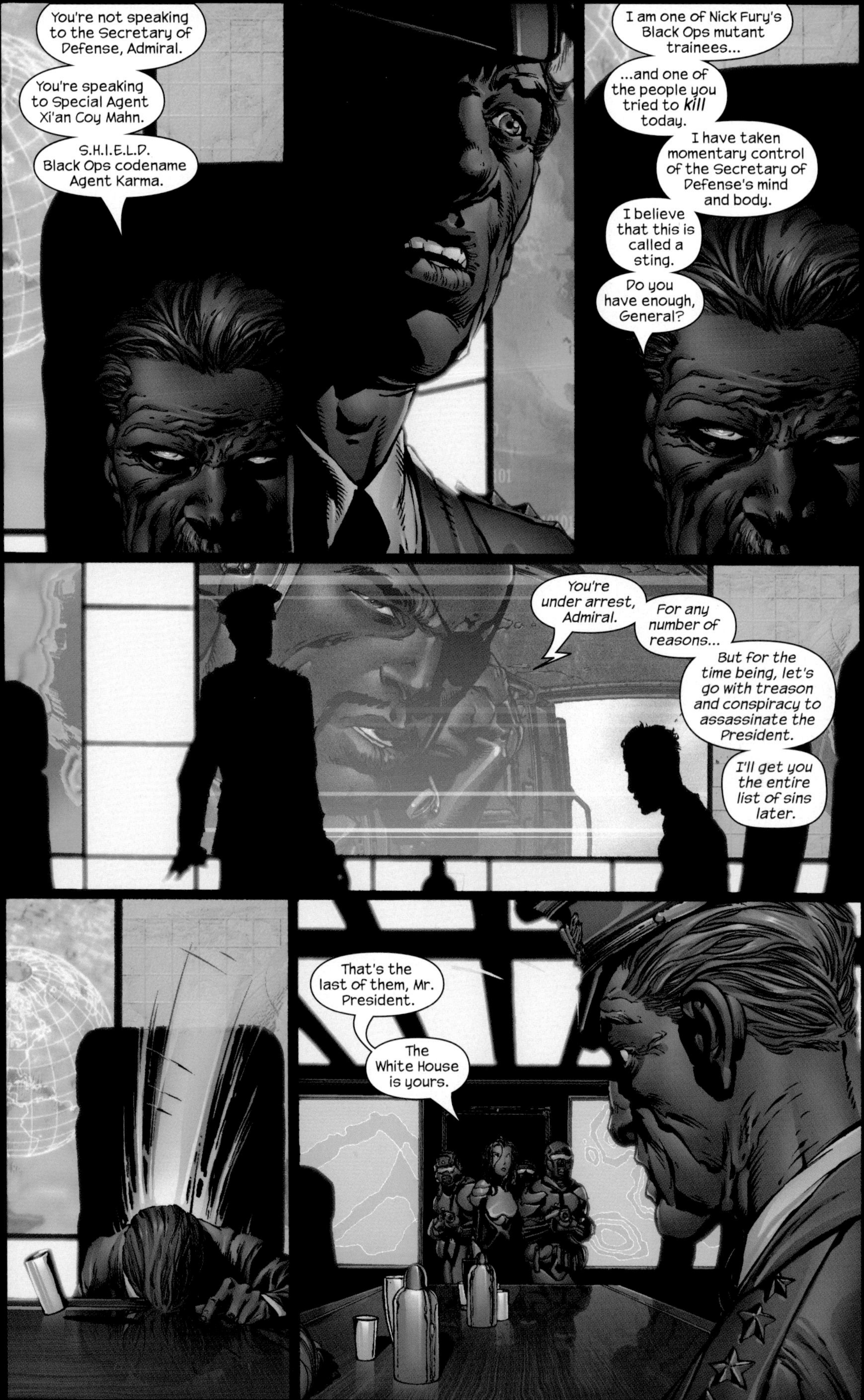
You're not speaking to the Secretary of Defense, Admiral.
You're speaking to Special Agent Xi'an Coy Mahn.
S.H.I.E.L.D. Black Ops codename Agent Karma.
I am one of Nick Fury's Black Ops mutant trainees...
...and one of the people you tried to *kill* today.
I have taken momentary control of the Secretary of Defense's mind and body.
I believe that this is called a sting.
Do you have enough, General?
You're under arrest, Admiral.
For any number of reasons...
But for the time being, let's go with treason and conspiracy to assassinate the President.
I'll get you the entire list of sins later.
That's the last of them, Mr. President.
The White House is yours.

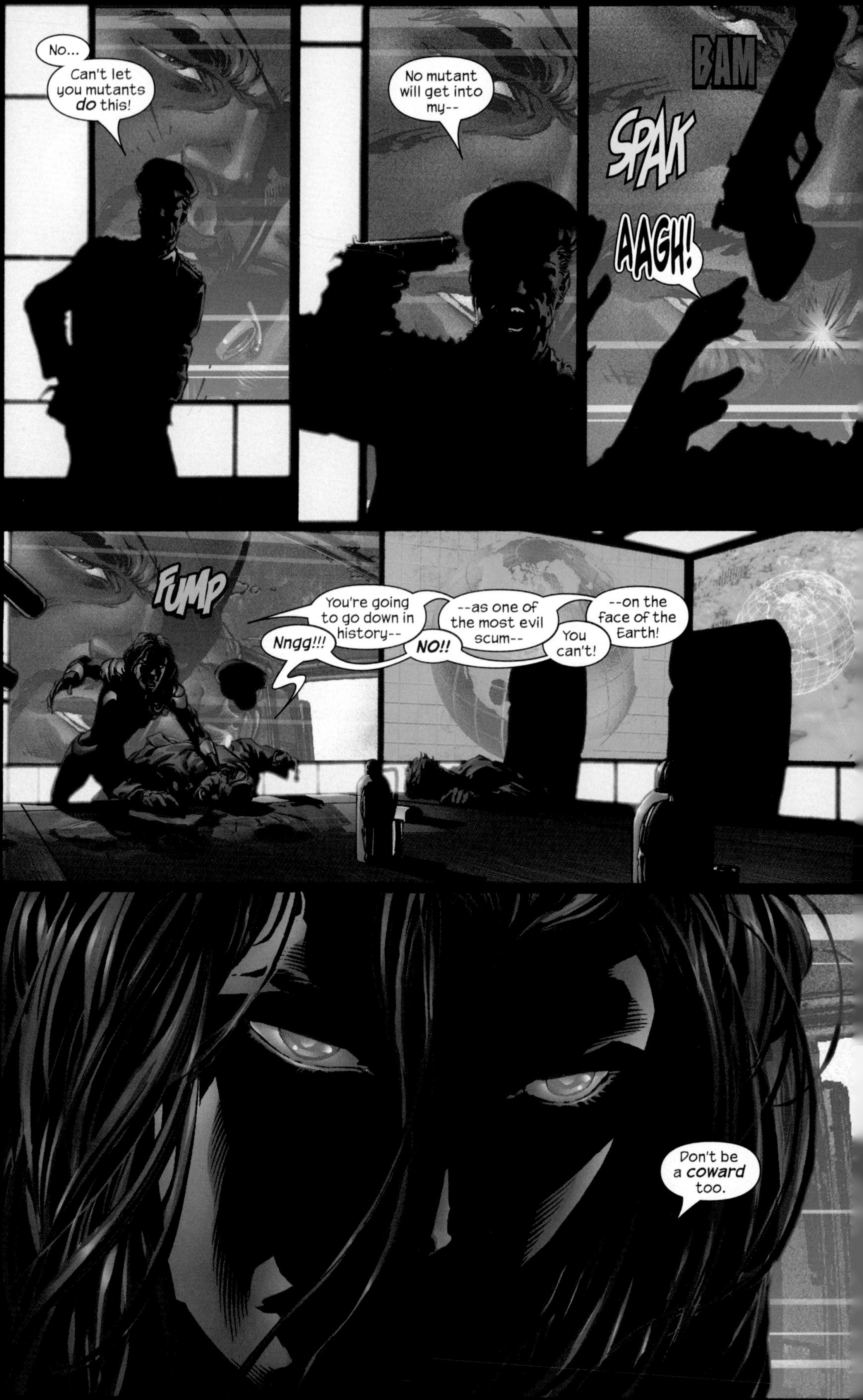
No... Can't let you mutants do this!
No mutant will get into my--
BAM
SPAK
AAGH!
FUMP
You're going to go down in history--
Nngg!!!
--as one of the most evil scum--
NO!!
--on the face of the Earth!
You can't!
Don't be a coward too.

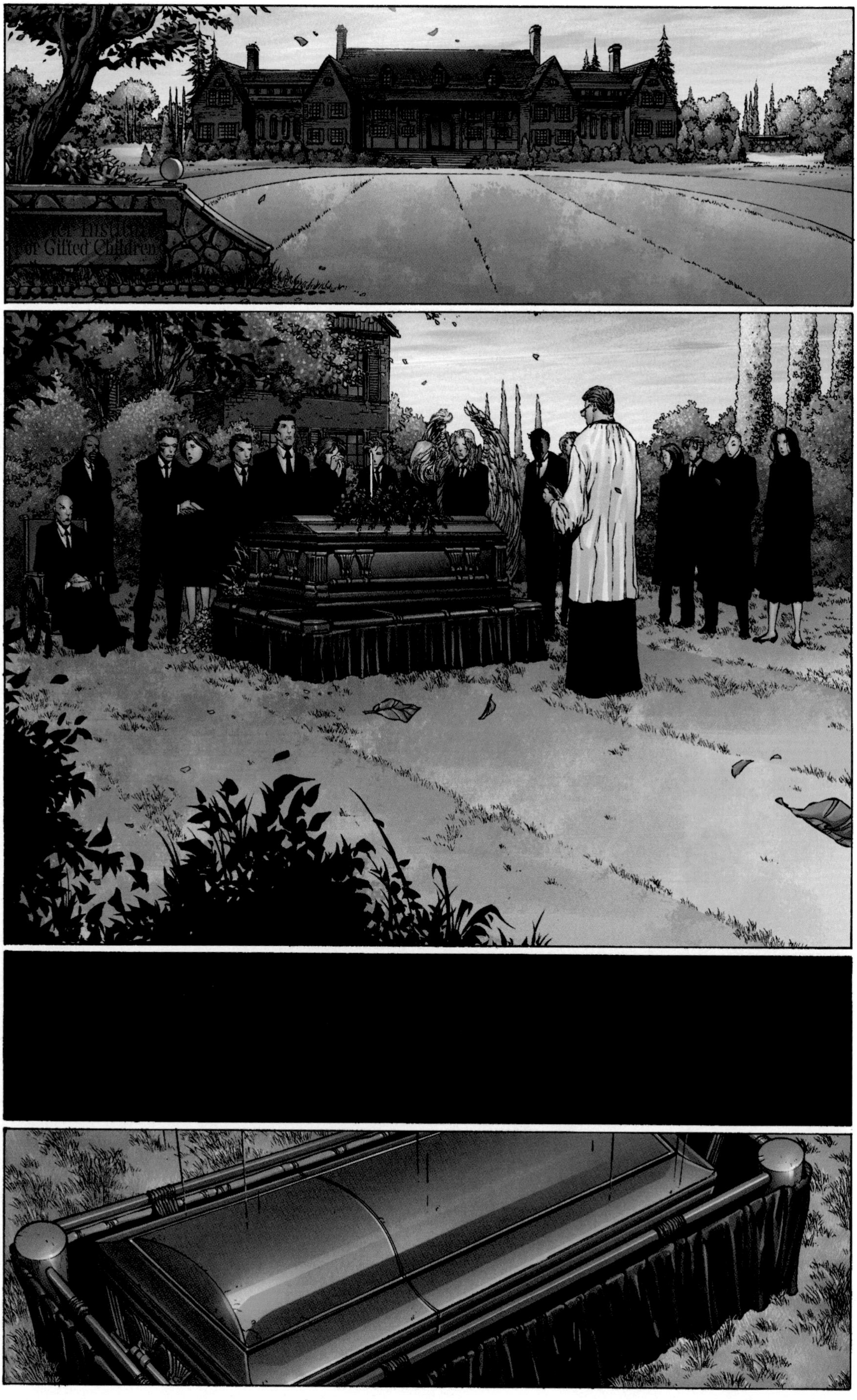
Gifted Children

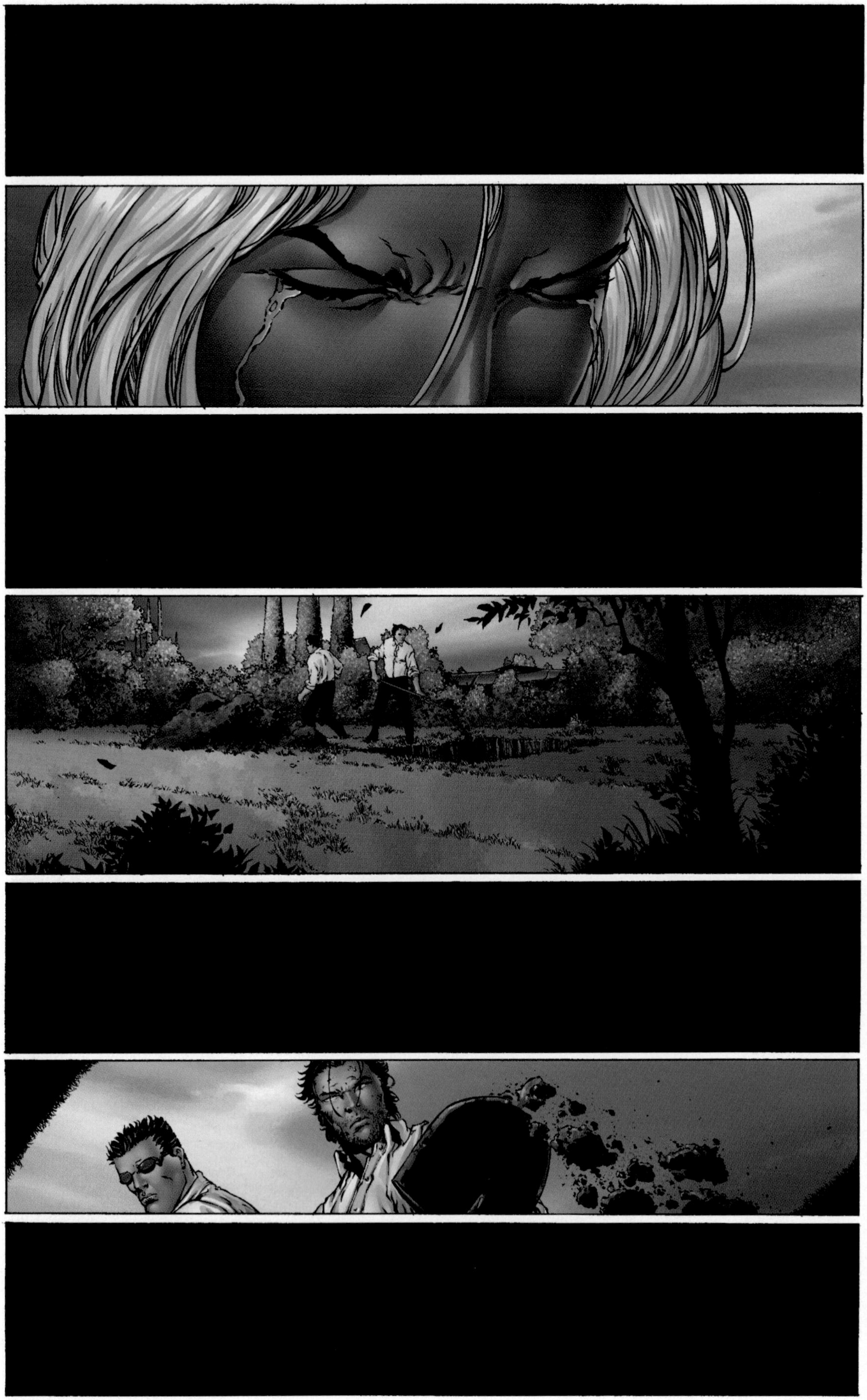

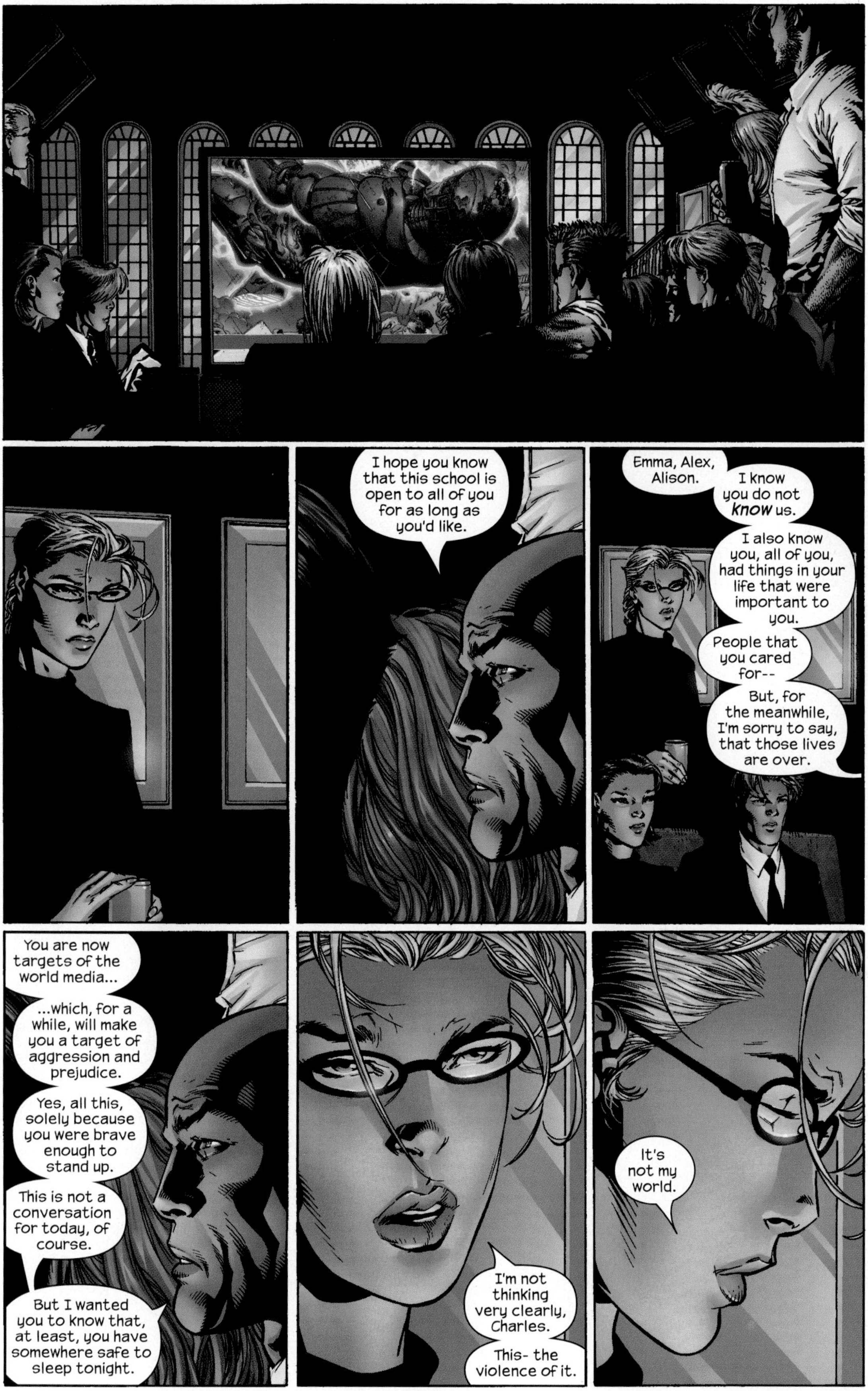
I hope you know that this school is open to all of you for as long as you'd like.
Emma, Alex, Alison.
I know you do not *KNOW* us.
I also know you, all of you, had things in your life that were important to you.
People that you cared for--
But, for the meanwhile, I'm sorry to say, that those lives are over.
You are now targets of the world media...
...which, for a while, will make you a target of aggression and prejudice.
Yes, all this, solely because you were brave enough to stand up.
This is not a conversation for today, of course.
But I wanted you to know that, at least, you have somewhere safe to sleep tonight.
I'm not thinking very clearly, Charles.
This- the violence of it.
It's not my world.

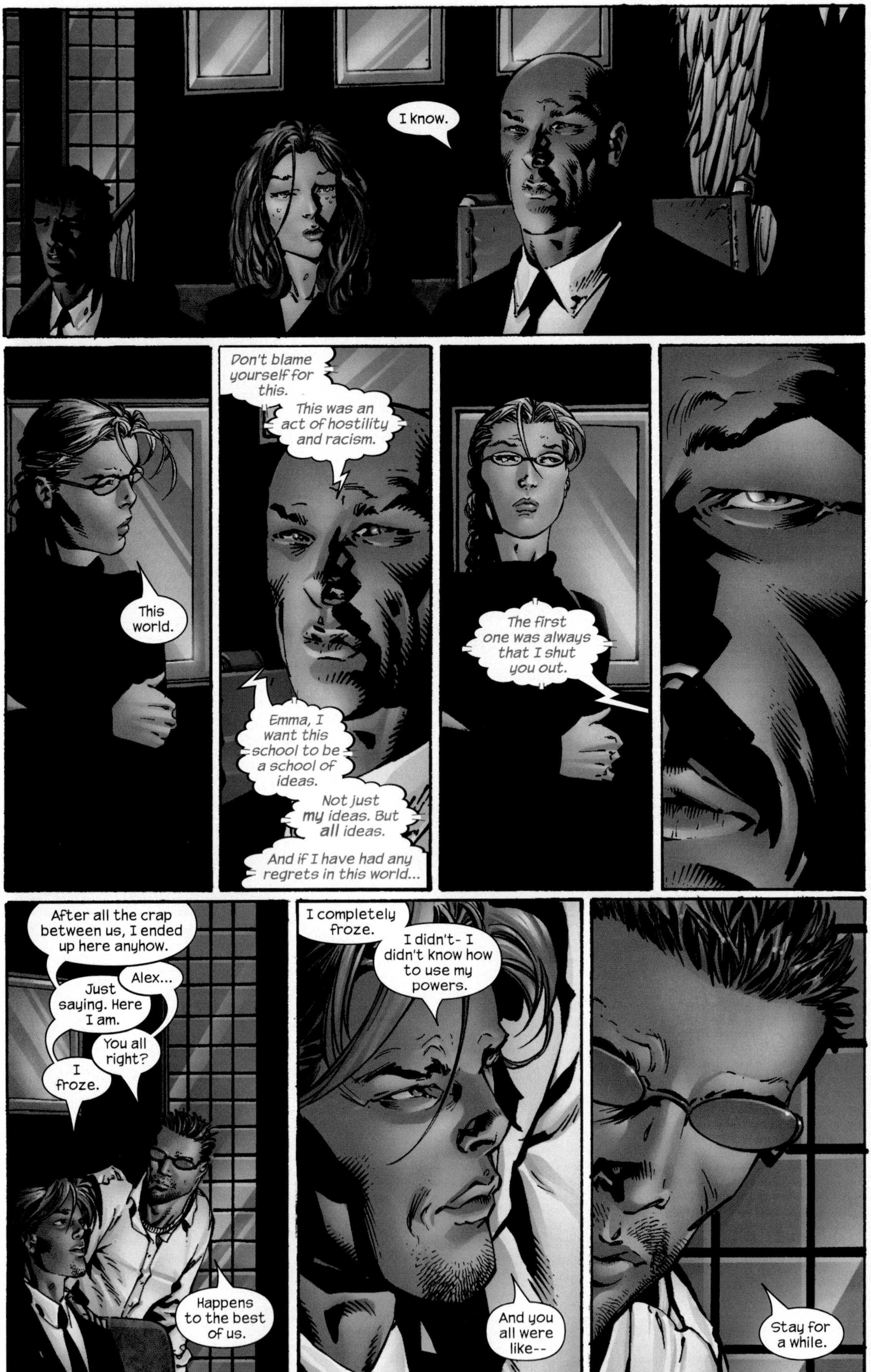
I know.
This world.
Don't blame yourself for this.
This was an act of hostility and racism.
Emma, I want this school to be a school of ideas.
Not just my ideas. But all ideas.
And if I have had any regrets in this world...
The first one was always that I shut you out.
After all the crap between us, I ended up here anyhow.
Alex...
Just saying. Here I am.
You all right?
I froze.
Happens to the best of us.
I completely froze.
I didn't- I didn't know how to use my powers.
And you all were like--
Stay for a while.

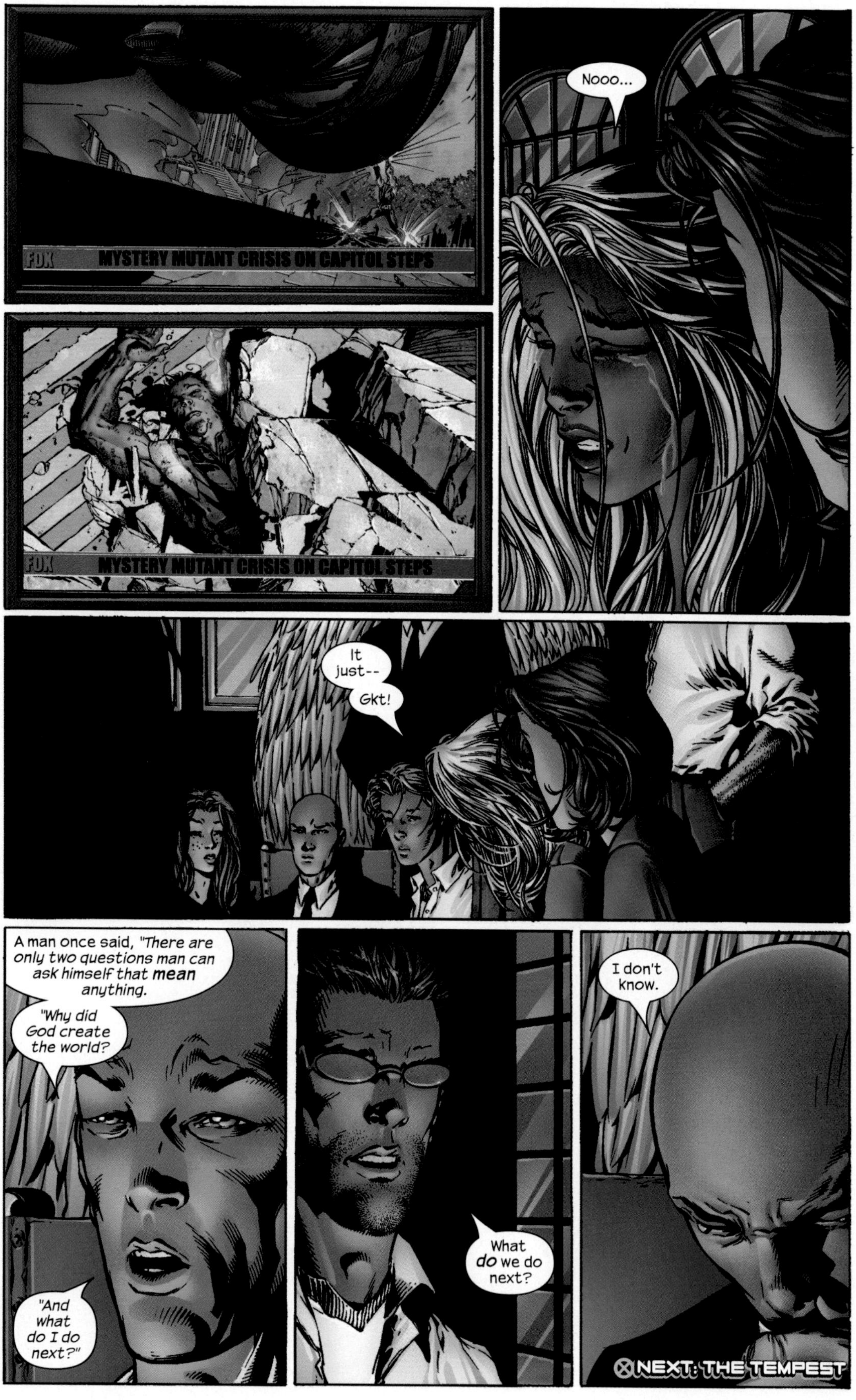
FOX
MYSTERY MUTANT CRISIS ON CAPITOL STEPS
Nooo...
FOX
MYSTERY MUTANT CRISIS ON CAPITOL STEPS
It just--
Gkt!
A man once said, "There are only two questions man can ask himself that mean anything.
"Why did God create the world?
"And what do I do next?"
What do we do next?
I don't know.
NEXT: THE TEMPEST

Ultimate X-Men #41
Cover Sketches

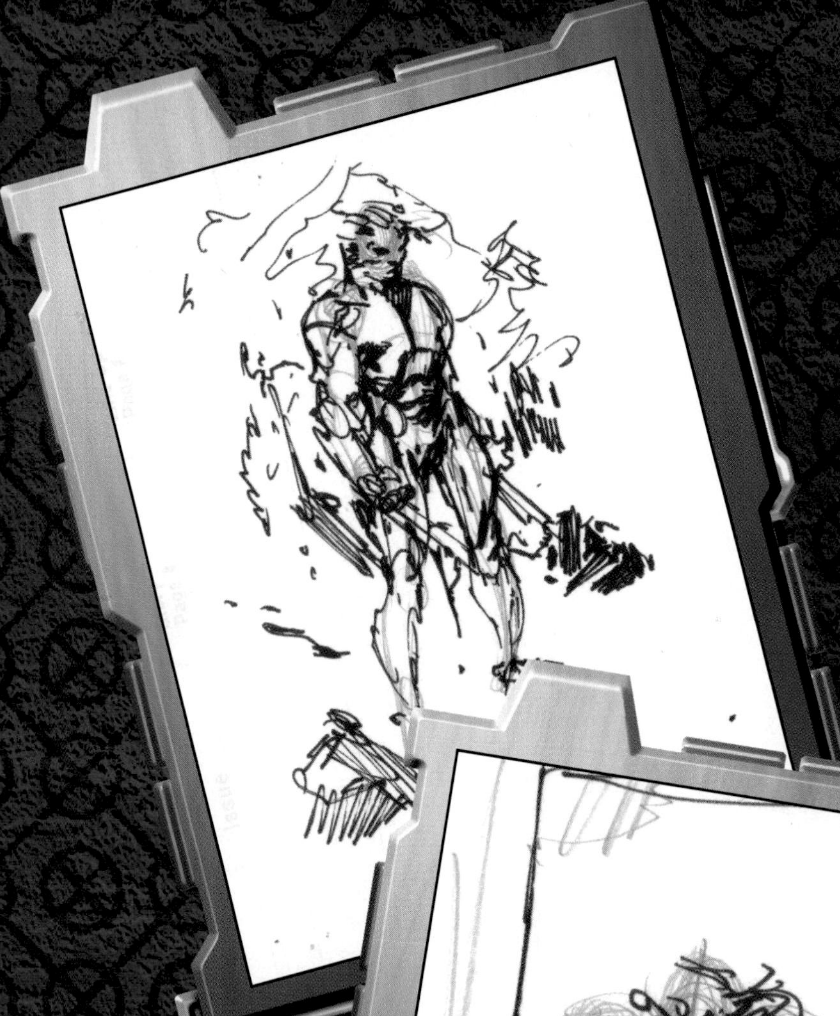

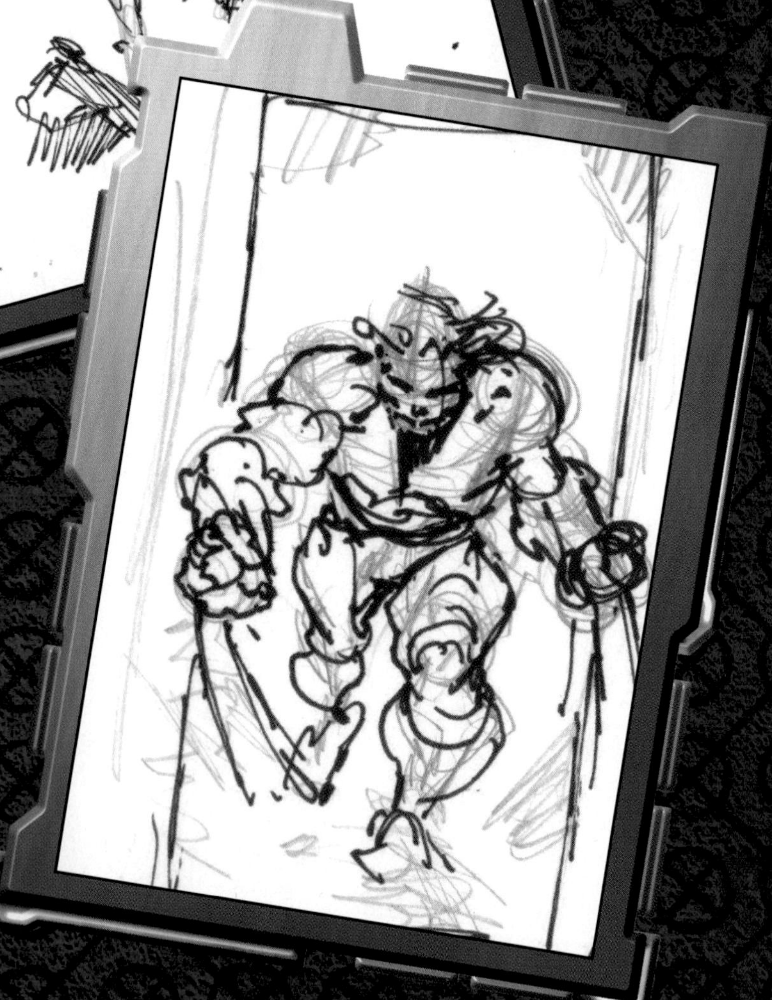

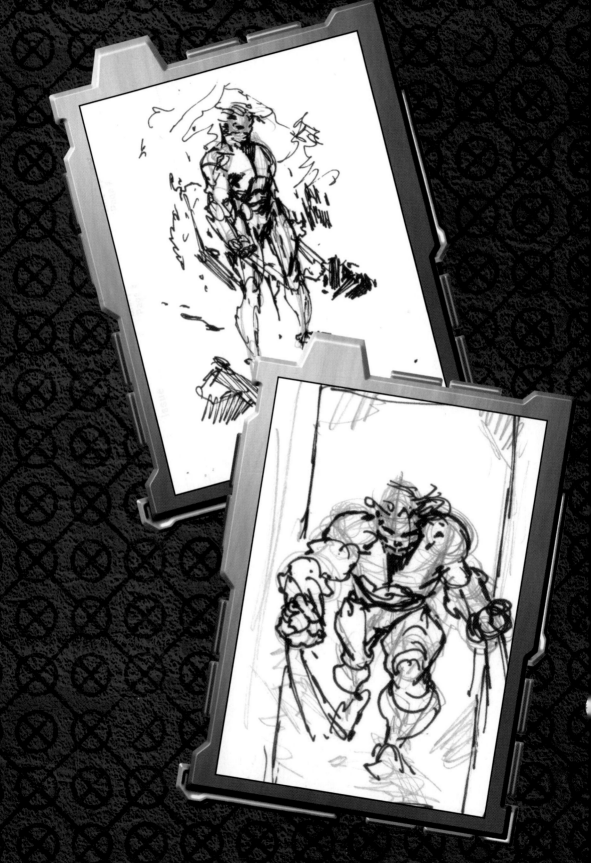

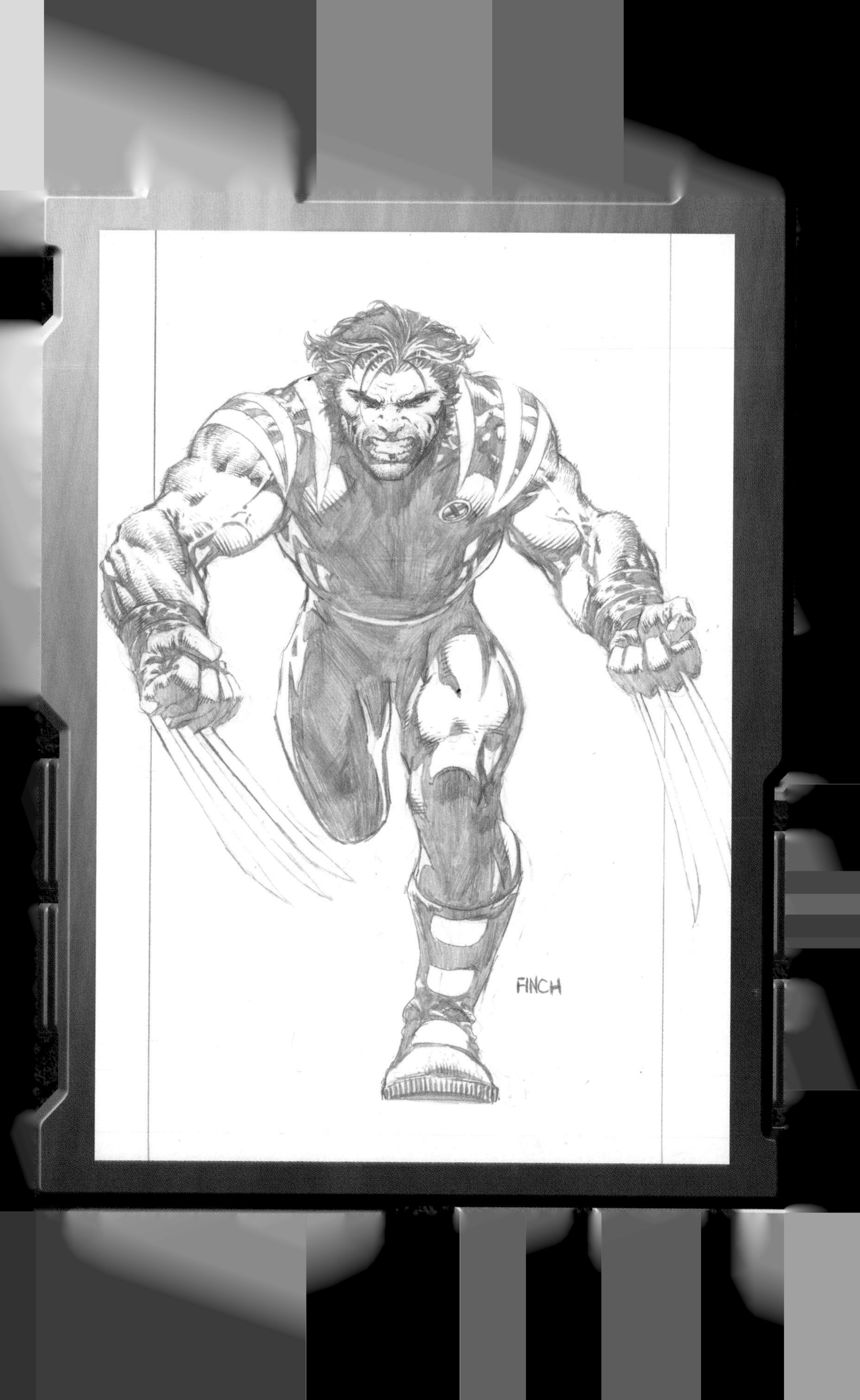
FINCH

Ultimate X-Men #40

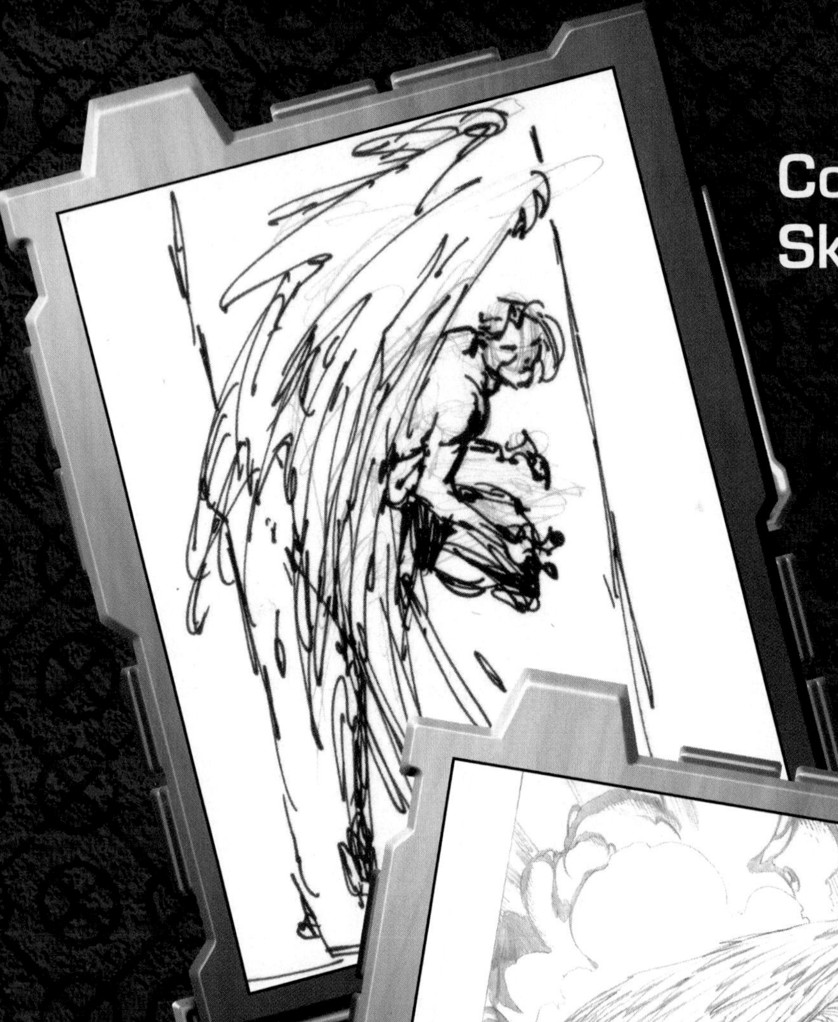

Cover Sketch

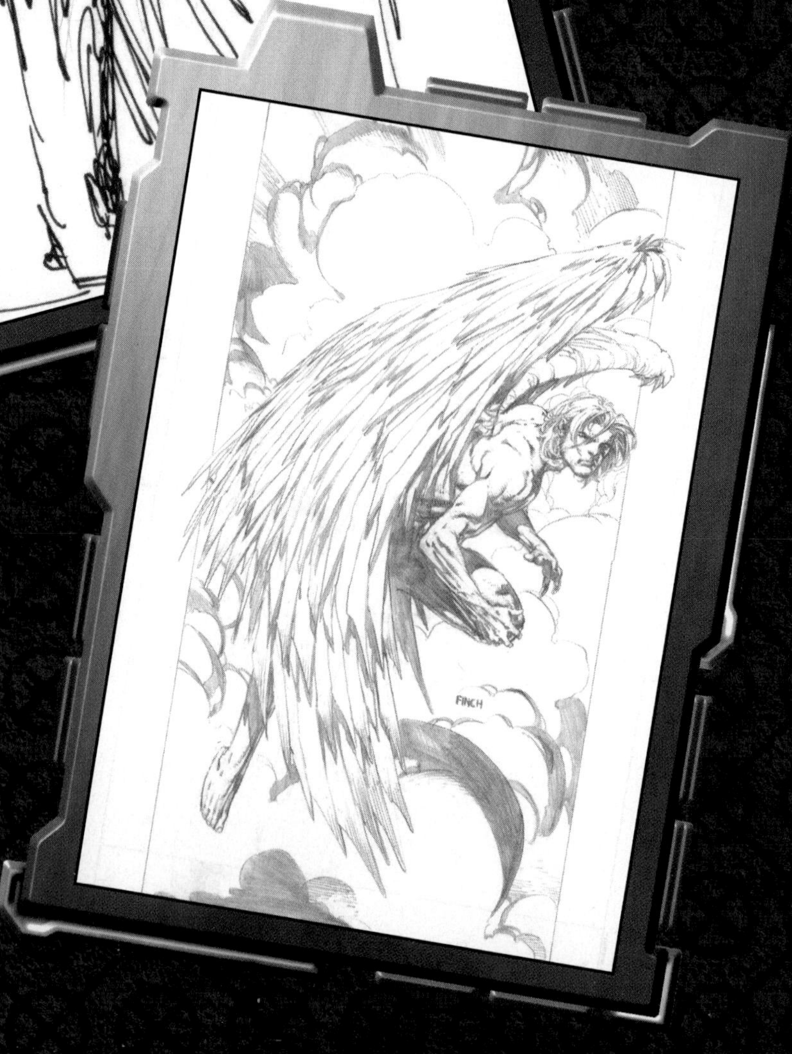
FINCH

Finished Pencils